MAD

THE BOLSHEVIKS AND THE RED ARMY, 1918–1922

THE BOLSHEVIKS AND THE RED ARMY, 1918–1922

FRANCESCO BENVENUTI

University of Bologna

Translated from the Italian by
Christopher Woodall

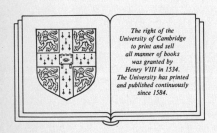

The right of the
University of Cambridge
to print and sell
all manner of books
was granted by
Henry VIII in 1534.
The University has printed
and published continuously
since 1584.

CAMBRIDGE UNIVERSITY PRESS

Cambridge
New York · New Rochelle · Melbourne · Sydney

Published by the Press Syndicate of the University of Cambridge
The Pitt Building, Trumpington Street, Cambridge CB2 1RP
32 East 57th Street, New York, NY 10022, USA
10 Stamford Road, Oakleigh, Melbourne 3166, Australia

Originally published in Italian as *I Bolscevichi e L'Armata Rossa 1918–1922*
by Bibliopolis, edizioni di filosofia e scienze s.p.a., Napoli
and © Bibliopolis 1982
First published in English by Cambridge University Press 1988 as
The Bolsheviks and the Red Army, 1918–1922

English translation © Cambridge University Press 1988

Printed in Great Britain at the University Press, Cambridge

British Library cataloguing in publication data
Benvenuti, Francesco
The Bolsheviks and the Red Army, 1918–1922. –
(Soviet and East European studies).
1. Soviet Union – History – Revolution, 1917–1921
2. Soviet Union – Politics and government – 1917–1936
I. Title
II. I Bolscevici e L'Armata Rossa 1918–1922. English
III. Series
947.084'1   DK265

Library of Congress cataloguing in publication data
Benvenuti, Francesco.
[I Bolscevichi e l'Armata Rossa 1918–1922. English]
The Bolsheviks and the Red Army, 1918–1922/Francesco Benvenuti:
translated from the Italian by Christopher Woodall.
        p.   cm. – (Soviet and East European studies)
Translation of: Bolscevichi e L'Armata Rossa 1918–1922.
Bibliography.
Includes index.
ISBN 0 521 25771 9
1. Soviet Union. Raboche-Krest 'ianskaia Krasnaia Armiia – History.
2. Soviet Union – History – Revolution, 1917–1921.
I. Title   II Series.
UA772.B38613 1988
322'.5'0947 – dc19   87-27839   CIP

ISBN 0 521 25771 9

CE

Our party discipline has developed from that inherited from the Narodnaia voliia party, from the proletarian discipline of the Russian proletariat (and, in part, from that of the German proletariat), and from the military discipline inculcated in us during the Civil War years.

S. I. Gusev, *Grazhdanskaia voina i Krasnaia Armiia*,
Moscow and Leningrad, 1925, 103

The proletarian state is a state of an absolutely particular kind which, just like our army, contains within itself the seeds of its gradual destruction.

N. I. Bukharin, 'Lenin kak markzist', in *Put' k socializmu v Rossii*,
New York, 1967, 238

Contents

Introduction

Despite its title, this is not a work of military history. The principal military operations of the Russian Civil War are not described and no attempt is made to present a comparative survey of the service structure of the Red Army. I have merely sought to highlight the ways in which the Bolsheviks, on seizing power, responded to the need to construct new armed forces, and the variety of attitudes that they adopted towards this issue between 1918 and 1922.

Attention has been focussed on the changes that the internal Red Army regime underwent, on its institutional position within the Soviet state, and on how the Bolsheviks themselves perceived these issues. To borrow from Soviet vocabulary an expression that was in common use at the time, this book is concerned with the 'military policy' (*voennaia politika*) of the Russian communist party (Bolsheviks) (RKP(b)) during the Civil War. It is my contention that this policy was much less clear-cut, unswerving, and consistent than contemporary Soviet and Western studies tend to suggest.

According to pre-1914 European socialist thinking, the nature of armies was such that the very features that reinforced their military power and operational capacity necessarily conflicted with their role as bodies of the state subject to the will of the people and to its legitimate elected representatives. Indeed, even in Jaurès' *L'armée nouvelle*, perhaps the boldest attempt by any socialist to confront orthodox military thinking, the overriding concern of the author clearly remained the democratization of the armed forces – which he presented as compatible with the demands of combat efficiency.[1] As late as 1912, 2nd International Congress resolutions repeated their appeals for the abolition of standing armies, along with their compulsory conscription, barracks training, and the authority of a caste of professional officers. They needed to be replaced by the 'universal arming of the people', a 'militia' army.[2] In *State and Revolution*, Lenin still drew attention to the constant threat of anti-popular repression that standing armies posed.[3]

Following their seizure of power, the Bolsheviks came to view the creation of a new army as indispensable to the very survival of the regime that they had established. Lenin stated that there was nothing in the experience of the socialist movement that could act as a guide to the construction of the armed forces of the revolution.[4] Moreover, the radical theories that the Bolsheviks, spurred on by the vigour of the spontaneous revolutionary movement, had developed during 1917, prompted many party members to reject all cultural and professional values other than the extremely general ones of revolutionary politics. They therefore opposed the restoration of institutional bodies potentially independent of the Soviets, and above all of the party: for only the party could guarantee that the revolution was buoyant and on course. Even those Bolsheviks who viewed the problems posed by reconstruction with a greater measure of realism were inclined to harbour suspicions about the new army, where each step in the direction of order and efficiency inevitably took a more accentuated and extreme form.

The clash between the advocates of the militia and of the standing army, or at any rate of versions of these two models, has already been illustrated by Soviet and Western studies.[5] But this was by no means the sole cause of internal tension during the construction of the Red Army. Bolshevik organizations in the units were undergoing a parallel process of transformation, which resulted in the emergence of a party structure of a very particular kind, the Political Administration of the Red Army of Workers and Peasants (PURKKA). This body operated in accordance with principles very different from those that continued to apply to civilian party organizations, and which were judged to be better suited to address the issues raised by the existence of a regular army. To this aspect, much less familiar, at least to Western readers, the present work devotes considerable space. The experience of party organization within the Red Army gave the Bolsheviks a chance to evolve forms of political leadership and administration that could later be introduced outside the military sphere.

The point at which the conclusions of this study differ most sharply from those of previous accounts is the assessment of the amount of influence that the men and the ideas of the so-called 'military opposition' of 1918–19 exerted on decisions affecting the structure of the Red Army and PUR. In my judgement, this influence was much greater than is generally admitted. The 'military opposition' differed in several ways from later Bolshevik internal oppositions. More than later opposition groups, it voiced criticisms and concerns that were shared by the party centre as well as by a majority of party members. Rather than constituting a clearly identifiable and homogeneous grouping, the 'military opposition' acted as an outlet for feelings that were widespread within the party. Its chief representatives were forced to act against a background of confusion and in a leadership vacuum, before new organizational principles had been fully implemented. The 'military opposition' was a composite phenomenon in which notorious 'left' opponents of post-October official policy rubbed shoulders with people of unquestionable political orthodoxy. Between these two groups there was a populous and anonymous middle ground, the political orientations of which were hard or impossible to identify. But like the grey area in a *chiaroscuro*, this intermediate mass shaded into the two clearer components of the drawing. The attempt to shed light on the existence of a whole variety of elements and to specify their nature is perhaps the second distinctive feature of this study.

I have also sought to trace the way some of the ideas of the 'military opposition' changed during the ensuing three years, at a time when this label had ceased officially to apply to any particular group or set of groups. I believe that this attempt to interpret the dispute in 1920–2 over the 'single military doctrine' in the light of the ideas of certain members of the 'military opposition' may also be claimed as an original contribution.

Lastly, the documentary evidence that I had the opportunity to examine seemed to disclose an image of Trotskii in which his qualities, already highlighted by I. Deutscher, as a great organizer and administrator, and a westernizing 'modernizer', emerged even more clearly than in the work of his distinguished biographer. In this connection, I find the profile that B. Knei-Paz has drawn of Trotskii's political personality most persuasive.[6] This particular aspect of Trotskii's thought and work struck me as the principal strength in his activity as a military leader, while at the same time marking his greatest limitation as a politician. It was also the chief cause of that feeling of foreignness and aversion that he inspired in so many army leaders and cadres. Some disapproved of his rigidly authoritarian approach to organization; others felt that he failed to take sufficient account of the original aspects of the Civil War experience, of which they deemed themselves to be the truest expression. I could not elude the impression that Trotskii was constantly isolated, not only within the party but even at top army level, both at the beginning and at the end of the Civil War.

Some of the issues that I have examined are already mainstream topics in Soviet history. Thus, while drawing attention to a number of points that have so far been neglected, I have probably also repeated conclusions (I hope at least from a fresh viewpoint) already reached by Western and Soviet scholars of military and political history. In several cases, e.g. G. Procacci's *Il partito nell'Unione Sovietica*,[7] the intellectual debt that the present work owes is much greater than the notes can possibly indicate. Obviously, however, I bear sole responsibility for any inaccuracies in the text as well as for any judgements and conclusions that I have felt fit to suggest.

I should like to express my gratitude to the Istituto E. Ragionieri Per La Storia Del Movimento Operaio for helping to make the publication of this book possible.

1 The disintegration of the Imperial Army

The process of democratization

The famous *Prikaz* no. 1, promulgated on 2 (15) March 1917 by the Petrograd Soviet, in response to pressure from the military units stationed in the city, was defined by Trotskii many years later as 'the single worthy document of the February revolution'.[1] This 'charter of the freedom of the revolutionary army' or 'soldier's Bill of Rights'[2] embodied the demands made by the most radical elements of the revolutionary movement in the Imperial Army. The Order was also the clearest possible indication that the disintegration of the Russian armed forces had now gathered a momentum that it would be hard to contain. The democratic and libertarian spirit reflected in the text rendered any attempt to reconcile it with the maintenance of a fighting army, depleted and exasperated by a series of bloody defeats at the front, purely illusory. More than anything else, it had been Russia's increasing involvement in the World War, in human even more than in economic terms, that had prompted the units in the firing line to follow the initiative taken by the soldiers of the Petrograd garrison. With a total of approximately 9 million men in uniform – over a third of the able-bodied male population – the Russian troops had long since ceased to be merely the nation's fighting arm. They were in fact a very representative slice of the country as a whole.[3] To sustain the war effort, it seemed that steps to militarize the rear would sooner or later become inevitable. The February revolution made sure that the opposite occurred: increasingly, soldiers ceased to consider themselves such, and the political concerns and psychological outlook dominant among the civilian population came to prevail over those at the front.

The regulations approved by the Soviet were mainly negative in character.[4] The Order sanctioned the existence of elected soldiers'

5

committees from company level upwards, and called on those units that had not yet held elections to do so. The weaponry at the disposal of each unit was to remain under the control of the committees and might under no circumstances be handed over to the officers. The most odious trappings of military discipline, such as compulsory saluting when off duty and the pompous titles of Russian officers, were abolished. Oppressive and brutal treatment of ordinary soldiers was prohibited. Officers were no longer entitled to address the men with the familiar 'ty'.

The Order also included a number of provisions that appeared to be the outcome of lukewarm concessions by soldiers' representatives. Their aim was to forestall any attempt to sanction the existence, at all levels in the military hierarchy, of a power structure opposed to that of the officers. This was true for example of the feeble attempt to limit the committees' sphere of authority to the unit's 'political activities'; and, equally, of the renewed insistence on the principle that 'during army service and in the fulfilment of their military duties, soldiers must observe the strictest military discipline'. Yet there was nothing in the wording of the Order to guarantee the enforcement of such rules. The document excelled for its evasiveness and lack of precision, the result of hesitations and conflicts within the Soviet.[5] The likely impact of the new principles on the existing military hierarchy, and the new relations within the army that they would bring about, were ignored.

Over the weeks that followed, the military authorities and the Soviet itself tried to spell out just what these measures meant. The Bolsheviks were the only political party who came out unanimously in favour of an extreme interpretation of the Order, opposing any move to limit its scope. They insisted that the soldiers' committees should have 'full power' (*polnovlastie*) within the detachments and units. They even argued that the officers should be elected by the soldiers, something which Order no. 1 had not specified.[6] Order no.2, issued a few days later, stressed that the previous Order only applied to the Petrograd garrison, and demarcated the committees' sphere of activity very narrowly, defining them as 'organs that enable soldiers to take part in the political life of the country and cater for the social requirements of each company or other unit'.[7] Those officers' elections that had already been held in Petrograd were, however, deemed valid. Order no. 2 was not published by the main Soviet organ. The product of a compromise between the War Ministry and the Soviet itself (in which, besides, it was a widely held opinion that Order no. 1

had gone too far), it had a very limited effect. The ban on holding
further officers' elections, and the territorial limitations on the validity
of the new regulations, were reiterated in a subsequent Order no. 3,
which, however, does not appear to have met with any greater
success.[8]

At the end of March, the Commander-in-Chief of the Imperial
Army wrote a 'temporary regulation' which, although it set out to
establish a hierarchical structure into which the elected committees
could fit, also sought to restrict the margins for discretion that Order
no. 1 had left open.[9] The committees were legalized and *korpus*, front,
and All-Army congresses were established. The All-Army congresses
were to be held at the Supreme Command Headquarters. Delegates
were elected from below, according to a system of indirect representation involving electoral colleges at the various levels in the army
hierarchy. On the other hand, the regulations stated that 'military and
training matters are in no way subject to discussion'. Committees
were free to appeal to the committee of their commanding unit but in
the meantime they were obliged to carry out every order that their
commanding officers issued. There was no comparable restriction on
the topics that the congresses at the various levels were allowed to
discuss, though they were only to be convened 'in cases of necessity'.
The regulation, lastly, attempted to enlist the elected committees in
the effort to increase fighting capacity: the soldiers on the committees
were 'expected to help reinforce discipline' in their detachments.

Committees were free to exercise full autonomy and freedom over
soldiers' 'education', including the circulation of newspapers, and
also over 'the internal life of the detachment'. The number of committee members was limited drastically to three, one of whom had
to be an officer. Congresses had to bring together officers' and
soldiers' representatives in the same proportions. Even bearing in
mind the range of positions assumed by the various front-line unit
commands, above all with regard to election regulations, the document produced by the general staff presumably marks a last line of
defence upon which the top military hierarchy sought to take up
position.[10]

Soviet authorities adopted a more open but also less clear-cut stance.
At the beginning of April an All-Russian Conference passed a resolution 'on the popular army'.[11] Without explicitly ruling out the involvement of soldiers in technical and military decision-making, the Conference insisted that the committees should become 'organs for
soldiers' self-management':

the purpose of company, regiment etc. committees is: a) to supervise the financial administration of the detachment; b) to reach decisions regarding the life and internal order of the detachment; c) to keep a check on elected functionaries and to take measures against any abuses by them; d) to defend the rights of soldiers as citizens; e) to organize educational and cultural work (*kul'turno-prosvetitel'naia rabota*) within the detachment; f) to develop a political consciousness amongst the soldiers of the detachment and to prepare them for the elections to the Constituent Assembly.

At least 'as a general rule', commanders, whether stationed at the front or at the rear, could not be elected. The elections that had already been held were, however, declared valid. It was recognized that units had the right to 'refuse' an officer, providing the grounds for such action could be clearly established.

Interestingly, this document does not confine itself to regulations regarding army life and officer–men relations: it sets out to impose discipline on relations between soldiers' committees and civilian Soviets in the district where troops were quartered. 'A close union' between the two sources of authority was prescribed. The Soviets, however, declared themselves to be 'the highest representatives of the political will and action of the mass of soldiers'. If the decisions of the special 'military sections' (*voennye sektsii*) of the Soviets did not possess the character of 'government orders' for the committees, the committees were nonetheless obliged to 'submit to the decisions' of the 'sections', in all matters regarding 'political action'. Representatives of local Soviets, 'without a special election', might sit with full voting rights on unit committees, if the detachment took a decision to this effect. In practice, this presumably meant that Soviets could appoint their own delegates.

The resolution revealed the fear that military organizations above detachment level might band together and run the soldiers' committees in a particular area 'separately' from the local Soviets. Above all, the establishment of committees at the *okrug* or brigade level was deemed 'inopportune', and the creation by the Soviets of special commissions, entrusted with the handling of the political life of all the troops in the area, was favoured.

The democratization of the army thus upset the new democracy of the Soviets just as much as it did the army High Command. The High Command was above all keen to restore discipline and the observance of rank, an issue on which the parties represented in the Soviets tended to remain evasive. But the growth of independent military organizations, all the more threatening for being armed, made the Soviets fearful of a break with the radical movement within the army, and prompted them to reassert the superiority of the civilian power that they themselves represented over the committees.

The October revolution and the army

Following the victorious insurrection, the first actions taken by Soviet power with regard to the armed forces had consequences similar to those produced by Order no. 1: they sanctioned and reinforced the already existing trends towards disintegration and democratization. The former of these trends had, however, progressed much further than the latter. General demobilization began on 28 October (10 November), with the discharge of the 1899 age class.[12] On 16 (29) December, two provisions introduced by the new civilian and military authorities, abolishing all remaining officers' titles and even their ranks, provided a clear idea of the form that democratization would assume. The principle that commanders should be elected was introduced in a legal form for the first time.[13] From the platoon to the regiment, commanders were to be appointed directly by the soldiers of their detachments; officers of higher units, on the other hand, were to be chosen by soldiers' congresses at the corresponding level. Technical specialist staff were to be selected by the committees, 'exclusively' from among candidates in possession of the relevant knowledge. This was one of the few limitations placed on the principle of election. Despite these radical innovations, other measures displayed a certain continuity with those which, under the Provisional Government, had sought to correct Order no. 1. A regulation issued on 30 November (13 December), although it began unambiguously by attributing 'full powers (*vsia polnota vlasti*) within each unit' to the soldiers' committees, went on to specify that the realm of activity of the committees within their units was confined to 'political life, educational and cultural activity, cooperation with civilian authorities, and economic management'.[14] On the other hand, 'those fields of activity that cannot be handled by the committees prior to the total reorganization of the army, i.e. operations, combat, supplies, and health, shall remain under the direction of the former organs, under the control of the committees and commissars, in agreement with which they shall make provisions and issue orders'.

Here we come across a principle, that of 'control', as distinct from those of 'management' or 'leadership', which the Bolsheviks were to develop considerably during their subsequent organizational activity. The document in question adds it to that right to 'self-management' that we have already encountered in the earliest documents produced by the Soviets and by the military authorities in February–April 1917. One can nonetheless detect a compromise with the soldiers' tendency to assume power automatically over every sphere of military life, as they were encouraged to do by the Bolsheviks themselves prior to the insurrection.

The formulation of the new principle of 'control' occurs alongside reference to 'commissars'. The powers and functions of these characters remained obscure throughout the entire period leading up to April 1918, when they were called upon to assume a crucial role in the organization and leadership of the newly founded Red Army. The commissars that the Provisional Government sent off to the combat units had been somewhat different from those in question here: more like high-ranking government agents occupying command posts than a dense network of control, agitation, and organization, reaching down into the smaller operational detachments. Even the commissars of the Provisional Government had been attributed a function of 'supervision' (*nadzor*) over the activities of commanders, in order to 'check that officers do not carry out and do not hatch counter-revolutionary plots'.[15] In many units these functions were probably assumed in a very much more informal way by the soldiers' committees themselves.

It was the 2nd Congress of Soviets, the same one that ratified the inauguration of the first Bolshevik-majority government, that ordered the immediate substitution of the Provisional Government commissars by others of its own choosing.[16] Under the same provision, army commanders were subjected to the authority of the new 'military committees' (*voennye komitety*), which from then on were principally referred to in the documents as 'revolutionary military committees' (VRK). Elected, or at any rate set up, following the seizure of power, in all detachments and units, they consisted prevalently of Bolsheviks and their sympathizers, whose aim it was to adjust the political climate within the army to the new regime.[17]

The post of commissar was not considered permanent, but rather 'necessitated by the exceptional nature of the political situation'.[18] As such, it was not remunerated. Nor were commissars necessarily appointed by the higher civilian and military authorities: there was a special procedure whereby higher military committees confirmed the election of commissars by their detachments. The commissars' powers were as broad as they were vague, evidently in view of the exceptional and transitional nature of the period in which they were called upon to operate. They had 'full powers' to dismiss from their posts any member of staff attached to the detachment or military institution; they could adopt 'the measures needed' to 'prevent any counter-revolutionary move, from wherever it might come'; and they had the right to arrest 'both those who violate the revolutionary order and declared counter-revolutionaries'.[19] This period also provides the first documentary evidence of the institution of commissars' counter-signatures on orders given by their corresponding commanders. Though commonly found in the rules issued by the committees of the various detachments, these counter-signatures were not prescribed by the central authorities.[20] On the other hand, the centre granted the commissars the right to determine 'which orders and provisions [might] be issued without their go-ahead'.[21] As a result, a number of soldiers' committees promptly decided to execute 'only those orders approved by the commissar'. The formal rule banning soldiers' committees from interfering in purely military and operational affairs appeared not to apply to the commissars. Although the central authorities had not provided any explicit formulation of this point, it was a view that soldiers and their committees evidently held. Here, for example, is how the VRK of the 42nd army corps (*korpus*) expressed itself in an *instruktsiia* to the commissars of that unit:

> The commissars supervise the provisions and activities of the officers from the service, social, political, economic and combat standpoint. The commissars must, as far as possible, be attached to the general staffs. All orders and directives must be confirmed by the commissars, without whose signature they are not deemed valid. In the case of disagreement between the officers and the commissar, the decision is up to the higher military organization.[22]

In another document, the VRK of the same unit states:

> 1 – All the organs and the members of the command and of the corps must remain at their posts and work in close contact with the organizations of the detachments, submitting without question to all decisions taken by the army VRK. They must also take every step to ensure that the normal life of the corps is not disturbed.
>
> 2 – No directive may be issued without the knowledge and approval of the VRK or the regiment commissars, who must be 'appointed' in each regiment in which they do not yet exist . . .
>
> 3 – All directives issued in the name of the military organs and

commanders must bear the approval of their commissars or of the representatives of the existing military organizations, in addition to the signature of whoever is issuing the orders.[23]

In this command structure, authority was extremely decentralized. The commissars were thought of as instruments of the soldiers' committees, and power was formally concentrated in one body, the VRK of the superior unit. The VRK itself was collegial in character and usually elective, albeit through a complicated system of indirect election.[24] Often the new VRK did not even appoint commissars as specific organs through which it could assert its own control over 'all operational and service orders issued by the officers'.[25] Other documents, however, specify that commanders' orders were deemed valid if signed by two VRK members, which suggests a certain division in functions within the committee.[26] Every VRK, especially those of the larger units, considered itself directly responsible for the observation of the laws of the Republic in the detachments under its control, and the guarantor of their enforcement by the lower-ranking committees.[27]

This outline, which only offers a glimpse of the range of different organizational models and of the variety of decision-making powers granted by the new revolutionary military bodies, gives a rough idea of the *komitetchina*, the 'committee regime', which put down strong roots in the crumbling Russian armed forces.[28] After the final demobilization of the old army, it was not hard to recognize the survival in the new one of the democratic and federative, often merely anarchical, organizational tradition which had developed during 1917.

The Bolshevik 'military organization' and the Red Guard

The political and organizational experience that the soldiers' committees had gained in the Imperial Army did not constitute the only precedent for the formation of the Red Army, when this got under way in the spring of 1918. It is worth taking a brief look at the structure of the Bolshevik organization that operated in the army over the same period. The main promoters of *komitetchina*, the Bolsheviks had also provided most of the leadership and regular officers of the revolutionary territorial militia (the 'Workers' Guard' or 'Red Guard'), which had been created in the main urban centres of European Russia following the February revolution.

In March 1917 the Petrograd party committee had at its disposal an organization based in the units of the garrison and Baltic fleet, which also controlled numerous cells of Bolshevik soldiers belonging to front-line units.[29] In April, this organization was placed under the direct control of the Central Committee. By June it had already gained sufficient strength to hold an All-Russian Conference of party military organizations active both at the front and in the rear.[30] A series of resolutions on the progress of army democratization were passed, while at the same time the Conference spelled out the general tasks facing the organization ('to create amongst the democratic-revolutionary elements within the army, who support and work for Social Democracy, a material armed backing for the revolution and for the demands that the revolution places on the agenda').[31] The Conference also formulated an internal regulation.[32]

Membership conditions were as indicated in the party statute for ordinary territorial organizations. The regulation specified, however, that its internal workings should be based on 'a broad elective principle': evidently the normal principle that leadership organs should be elected was in this case subject to unspecified restrictions. Otherwise, the party's military organizations were shaped in accordance with a pattern of formation that faithfully reproduced that of its civilian organizations. Cells existed from the company, squadron, and century levels upwards; they elected their own executive body and worked under the direction of the party committees of their superior unit. The Bolshevik military organization among the troops stationed in a particular district was to become 'a part' of the local town party organization. During the course of a general assembly, Bolshevik soldiers elected their own representatives, who would then sit on the territorial committee with full voting rights. Lastly, the regulation specified that 'in purely military matters the military organization is independent, but in general work it is under the direction of the town workers' organization'. Probably the requirements of undercover work in such a delicate sector had suggested the expediency of a number of statutory exceptions and of a certain independence of action.

By means of a hierarchical series of conferences and congresses, the military organizations elected a *biuro* (known as a *voenka*), which could send a representative to sit on the Central Committee with a consultative vote only. The *biuro* directed the activities of Bolshevik soldiers 'in the closest possible contact with, and according to Central Committee instructions'. It was also the task of the Central Committee to arbitrate in any type of 'disagreement and friction' that might arise either within the military organizations or between these and the party's civilian organizations.

Thus, by adhering to the structure of the Imperial Army, the Bolshevik military organization reproduced the democratic hierarchy of committees at work within it. Furthermore, in its work orientation, the pre-eminence of civilian and territorial structures was also asserted: a point which was forcefully underscored at the 6th Party Congress (26 July–3 August/8–16 August 1917), probably as a result of the excessive independence from the Central Committee shown by the Bolshevik military leaders during the crucial July days. On 31 August (13 September), in response to the vigorous protests of the Bolshevik military leaders against the new measures of control adopted against the organization that they headed, the Central Committee curtly explained that the military organization was merely a 'military commission attached to the Central Committee' and that 'all [its] work ... was performed under the direction of the Central Committee'.[33] All things considered, the Bolshevik organization was determined to maintain certain fundamental principles of 'democratic centralism' even in the military sphere.

The technical and organizational experience of military cadres was turned to account in the organization of the Red Guard. These retained their militia character right until their final disappearance in the spring of the following year.[34]

The Soviet of the Vyborg district of Petrograd was one of the first to take steps to create its own armed force. The regulations that it drafted served as a model for the organization of the Red Guard at town level:

> Any worker, whether man or woman, as well as any member of a socialist party or trade union, is entitled to join the Workers' Guard, on the recommendation or appointment of a general factory or detachment assembly.
>
> 1 – All members of the Workers' Guard belong to *desiatki* [groups of ten] which elect *desiatniki* [group leaders].
>
> 2 – The *desiatki* are organized into *sotni* [centuries], led by *sotskie*.
>
> 3 – Ten *desiatki* make up a 'Workers' Guard battalion', headed by an elected commander and two assistants (*pomoshchniki*).
>
> 4 – The *sotskie* of each battalion, together with the commander's assistants, and under the commander's presidency, constitute the 'Battalion Soviet'.
>
> 5 – The Battalion Soviet receives all instructions and orders from the 'Soviet of the Workers' Guard', which is elected by the district Soviet of the worker-deputies and soldiers, and includes five people: a president, two president's comrades and two members.
>
> 6 – When on duty, members of the Workers' Guard observe rigid and conscious comradely discipline (*tovarishcheskaia*).[35]

During the same period the Petrograd committee of the Social Democratic Workers' Party of Russia (RSDRP(b)) issued its own directives for the creation of similar formations. In place of the battalion was envisaged the *otriad* (squad), above which there was a further grouping, the *druzhina*, the name of which recalled the revolutionary armed squads of 1905. The biggest contrast with the previous regulation was that in this instance only the commander of the *desiatka* was elected directly by the militia soldiers, whereas all his superiors were elected by lower-ranking commanders. Furthermore:

> 4 – Attached to the commander of the Red Guard and the commanders of the *druzhiny* and of the *otriady*, there are elective Soviets, with full voting rights.
>
> 5 – In combat actions, the commander assumes full command and all orders are issued by him.

The second regulation was thus stricter than the first, which had not been drafted throughout by a Bolshevik organ. In both cases, however, reference was made to people, institutions, and forms of operation that on the one hand derived from *komitetchina* experience, and on the other provided a foretaste of institutions that were to emerge later on in the Red Army. The most obvious example of this is collegial command, which made its appearance in the Petrograd committee regulation. Unlike regulations governing soldiers' committees in the Imperial Army, we encounter in both cases the attempt to reconcile a democratic leadership of the armed forces with authority of command. Lastly, it is symptomatic that, out of hatred for the methods of regular armies, the second regulation even laid down the kind of tactic that should be pursued by the Guard: 'partisan struggle'.

We also have a series of documents regarding the organization of the Red Guard in Petrograd just prior to the Bolshevik insurrection. At the 3rd City Conference of the RSDRP(b) (7–11/20–4 October), and the Conference of the representatives of the city's Red Guard (22 October/ 4 November), the need to establish a number of general principles was registered once again.

The Party Conference considered the Red Guard 'an organization without a party', except, significantly, that the hope was voiced that there would be 'a predominant influence of our party' among its ranks.[36] This definition was not taken up by the representatives of the Red Guard, who declared that its detachments took orders from the Petrograd Soviet. Even at district level, their squads were under the authority of the corresponding Soviets, flanked by other special bodies (*komendatury*). These bodies consisted in part of militia soldiers elected by the detachments and in part of civilians. Also, the detachments were dependent on the authority of the factory committees which had formed them. Elective command was confirmed, even if on this occasion there was the proviso that commanders had to have undergone 'specific preparation' and that, if they had not done so, they would have to be 'compulsorily trained' by the central *komendatura* of the Guard. Moreover, the district Soviet was entitled to 'refuse' a commander elected by its corresponding detachment.

Lastly, this set of regulations featured a significant definition of the type of discipline that should reign in the squads. One can detect both the wish to safeguard the democratic and revolutionary nature of the organization and a desire to ensure its combat efficiency, a requirement all the more comprehensible if one considers when the regulations were drafted:

> The strict observation of discipline and the unconditional submission to the elected institutions is based not only on the force of blind obedience but on the consciousness of the importance and extraordinary responsibility of the tasks of the Workers' Guard, and also on a wholly free and independent democratic organization.[37]

Widely differing concepts rub shoulders in a wordy and confused form, reflecting a certain embarrassment about taking a forthright stand on the issue of the construction of an armed force. Formulations of this type certainly provide few clues as to the reasons for the Guard's success during the heroic days of the revolution. Instead, these ought to be sought in the cohesion provided by the social homogeneity of those engaged in combat and by the considerable number of Bolshevik party members among them. An overwhelming emphasis on class background may be detected even in the documents that we have examined here. In Petrograd, 'at the beginning of 1918', up to 70% of commanders were communists; of the troops, 50%.[38] The effect of party discipline, added to the voluntary character of the formations, and to their relatively small numerical size, are in fact the other factors that help to account for the organizations' thrust and compactness, on which the Soviet authorities counted following the insurrection. It seemed that the democratic principles, whose spread played an important role in the disintegration of the Imperial Army, and which were enshrined in the Bolshevik military organization and the Red Guard, were to prepare the ground for an alternative military model.[39]

The volunteer army

The threat of the German advance made it impossible for the new government to elude for long the problem of organizing the defence of the country on a more adequate basis. An armistice was signed on 2 (15) December 1917.[40] Over the weeks that followed, the Soviet authorities considered the possibility of using part of the old armed forces while they waited to launch a new kind of system which, in accordance with the traditional socialist conception, would have to be a territorial militia based on universal conscription.[41] This final goal had been reconfirmed by the June–July Conference of Bolshevik Organizations, which had included among its resolutions the intention to struggle 'for the immediate and complete liquidation of standing armies and their replacement by a militia of the whole people and the universal arming of the people'.[42]

The plan to reorganize one part of the existing regular units had to be rapidly abandoned, however, due to the startling rate at which men were deserting from the front.[43] Interest then switched to the idea of forming volunteer units from the remaining detachments of the regular forces. The catastrophic collapse of the Rumanian front made it essential to accelerate this initiative and turned it into the founding principle of the new army. At the end of December (mid-January), talk began of a 'socialist army', as of a new entity independent of the old one.[44] In an order given by Krylenko on 25 December (7 January 1918), it was stated that 'the old army that has existed until now is not in a position to undertake this task [the defence of the country]. A new army of the armed population must be formed to this end. I call upon all those to whom freedom is dear to enter this army, the embryo of which is the workers' Red Guard.'[45] From 13 (26) January onwards, the use of the term 'The Workers and Peasants Red Army' (RKKA), which appeared in the All-Union Central Executive Committee (VTsIK) document on 'the rights of the people', began to gain currency.[46] The troops at the front were instructed to form the new volunteer units around the soldiers' committees, while those in the rear were to consider the Guard squads as the nuclei.[47] The final decree which is usually pointed to as the birth certificate of the Red Army (issued by VTsIK on 15 (28) January 1918) provided for the setting up of a national *kollegiia*, with the job of presiding over the organization of the new army. The Collegium included not only representatives of the War Commissariat, but also members of the Red Army general staff.[48] The 'All-Army Demobilization Congress', which assembled the representatives of the committees of the regular units, launched an appeal to 'soldiers, workers, and poor peasants' to create a 'socialist armed mass' consisting of 'several million men': not with a view to following the example of Napoleon 'who marched across the breadth of Europe with iron and with fire', but in order to defend the revolution from its enemies.[49]

This approach, adopted under the pressure of circumstances, was to prove anything but final. The founding deed of the new army betrayed its provisional and compromise character. The stipulation in the introductory paragraph of the decree of 15 (28) January, that the army had to consist of 'the most conscious workers and peasants', has appeared to some as an implicit rejection of the principle, widely asserted by Red Guard members, whereby recruitment for the armed force of the revolution should be narrowly class-based. Lenin himself apparently insisted that a clause of this type, open to broader interpretation, be included in the text of the decree.[50] Regulations submitted for acceptance to recruits on joining the army, however, reveal a clear continuity with the recruiting criteria that, as we have seen, applied to the Red Guard:

> To enter the ranks of the Red Army, applicants must have recommendations from: the committees of the sections and democratic social organizations that share the platform of Soviet power; party or union organizations or from at least two members of the said organizations. For the incorporation of entire detachments, collective responsibility (*krugovaia poruka*) as well as individual voting is demanded.[51]

The main feature of continuity with previous experience was that the commanders were still elected and there were still soldiers' committees, also elected.[52] The first formations of the volunteer Red Army inherited also the concept of discipline proper to the Red Guard and to the committees formed in the Imperial Army. Speaking of the need to maintain order in the detachments, these committees also took care to specify that such order could not but be grounded on 'conscious discipline'.[53] The decree issued on 30 November (13 December) 1917, regarding the thorough democratization of the Imperial Army, demonstrated a similar confidence in the possibility that 'rigid discipline' might be ensured by 'the strength of influence of the comrades, and by the authority of the committees', and only in the third instance by that of 'comrades' tribunals'.[54] Besides, from the military standpoint, these tribunals had the same organic defect that afflicted the committees, i.e. that, being elected, they were accountable and could therefore be revoked by those whom they were supposed to judge.[55] Even under the mortal threat of the German march on Petrograd, at the end of February 1918, the more influential of the hastily appointed Red Army leaders upheld the same principle as against the 'discipline of the rod' (*palochnaia distsiplina*), which some would have liked to have seen imposed by machine gun fire.[56] Despite the institutional importance that the new political and military authorities attributed to the promulgation of the decree of 15 (28) January, the first Soviet armed forces retained a highly politicized (and therefore non-military) conception of discipline, and a consequent conviction that in revolutionary conditions armed service could not help being rigidly elitist. The volunteer army retained and united both the anarchic tendencies of the democratization process that had affected the old Imperial Army, and the tight-knit party political character of the Red Guard. The scattering of the revolutionary detachments in the face of the German advance, and the small number of volunteers who joined the Red Army before and after the peace of Brest (which must have appeared disappointing to the highest-ranking members of the Soviet government), demonstrated the dramatic inadequacy of the volunteer army.[57] While Soviet power was coming to identify itself increasingly with the power of a single party, several of the fundamental problems that both the Soviets and the military organs of the Provisional Government had encountered were about to present themselves anew to the inner core of the Bolshevik party.

2   The birth of the Red Army

Towards a regular army

The decision to work towards a mass centralized 'regular' and professionally trained army began to take shape in the days immediately after the signing of the Brest–Litovsk peace treaty. New principles were not, however, adopted all at once. It was a slow and gradual process lasting until December 1918 at least. Over this period, almost every new decree issued by Soviet power on military matters chipped away at the organizational principles that had still prevailed at the beginning of the year. The apparent reluctance with which the new course was embarked upon was partly a result of unavoidable conditions: recruiting, for example, proceeded with difficulty and this was a symptom of the exhaustion of the population and its potential discontent. There were also various political factors that counselled circumspection. A notable resistance could immediately be felt within the Bolshevik party itself. Moreover, until late autumn 1918 Soviet leaders must have been uncertain whether their main armed adversary would be internal counter-revolution or German occupation. Nor was it clear what forces the enemy would be in a position to field. There was therefore a preference for consolidating each newly adopted measure rather than attempting to set up a whole new scheme from scratch.

Lenin's exhortation to the 7th Party Congress, on 7 March 1918, to 'learn the art of war properly', was probably the first significant indication that a change of course was in the air.[1] The task of organizing the defence of the country had become top priority since it had been observed that well-armed and disciplined foreign armies had been able to impose on the Soviet Republic the extremely hard terms of the peace treaty. The Congress included among its own resolutions a point that spelled out the need 'to train systematically and com-

20

prehensively in military matters and military operations the entire adult population of both sexes'.[2] These indications were still very ill-defined. The following day, Lenin spoke again, in vague terms, of the future 'armed force of workers and peasants, one least divorced from the people' as of something synonymous with 'the armed workers' and peasants' Soviets'.[3] The traditional concept of the 'militia' was still attractive, even though recourse to 'regular' models was not explicitly ruled out. It was in any case clear that the military preparation of numerically large nuclei was favoured, and this in itself seemed a new departure. That this objective was not solemnly and clearly expressed by the authorities at the beginning of March may be accounted for by the fact that the treaty of Brest–Litovsk provided for the 'thorough demobilization' of the Russian armed forces, 'including the detachments that have been newly formed by the present government'.[4]

As early as 2 March, an appeal was made to the officers of the old army to place themselves at the disposal of the authorities and to furnish the volunteer formations that were bound for the front-line with 'a minimum of knowhow'.[5] Only two weeks later a first page article in *Izvestiia* urged the 4th Congress of Soviets that was then in course to take into serious consideration the possible construction of an army founded on compulsory recruitment and on the systematic employment of 'military specialists' (*voenspetsy*), and called upon delegates to demonstrate 'realism'.[6] Addressing a meeting in Moscow on 21 March, Trotskii (who had been made People's Commissar for War on the 4th)[7] stated that for the time being only volunteer detachments would be formed but that before long 'every worker and peasant' would undergo military training and that 'officers and non-commissioned officers of the old command corps' would be made use of as 'instructors'.[8] In effect, he went so far on this occasion as to outline the role that the former officers would play in the Red Army. As if to head off any opposition to this approach, Trotskii specified that the former officers would be in charge 'of the technical and strategic-operational side, while responsibility for the overall apparatus, its organization and internal structure, [would] be entirely in the hands of the Soviets'. To sweeten the pill, the newly appointed War Commissar assured his listeners that there would not in any case be a return to the regime that had governed the Imperial Army prior to its disintegration: 'As far as discipline is concerned, it must be that of men united by a single steadfast revolutionary consciousness, a consciousness of their socialist duty. It shall not be based on directives

from above, like officers' stick-wielding discipline, but rather a frater-
nal, conscious and revolutionary discipline.'

At a meeting of military representatives in Moscow, at the end of
the same month, Podvoiskii made what has been considered the first
explicit reference to the future form that the Soviet armed forces were
to assume.[9] What was being aimed at was the construction of an army
of 'a million and a half men', a goal which implicitly ruled out the
maintenance of the principle of voluntary recruitment. Widespread
use would be made of 'specialists, ... generals, officers and engineers'. To allay the doubts of those who protested about the 'counter-
revolutionary' sentiments of such people, Podvoiskii gave advance
indication of the remedy that a few days later was to be adopted: 'two
political commissars' would be detailed to work alongside commanders and former officers of the old army. The structure of the units,
which the Red Army had also inherited from the Red Guard, would
be modified: no longer would there be small, poorly coordinated
squads, but instead 'divisions, divided into brigades, regiments, bat-
talions and companies'. An army 'equal to the German and Japanese
ones' had to be set up.

As has been seen, the attachment to commanders of commissars
(defined apparently interchangeably as 'political' or 'military') was not
a Bolshevik innovation. Judging by what Podvoiskii said at the end of
March, the possibility of introducing commissars into the new Red
Army had been discussed as early as 5 March. This was the date of the
decree that brought into being the 'Supreme Military Command'
(VVS) of the Republic, located at the War Commissariat and consisting of one 'specialist' and two commissars (M. D. Bonch-Bruevich,
P. P. Proshiian and K. I. Shutko respectively).[10] The same document
established a system of 'screens' for troops in the western front area,
commanded by similar collegial bodies.[11] Lastly, on 6 April, an order
appeared, bearing Trotskii's signature alone, in his dual capacity as
War Commissar and VVS President, in which the commissars' tasks
were specified.[12] This document remained the only instruction from
the centre on this subject that is known about during this period and
the most complete of all those issued during the course of the Civil
War and the years immediately following.

The commissar was defined as 'the political organ of Soviet power
within the army': not therefore a party man. His job was 'to make sure
that the army does not itself become an independent force, and break
away from the Soviet regime, and to prevent individual Soviet institutions from becoming hotbeds of conspiracy and tools that might be

used to struggle against the workers and peasants'. Commissars were at the same time to liaise between the central and local organs of the Soviet state and the army, 'ensuring' that the former 'cooperate' with the Red Army.

Last of all, the document included a definition of correct relations between commissars and army commanders, which was to become a source of numerous subsequent conflicts:

> Orders are valid only if issued by military councils [*voennye sovety*: bodies consisting of commissars plus the commander, at the command of the detachments and the higher units], and providing they are signed, as well as by the military commanders, by at least one commissar.
>
> All work must be carried out in full view of the commissar, but the specifically military running of the camp is the job not of the commissar but of the military specialist, who works in close coordination with the commissar.
>
> The commissar is not responsible for the expediency of purely military, operational, or combat orders. The military leader alone must account for these. The signature of the commissar beneath an operational order means that he vouches for this order, insofar as it was dictated by considerations of an operational (and not of a counter-revolutionary) character.
>
> Should he not approve of a purely military instruction, the commissar does not prevent its execution, but merely reports his lack of approval to the superior military council. The execution of an operational order can only be prevented if the commissar has sound reasons to conclude that it has been dictated by counter-revolutionary designs.

The carefully weighed wording and apparent bureaucratic precision of this document distinguish it from those written by the soldiers' committees of the old Imperial Army. It is clear, however, that the relations with which it is concerned are not in fact subject to very strict discipline. The fundamental weakness was that the commissar's task of surveillance could, at his own discretion and at any point, involve his direct assumption of 'purely military' responsibilities.

While the central leading body of those commissars who had worked in the Imperial Army following the October revolution was being disbanded, a new 'All-Russian Office of Military Commissars' (VBVK) was set up.[13] The embryo of the future political apparatus of the Red Army began to take shape. At the same time, the centre sent another type of political organizer to cooperate on the formation of

armed detachments in outlying areas: these were the *agitatory* of the
'section for agitation' of the Vserossiiskaia kollegiia, which was in
charge nationally of the training of the Red Army.[14]

On 8 April, a new decree decided upon the formation of a system of
'military commissariats' at the *volost'*, *uezd*, *guberniia*, and *okrug*
levels.[15] As with trained field detachments, a council of two commissars and one 'specialist' was placed at their head. It was up to these
bodies to see to the recruiting, arming, and training of the conscript
troops, a task which was thereby removed from the 'military sections'
of the local Soviets. A previous decree of 25 March had in fact seemed
to satisfy the aspirations of the latter as regards the organization and
leadership of the armed forces,[16] but the order of 8 April provided a
clear outline of a military organization with an independent and
centralized structure. Local powers immediately demonstrated vigorous resistance to its enforcement.[17]

On 22 April VTsIK adopted the decree on compulsory conscription
for all citizens between the ages of 18 and 40: the only limitation was
that 'in the near future, the transitional era, ... only workers and
peasants who [did] not exploit the work of others' would be called
up.[18] Compulsory service was introduced on 29 May.[19] However well
ventilated by the authorities over the previous weeks, the measure
was probably adopted under the pressure of the revolt of the Czechoslovakian Legion (26 May) and of the news that in Kuban the White
generals Krasnov and Denikin had begun forced mobilization in areas
controlled by their 'Volunteer Army' (second half of May).[20] Drafting
was scheduled to begin on 12 June in the *guberniia* (province) of
Moscow, and was to continue in other provinces throughout the
central area of the country through till August.[21] Mobilization did not
take place on a larger scale until September, in response to the
growing demands for men from the fronts that had already been
formed. Throughout the summer, conscription was experimental in
character, and was enforced with caution: lacking any call-up lists, in
the cities it was above all factories that were relied upon. A series of
revolts in the country areas, an expression of the resistance of the
rural population to the reintroduction of compulsory service,
appeared to confirm the fears of those who had formulated the decree
in socially restrictive terms. In any case, the new army could hardly
maintain for long its desired proletarian purity. With increasingly
wholesale mobilization, the class character of the armed forces rapidly
blurred. It is symptomatic that until the end of July conscription
registers and recruitment instructions made no explicit mention of the

'social origin' of those mobilized, nor of whether or not they belonged to political parties.[22]

Two successive decrees, of 21 March and 22 April, signed by VVS and VTsIK respectively, abolished the election of officers by their troops.[23] At the same time, the authorities called upon the command cadres of the old army to enrol in the new one: indeed, the first such appeal was dated 21 March.[24] The division commanders and their superiors would be appointed by the Commissariat for War, with the go-ahead of VVS, and subject to information from the Council of People's Commissars (SNK). The appointment of commanders below divisional level was left up to territorial military commissars, whose task it was to examine closely the lists of candidates put forward by the Soviets and by other local social organizations.

The way in which the decision to resort to professional soldiers gained support within the party remains shrouded in mystery. There is evidence that in March a crucial meeting was called during which leading Bolsheviks in charge of military affairs set out the reasons for their opposition to the introduction of 'specialists' into the Red Army.[25] Problems were apparently discussed that had to do with 'compulsory military service, the role of communists in the army, commanders and commissars, and the relations between them'. Lenin seems not to have expressed an opinion on this occasion, referring a decision to the Central Committee. Meeting on 31 March, the supreme organ of the party decided in favour of the employment of former Tsarist officers. Regrettably, it is not known how the Central Committee proposed to tackle the other problems on the agenda, even though these were all closely related to the central issue. An approximate idea of the main features of the line that eventually emerged may be gained not only from some of the documents already examined but also by Lenin's famous article on the 'Immediate Tasks of the Soviet Government', of which the main ideas were discussed at the new sitting of the Central Committee on 7 April, and which was published on the 28th of the same month. Lenin argued the need to move towards an administrative and economic regime based on discipline and efficiency. In particular, '"Red Guard" methods' were contrasted with the course that Lenin proposed: the 'utilization of bourgeois specialists' in all fields.[26]

It is quite surprising that the initial steps taken to set up the Red Army did not include instructions regarding the organization of the party within its ranks. As we shall see, these were the achievement of a considerably later phase. Both the abolition of the old soldiers' committees,[27] following the completion of demobilization, and the disbanding of the Central Committee's military organization,[28] were decided upon during the first half of March. Thereafter, as far as is known, no decision was reached that addressed the problem of forming political soldiers' organizations within the new army. The cells that formed the base of the disbanded Bolshevik military apparatus were invited, in their turn, to join the territorial party organizations. By now, it was argued, 'the soldier's coat has ceased to be the symbol of a separate political and social class'.

At this juncture, almost the only condition that Lenin felt it necessary to impose was that steps should be taken to ensure that 'at least one in ten soldiers [were] persons recommended by the Russian communist party, by the Left Social Revolutionaries, or by the trade unions'.[29] Elected party and committee cells came into existence, however, during the very first days of the Red Army, whereas non-party or multi-party committees probably became a much less common phenomenon.[30] As long as the detachments had not started being sent to the front, their political bodies retained their links to the territorial Bolshevik organizations, which had often played a prominent role in their recruitment and training. This incoherent and ill-defined structure was the direct heir to the organizational tradition created by the soldiers' committees in the Imperial Army and by the Red Guard squads. In the resolution passed at the end of April by the conference of the Petrograd party 'collectives', the line of succession was clearly discernible.[31] The collectives gave themselves the task of upholding discipline in their detachments, of directing 'all aspects of political, cultural, and economic life', and of 'proposing and gaining approval for party candidates to all the elected offices' of the detachment. Even in its aspiration to gain a monopoly of power, the party committee and the cells that it directed claimed the right to represent the *komitetchina* principle of soldiers' 'self-management'.

The commissars soon became the main obstacle in the committee's path. In June, at the close of the first 'Congress of Military Commissars', a set of regulations was approved which subjected the activity of unspecified 'military committees' to the commissars' 'control'. Commissars were empowered to dissolve soldiers' organizations, if they deemed the orders that these gave to be 'clearly damaging and in violation of the order of the detachment, or to constitute a refusal to submit to the legitimate request of the officers'.[32] The party collectives, on the other hand, engaged in only 'close contact' with the commissars, and considered themselves, as party bodies, to be answerable to their corresponding territorial party committees only.[33] As for relations between soldiers' political organizations and officers, as early as the summer months of 1918 Supreme Military Inspection stigmatized the habit of the 'soldiers' committees' of meddling in matters of 'operational leadership', and allotted control over this to the 'central power' and to its representatives on the spot.[34]

First reactions

On 14 March *Izvestiia* published an SNK resolution that made Trotskii, already Commissar for War, President of VVS. This document also announced that Podvoiskii had resigned from the Commissariat, Shutko had been expelled from VVS, and that Krylenko, the Commander-in-Chief of the armed forces of the Republic since the October insurrection, had proposed outright that the office that he held be scrapped. The same issue of the newspaper carried, on another page, a letter to the editor from Krylenko, explaining that he had handed in his resignation as Commander-in-Chief and that he had delivered his reasons for so doing, in writing, to the government. In Krylenko's view, 'the approach to work that has lately been adopted' by the military administration made it impossible for him to continue to occupy any post of responsibility on its staff. He would therefore wait for SNK to resolve as soon as possible 'the point of principle in this issue' (probably set out in his letter of resignation, which has not been made available). Until such time, he ruled out any possibility that he might assume military functions.

It seems that the arrival of Trotskii at the Commissariat for War had caused a major upheaval among the high Soviet military authorities, in particular among the party men. Podvoiskii and Shutko remained at their posts, but Krylenko chose not to.[35] The reasons for his protest may perhaps be related to certain statements he made in one of his last appeals, sent to the soldiers of the old army while he was still in office. Reread only two weeks later, the hope he expressed on 5 March that a 'free universal army of free men' might be imminently established, would have seemed a glaring anachronism, as would his explicit rebuff of the prospect of any form of 'standing' army, on the grounds that it would be of no use to a population that was already armed.[36]

The debate at the 7th Party Congress (6–8 March 1918), convened to discuss and ratify the Central Committee's decision to reach separate peace terms with Germany, demonstrated that it was above all those party members who remained critical of the Brest treaty who also felt uneasy about a reorganization of the armed forces along orthodox and unilateral lines, and who lacked confidence in the Republic's ability to succeed in such an attempt. Bukharin predicted an impending revolutionary explosion in the countries of Western Europe and an imminent confrontation on a world scale. This, he argued, would oblige Soviet power to unleash a 'revolutionary war'.[37] Although Lenin studiously avoided any reference to the immediate scheme for military reorganization, his insistence on the need to 'learn from the Germans' how to wage war no doubt wounded the theoretical sensitivity of the most eminent leaders of the 'left communists'. Bukharin rejected the two-stage policy outlined in the party leader's cautious address. In his opinion, Lenin's plan was to take advantage of the breathing-space that the Brest peace afforded revolutionary Russia in order to fit out an army 'following all the rules of military art' and to postpone declaring hostilities with any enemies until a later date. In Bukharin's view, the armed forces of the revolution should be organized during 'the revolutionary war' itself, making use of forms of combat that the peasants in the Ukraine and in Bielorussia had adopted against the foreign invader: guerrilla warfare, partisan struggle. History would not leave Soviet power enough time to build a military machine of the 'bourgeois type': that was 'utopia'. It was 'just this *muzhik*', in his struggle to preserve the land gained through revolution, who would 'save us'.[38]

This confidence in the ability and willingness of peasants to do battle, used as an argument against the formation of an army of a regular type, was exceptional among the 'left communist' group. In subsequent debate, it played no major role in the arguments of those opposing official policy. On 19 March, at a meeting of the Moscow Soviet which Trotskii attended, Iaroslavskii clearly spelt out what was to be one of the principal arguments of the opposition throughout the ensuing period: 'the group best suited to the struggle against imperialism is the urban proletariat, which cannot be said of the population of the villages and country areas'. Iaroslavskii capped this thinly-veiled criticism of the approach then in favour among the highest circles to the institution of universal and compulsory military service with a warning regarding the forms of participation of former officers in the leadership of the new army that could be considered tolerable: 'While labelling all these staff generals and commanders experts in military affairs, in their capacity as specialists, we must remember that the detachment leader must be a person who enjoys

the full confidence of the ordinary soldier.'[39] The reservation
expressed here had to do with the nature and extent of powers that
were to be granted to the commanders of the old army.

On this occasion, as on others during this initial period, Trotskii
avoided tackling head-on any displays of ill-concealed hostility
towards the policy that he embodied, preferring to alternate bland
reassurances with more resolute expositions of his own scheme. At
the meeting of the Moscow Soviet, he replied indirectly to Iaroslavskii
in such a way as to satisfy him: there would be a great number of
commissars in the new armed forces and 'their powers will be unli-
mited'.[40] It should be pointed out that at this point the instruction
which, if interpreted to the letter, placed fairly narrow limits on the
ability of commissars to intervene in operational matters, had not yet
appeared. However, Trotskii also stated that 'it is not our party that
has broken up the Russian army, the war itself has led to its complete
disintegration. Even without the party's intervention, we had already
been reduced to the bone and extenuated by the bourgeois plunder-
ers.' By denying any such responsibility, Trotskii seemed to be repu-
diating, at least in part, the past activity of Bolshevik military organizations. Above all he elaborated a line of argument which he would
then be able to use in his dealings with the old command corps, who
considered the Bolsheviks principally to blame for the defeat of the
nation.

At the end of March, in an interview in *Pravda* (which he was careful
not to include five years later in *Kak vooruzhalas' revoliutsiia*), the War
Commissar set out in a particularly trenchant form the main points of
his programme:

> Within the context of the tasks that politics entrusts to the military
> sphere, the specialists will find ample space for the employment of
> their energies, and, for my part, I shall take every possible step to
> remove from their path the tensions that spring from inner tensions,
> from the Soviet organizations, from small-minded suspicions,
> etc. . . .
>   I see my main task as that of encouraging the introduction into the
> field of army and naval leadership and into that of their administra-
> tion of the old military rule: 'Execute and report'.
>   The Tsarist legacy and deepening economic disarray have under-
> mined people's sense of responsibility. A psychology has been
> created whereby it seems that an order that is not carried out might
> not be of importance to the interests of the country. This has to stop.
> In the army as in the Soviet fleet, discipline must be discipline,
> soldiers must be soldiers, sailors sailors, and orders orders. Red

soldiers and sailors understand all this with increasing clarity, having gained an experience of a chaotic democracy. This is why there is a growing trend towards revolutionary Soviet order, towards firm discipline, and I hope I shall encounter psychological support for the work of refounding the army and the fleet.[41]

As can be seen, this is a full-fledged guarantee to the officers of the Tsarist Army. The organization of the Red Army is even presented as a 'refoundation' (*vossozdanie*) of the old armed forces. Soviet power seemed to be declaring, along with Trotskii, that it had adopted the viewpoint of the professional soldiers. Trotskii never repeated, at least not in such one-sided terms, the concepts set out here. Obviously, it was the need of the moment that rendered it expedient to give both career soldiers and the new Soviet authorities a shock that would persuade both sides to tread the new path. The interview reflected an attitude which within a few months a large section of the party would seek openly to combat and would attribute exclusively or principally to Trotskii. It is still too soon to ask whether such an accusation was well-founded. For the time being, it is enough to point out that a good many Bolsheviks, both leaders and ordinary militants, must have been appalled by the way that Trotskii presented himself as a bulwark of the rights of the officers' corps. They must have been equally taken aback by his bald reassertion of a traditional concept of military discipline, in open conflict with the 'chaotic' regime that, according to him, had distinguished the first heroic steps taken by the revolution.

What was the opinion of the other group that was directly affected, the demobilized former officers? A letter that one of them sent during the second half of April to *Izvestiia* demonstrates that, despite the sense of scandal felt by some party members, the initial measures taken in spring 1918 were still very far from giving the professional soldiers the kind of army they would have liked to see.[42] The anonymous officer wrote that he belonged to the 'majority' of career officers, 'honest citizens who love their fatherland', and who deemed it their duty to answer the call of the Soviet government. However, he observed, the slow response to this appeal should give pause to consider the reasons for the former officers' diffidence. The hypothesis that they might be committing intentional 'sabotage' must be ruled out straightaway. The real problem was that 'in the plan for the new army, nowhere is there a list *of the rights and the duties of the service*, precisely laid down by decree'. If they wished to avoid 'falling again into the same error committed in the first months of the revolution' (when 'the promulgation of a decree on the rights of the soldier-citizen, without mentioning his rights', had led 'to the complete disintegration of the army') steps had to be taken at the earliest opportunity: 'The lack of essential underlying principles, necessary to the formation of an army, induces the majority of officers and soldiers, against their own instincts, to abstain from entering its ranks.' This was an appeal solemnly to sanction, 'by decree', the establishment of a regime of discipline, such as the Soviet government was advocating – in word if not in deed. But how could relations involving, for example, the deliberately vague and informal office of 'political commissar' be given a precise definition? And again, from the Bolsheviks' standpoint: would the loyalty of the former Tsarist officers bear the strain when the new army came to fight not 'external attempts at restoration' (the only eventuality of war taken into account in the anonymous officer's letter) but a civil war? The Red Army inevitably bore the birth marks left by the uncertain replies these queries received. Trotskii himself appeared brutally to contradict his own enticing appeals to the old command corps when, on 20 June 1918, he bore witness against the commander of the Baltic fleet, Shastnyi, before the 'revolutionary tribunal' of VTsIK.[43] The trial imposed the death sentence on the commander, who had been accused of engaging in 'counter-revolutionary' agitation among the men and of a presumed attempt 'to turn [the fleet] against' the Soviet regime, and to hand the ships over to the Germans. The charges included the accusation that he had sought to alter relations between the fleet commander and the higher political commissars, with a view to restoring the 'previous' command structure.[44] Shastnyi's name became synonymous with the merciless response that would meet every act of betrayal, real or presumed, by former officers.

Far from being accidental, the blurred character of relations within the Red Army was one of its essential features. A more solid and coherent structure would only emerge once the party cadres in the army had themselves been persuaded, or forced, to accept the arguments for discipline and military efficiency, and once those officers willing to cooperate had provided sufficient evidence of their loyalty. For the time being, that remained a very distant prospect.

In a wide-ranging manifesto published on 20 April in *Kommunist*, the 'left communists' saw in official military policy 'a deviation towards the re-establishment of nationwide (including the bourgeoisie) military service'.[45] Recalling the former officers to arms amounted to a renunciation of 'the task of creating a proletarian command corps'. What was happening was that 'the old officer corps and the command structure of the Tsarist generals' were being re-established:

> Attempts to restore general military conscription, insofar as they are not doomed to failure, would in essence lead to the arming and organization of petty bourgeois counter-revolutionary forces. This is still clearer with regard to the restoration of the old officer corps and the returning of Tsarist generals to command power, insofar as their use is not accompanied by the most energetic efforts at creating proletarian cadres of a revolutionary officer corps and the establishment of vigilant control over the Tsarist command corps in the transitional period. 'Nationwide' (and not class) armed forces headed by the old generals cannot be penetrated by a revolutionary class spirit, and will inevitably degenerate into a declassed soldiery and cannot constitute a support for armed intervention of the Russian proletariat in the international revolution.[46]

This necessitated the adoption of the following organizational measures:

> the creation of a cadre of instructors and commanders of rapidly mobilizable units from among the workers of the evacuated regions, who remain without productive occupation; the use of Tsarist officers to train these instructors, the creation of a proletarian and revolutionary, and not intellectual and bourgeois reserve officer corps; the training in military matters of workers and poor peasants only, the organization of real control over the Tsarist generals and the preparation of a higher command staff from among the party comrades who already have military experience, but are as yet without theoretical training.

Lastly, there was a proposal to launch against the Germans (the 'left communists' remaining stubbornly opposed to the Brest–Litovsk peace treaty) 'partisan' rather than regular type units, should the need arise.

The confidence that they had enough time at their disposal to train a new officer corps and adequate 'class' forces may have been buoyed up by the conviction that the military phase of the revolution was virtually over. These positions seem to me, however, to be based on considerations of a largely ideological character. As we shall see, they acted as a precedent for almost all future forms of opposition from within the party to its military policy, and at the same time provided a summary and a theoretical formulation of the Bolsheviks' experience of revolutionary armed organization from the February revolution onwards. The demands of the 'left communists' were essentially twofold: the application, in the recruiting of both ordinary soldiers and commanders, of strict class-based criteria which would let in peasants only if 'poor'; the guarantee of 'real control' over former officers. The opposition of the 'left communists' to the new military approach was of a different nature from that of the supporters of the 'militia', among whom the ideas and socialist schemes of the period of the 2nd International still flourished. The 'left communists' were indifferent to the 'militia' or, if it was synonymous with a watering-down of the class-basis of the revolutionary armed forces, downright hostile. Moreover, they considered the powers granted to political commissars to be blatantly and wholly inadequate. This twofold concern – to uphold the proletarian purity of the armed forces and to strengthen the leading role and influence of the party – was a faithful reflection of an important strand within the Bolshevik ideological tradition. One last political feature of this document was that it presented itself more as a court of law set up to cross-examine the aims of the creators of official military policy than as a precise analysis of the Soviet government's recent measures and an alternative platform to them. The 'left communists' declared that they could expect nothing better from people who had been willing to put their names to the 'shaming' Brest–Litovsk peace treaty. Lenin seemed to appreciate the prevalently admonitory character of the manifesto and, in his thorough criticism of it, he made no reference to its military section, concentrating his energies on attacking those parts devoted to economic and foreign policy.[47] This may perhaps be considered proof that, at that date, not even the highest Soviet authorities possessed a clear idea of the form that the new armed forces would take. In any case, Lenin's evasiveness on this occasion is only the first example of the strict circumspection that he unfailingly observed over the following years each time he had to make a pronouncement on issues of military organization.

By the beginning of April it was already apparent that the arguments of the 'left communists' merely gave a systematic appearance and theoretical dignity to widespread party feeling. Their platform represented more than the theorizing of a well-defined political grouping of intellectuals and prominent leaders. The Petrograd Regional Party Conference passed, for example, a resolution on the construction of the Red Army which had many points in common with the manifesto printed in *Kommunist*.[48] Their resolution forcefully restated the principle that the new army should be formed on 'class' lines. More than that, it specified that the army should be run in accordance with 'democratic centralism', i.e. with the same framework that regulated relations between lower- and higher-ranking organs within the Bolshevik party. In this particular case this stipulation doubtless represented a preference for administrative decentralization. The cohesion of the troops had to be ensured exclusively by means of 'the severest self-discipline'. These democratic and federalist viewpoints were tempered by the vague precept that the 'general management' of the armed forces should be the responsibility of 'central Soviet power'. 'Military specialists' ought to be used only as the 'instructors' of new command staff. One section in particular revealed the disagreement over the order abolishing the election of officers: 'Owing to the absence of military specialists among the workers and peasants, the principle of electivity to positions of command must be balanced, for reasons beyond our control and on a temporary basis, by that of recommendation and confirmation by the leading organs of Soviet power.'

It should be added that Zinov'ev, Petrograd party secretary, took exception to the administrative centralization implicit in the system of territorial military commissariats. During this period he made a series of declarations in favour of a notable restriction of the role that former officers might play in the Red Army.[49]

Nor were unfavourable reactions slow to materialize from the other parties represented in VTsIK. At the session on 22 April, Trotskii explained that the reintroduction of the old officers made it necessary to suspend the orthodox 'one-man command' (po tipu edinachaliia) model, and instead 'to split the authority of the military leader', by attributing 'the purely military, operational, and combat functions' to a professional officer, and 'the work of political and ideological instruction' to the commissar.[50] The 'extreme restriction' placed on the principle of the election of commanders was presented by Trotskii as a highly important constitutional guarantee, designed to safeguard the army and above all the Republic from the phenomenon of 'military syndicalism' (armeiskii sindikalizm): in other words, from the danger that 'the army might come to consider itself an independent entity, entitled to establish its own laws'.[51] The fact that the local Soviets took part in drawing up the lists from which the central military authorities were to select the higher-level commanders was pointed to by Trotskii as a sufficient guarantee that the command corps selected would be politically reliable: 'Therefore, comrades, the so-called democratic principle is not prejudiced in any way; on the contrary, it is placed on a more elevated Soviet basis.'[52]

For the opposition, Martov opened fire on the decrees that Trotskii had advocated, alleging that they marked the start of a more generally authoritarian phase of Soviet power. In Martov's view, peasants enrolled in a regular standing army represented a greater threat to Soviet power than if they formed part of a territorial militia. But even a rigidly class-based army might act as an 'anti-revolutionary and anti-socialist' instrument.[53] He therefore proposed an alternative motion to Trotskii's address, in which the class basis was counter-balanced by a 'democratic militia' founded on the 'arming of the entire people'. Moreover, Martov's motion contested the principle whereby the commanders would be appointed by the Commissariat for War and not by the legislative organs of the Republic, on the grounds that this would have meant running the risk of 'a restoration of closed militaristic general staffs', synonymous in every time and place with political restoration.[54] Lozovskii also declared that the decree abolishing the election of officials was full of 'anti-democratic elements' and proposed that the army take an oath of allegiance not to SNK but to VTsIK.[55] Il'in coined the contemptuous label of commanders' 'archangels' for the commissars,[56] and Dan' said that they in no way constituted a safeguard against political reaction: even though the generals of the French revolution were all 'ardent republicans', it was from their very midst that Napoleon had sprung.[57] Martov also expressed the fear that the introduction of commissars might be a prelude to the employment of the army in internal political repression.[58]

At the session on 29 March it was Sokol'nikov's turn to defend government policy. Martov and Dan' attacked the Red Army as an 'arm of the regime' that might be used against the disaffected. They set out their own plan for a militia that would be the 'equivalent in the military field of the dissolved Constituent Assembly'.[59] Kogan-Bernshtein contrasted the new 'Praetorian army' with an ideal 'people's army'.[60] To head off criticism from opposing parties, which expressed in plain terms opinions also held by many Bolsheviks, a Bolshevik such as Iaroslavskii, sceptical about official military policy, nevertheless felt compelled to speak out. The accusation levelled by Dan' – that with the latest military decrees the Soviet government was restoring 'the old order' – were roundly dismissed.[61] Yet in *Kommunist*, Radek openly stated that he shared the Mensheviks' anxiety about the possibility that a 'Praetorian clique' might form. He also said that he was sceptical about Trotskii's optimism that the old officers would be willing to cooperate.[62]

In actual fact, as we shall see, the idea of a militia disappeared neither from the long-term plans of the Soviet military authorities nor from the party programme. Indeed, at the 8th Congress, in March of the following year, it was reconfirmed as the ultimate goal of military policy. Nor did the decision to proceed with the formation of a regular army rule out certain aspects typical of the militia model, such as the widespread recourse to non-barracks training prior to enrolment in the fighting units. This in fact was sanctioned by one of the decrees promulgated in April 1918. Like many others, Podvoiskii, in charge of the machinery responsible for this form of training (Vsevobuch), had no difficulty in converting himself in plenty of time to the orthodox military principles that Trotskii had restored, viewing the construction of a centralized Red Army run and commanded by regular officers as a purely temporary phenomenon.[63] But even at the 1st Vsevobuch Congress in June 1918, some of Podvoiskii's collaborators voiced serious reservations which recalled criticisms formulated above all by the Mensheviks and the Social Revolutionaries. One of the speakers noted with satisfaction that 'all' military specialists were in favour of a regular army, clearly implying that this in itself was an excellent reason for revolutionaries to fight against it.[64] Another did not hesitate to declare that, 'however prudent we may be and however much confidence we may possess in those whom we place at the head of the army, we can never be absolutely certain of our freedom and of our safety from Boulangism and from surprise military assault. The only safeguard against these is the universal arming of the population.'[65] Later on in the debate, the same speaker displayed profound hostility towards the 'specialists' and showed that in his view a regular army was in itself an anti-democratic institution: 'The more democratic a country, the more practicable is the militia system.'[66] The citing of Switzerland was one of the most frequent commonplaces during the proceedings.

Among the reactions of discontent to the course followed in March by the top military authorities, it is worth mentioning a number of other episodes, expressions perhaps of states of mind less politicized than those recorded so far, but necessary nonetheless to complete the picture. On 5 March, the Petrograd Revolutionary Military Committee, the moving spirit behind the October insurrection, was abolished and replaced by an office of the military okrug, in accordance with a new scheme for the territorial organization of the non-combatant army. One of the first measures taken by the new administration was to send a dissolution order to those detachments of the garrison that had belonged to the old army and which had remained in existence until that moment. The Preobrazhenskii regiment refused to disband and clashed with the Red Guard squads which had been sent to disarm it and to arrest its officers.[67] Before surrendering, the soldiers' assembly declared indignantly that 'only' thanks to the soldiers of the Petrograd garrison had the two revolutions of February and October been possible. Evidently, a combination of revolutionary pride and of a more traditional *esprit de corps* had prompted these men to attempt to prevent the revolutionary traditions of the soldiers of 1917 from being finally erased.

Nor was it long before there were signs of discontent and dissatisfaction among the first volunteer units sent to the front in the summer. As was to be expected, common soldiers were disconcerted and embittered by the reappearance of the old officers. The military leaders were well aware that the old command corps, 'discredited by us during the destructive period of the revolution, will not for a long time enjoy any influence over the men'.[68] In August 1918, an important military leader on the northern front reported to the Commissariat for War that the men were demanding that the commands consist of 'a majority of comrades . . . and were expressing distrust of the command staffs'.[69] He therefore suggested that 'the best use for the generals, commanders, and members of the general staffs is not as military leaders but rather as specialist advisers'. According to the same source, who in this way displayed his own bias against official policy, 'this would enable volunteers to adopt a very different attitude towards officers; it would render control over the officers a concrete fact rather than merely being on paper, as it obviously is today with the institution of political commissars'.

Lastly, there was a significant motive for the strained relations that existed between the Republic's organs of government, and the high-ranking officers, who played a decisive role in drawing up the initial measures to reorganize the army. Promulgated on 31 March, the first order relating to the establishment of territorial commissariats made the military leader the greatest authority within their command organs. SNK, on the other hand, issued a decree on 8 April which stated that that role was to be assumed by one of the two political commissars. It therefore seems that even at this early stage there was a difference of attitude regarding the powers that the 'specialists' were to be granted, between Trotskii (who, as Commissar for War, had signed the first order) and the majority of his government colleagues.[70]

3   Reorganization on the battlefield

The first stage: the eastern front

The creation of regular army units, anticipated in the decrees of the spring, was finally sanctioned by the 5th Congress of Soviets in July 1918. The Congress announced the end of 'improvised and haphazard' squads, and proclaimed the centralized leadership of the armed forces. It also ratified the institution of commissars and indicated the need for a regime of discipline, for which both commanders and commissars would be held responsible.[1] In his conclusions, Lenin lent his authority to the first steps taken in that direction, by ridiculing the illusion (which he attributed above all to the Social Revolutionaries) that 'a regular Imperialist Army' could be defeated by 'guerrilla detachments'.[2] Those who advocated the formation of such detachments argued that there were insufficient time and resources to organize a more powerful force.

This view was not unfounded. It was a reflection of the military situation of the new Republic. Throughout the early summer months, the Red Army remained in fact a numerically small body with ill-defined structures, owing to the lack of any elementary coordination of the activity of the various organs of the High Command.[3] Autonomous regional nuclei of armed detachments still existed alongside those trained and sent out by the centre.[4] It was only the 'baptism of fire' constituted by the battle for Kazan' that made it possible and imperative to implement the theoretical principles that the Soviet military authorities had been asserting ever since March. In the Urals, the Red forces once again came up against an adversary superior in both weaponry and training. In John Erickson's telling image, 'on the way to the salvation of realism, Brest–Litovsk was only one half of the story; the eastern front was the other'.[5]

On 26 May 1918, with the seizure of Cheliabinsk by units of the

Czechoslovak expeditionary force, the Civil War turned from latent threat into reality.[6] The Czechoslovaks rapidly gained control over a huge zone, including much of the Volga region, the Urals, and Siberia. Soon their struggle acted as a catalyst on other anti-Bolshevik forces in the area. Under assault from these units, the detachments that the local party committees had hastily improvised and the initial reinforcements dispatched by the centre reproduced the scenes of chaos and panic that had met the German advance on Petrograd at the end of February. On 6 August, the town of Kazan' fell, laying the road to Moscow open to the enemy.

Having set up his headquarters at Sviiansk, Trotskii took energetic action to reinforce and reorganize the defeated Soviet formations that were fleeing towards the west.[7] The chief organizational experience gained at Sviiansk consisted in the relentless adoption of repressive measures against fleeing units and their military and political leaders. The very day he arrived, Trotskii wrote to Lenin that 'there is no hope of maintaining discipline without revolvers'.[8] Special squads were created to contain and halt the disorderly retreat.[9] The revolutionary military tribunal, installed on the War Commissar's armoured train, worked full-out against 'enemy agents', striking 'with still greater severity' at those Soviet citizens guilty of grave shortcomings.[10]

At the same time, huge efforts went into restoring proper troop morale, the needful counterpart to a formidable repressive apparatus. On 15 August, Trotskii informed Lenin that the army had to be prepared for a long war. It had to be turned into 'a popular war' (*populiarnaia*), and imbued with the atmosphere of a grand epic.[11] Trotskii and the High Commands were also struck by the positive effect that a massive injection of well-disciplined communists could have on the units' fighting spirit and capacity to resist. When Kazan' was retaken on 10 September the War Commissar did not hesitate to draw the necessary conclusions.[12] From that point on, the party would be the backbone of the Red Army's organizational skeleton, as well as of its single units.

During the very days when the battle for Kazan' was being decided, the Republic's supreme organs of command were submitted to thorough reorganization. On 2 September, a unified centre of military direction, the 'Revolutionary Military Council of the Republic' (RVSR), was established. Its purpose was to bring all Soviet armed forces, wherever they might be posted, under the same command, and to concentrate in a single organ powers that until then had been spread over a wide variety of bodies responsible for different areas and tasks.[13] The creation of RVSR was accompanied by the granting of sweeping powers to the Supreme Commander. This is what may be gathered both from a memorandum addressed by Egorov to Lenin and Podvoiskii, in which the issue was placed on the agenda for the first time, and from Trotskii's address to the VTsIK session of 2 September.[14] The arguments that Egorov fielded went far beyond the question of unifying and centralizing command. Indeed, they amounted to a plea for a revaluation of the powers and rights of military commanders: 'The necessity and feasibility of a one-man command (*edinolichnoe upravlenie*) for directing warfare, in a word that the military leader must be given full power, has been demonstrated by centuries-long experience.'

Trotskii stated that he was in favour of the institution of both a Commander-in-Chief and a supreme collegial organ, but he stressed that the creation of the latter must not lead to the replacement with communists of the members of the old High Command, most of whom had remained active in the organs of the Commissariat for War:

> Those who clamour the loudest against making use of officers are either people infected with panic or those who are remote from the entire work of the military apparatus or such Party military figures as are themselves worse than any saboteur – such as are incapable of keeping an eye on anything, behave like satraps, spend their time doing nothing and, when they meet with failure, shuffle off the blame on the general staff officers.[15]

The broad powers granted to the Supreme Commander were set out in a regulation (*polozhenie*) promulgated by VTsIK on 30 September. This crucial document also outlined the structure of RVSR and how it should function. In particular, section 5 ran:

> The Supreme Commander shall possess full authority in all strategic-operational matters. The orders of the Supreme Commander shall be validated by the signature of a member of RVSR. Regarding all other matters [i.e. those not of a 'strategic-operational' character], the Supreme Commander enjoys the same rights as other members of a *kollegiia*.[16]

As may be seen, this went further than merely sanctioning the reintroduction of the office of commander of all the armed forces. For the first time in a document of an institutional nature, the rights of an exclusively military leader were established in positive terms rather than merely as a restriction on those of the political commissar. This appears all the more noteworthy if one recalls that at this time and for several years to come the terms 'military leader' or 'exclusively military' were synonyms for 'former Tsarist officer'. These instructions should in fact be compared with the order issued on 13 June by SNK and the People's Commissariat of Internal Affairs (NKVD) regarding the establishment of the 'Revolutionary Military Council for the direction of all operations against the Czechoslovak rebellion.' It was from this order that the Supreme Unified Command of the Republic eventually emerged. This document stipulated that 'All commanders of single front-line units, as well as all commanders of single detachments, are fully and unconditionally subject to the Revolutionary Military Council. All operational orders are issued by the Commander-in-Chief Murav'ev and are validated by one of the commissars.'[17] The powers of the High Command were therefore defined with greater generosity here than in the document that VTsIK approved on 30 September, notwithstanding certain dramatic circumstances. Murav'ev at the beginning of July had committed an act of treason by refusing to continue to fight the Czechoslovaks and by declaring war on the Germans.[18] Nonetheless, the Soviet government determined to reinforce the office of Commander-in-Chief. Clearly, the experience of reconquering Kazan' impressed upon the Soviet authorities more the salutary effect of the reintroduction of traditional military principles and methods on the fighting spirit of the troops, than the dangers dramatically illustrated by the act of treason committed by a high-ranking 'military specialist'. In this context, the resolution passed by the Central Committee on 29 July, 'On the measures for reinforcing the eastern front', clearly did not view the imposition of restrictions on the power of the 'specialists' as the best way of preventing further acts of treason:

> The military commissars do not know how to keep a vigilant check on the officers. The full weight of responsibility for the flight of Makhin, the arbitrary transfer of Murav'ev from Kazan' to Simbirsk, the flight of Boguslavskii etc., fall on the respective commissars. A more vigilant and constant check must be maintained on insufficiently reliable officers. Commissars must be subject to the most severe punishment, even to the firing squad, for the flight or treason of commanders.[19]

The tough line taken here was echoed almost word for word by Trotskii, in an order issued on 18 August (and printed in *Izvestiia*), in which, in the case of the 'unjustified' retreat of a detachment, the commissar should be 'the first' culprit to face the firing squad, the commander 'the second'.[20]

The Central Committee resolution placed almost exclusive stress on the responsibility of the commissar. This is further evidence that, despite the disquieting cases mentioned in the resolution itself, by the beginning of September the Soviet authorities had begun examining the idea of effecting a sharp increase in the powers vested in the 'specialists'.[21] Therefore, as regards the ambiguous regulations governing the functioning of collegial command, the practice of combat seemed to have tipped the scales in favour of the military leaders. In principle, however, RVS authority was not undermined. On the contrary, it was extended to army command level. Adopted by the communists of the 5th and 3rd armies, this move was ratified by the Commissariat for War, in the face of opposition from the front commander.[22]

On 6 September, Vatsetis was appointed Supreme Commander.[23] He had occupied the post of commander of the Czechoslovakian front since 12 July, following the dismissal of Murav'ev.[24] It is worth noting, in view of subsequent developments, that although Trotskii was undoubtedly the principal force behind the entire effort at reorganization, Vatsetis' candidacy was in actual fact first put forward by Lenin, in a communication to Trotskii prior to 20 August.[25] This did not prevent the head of the government from urging Trotskii, in a message written a few days later, not to hesitate to have the newly appointed Supreme Commander shot, should he fail to obtain rapid and decisive successes.[26]

Buoyed up by the brilliant operation that had secured the Red Army's first decisive military triumph, Trotskii now set to work to apply on a vast scale the lesson that he had learnt:

> Now that Kazan' is in our hands and impeccable order prevails in the town, I consider it my duty to reaffirm with renewed force what I reported at the commencement of the operations against Kazan'. The soldiers of the Red Army constitute in their overwhelming majority superb combat material. The failures of the past months took place as a result of the lack of proper organization. Now that the organization has taken shape under fire, our units fight with incomparable valour.[27]

The second stage: the southern front

Following the creation of RVSR and the appointment of a Supreme Commander, the next step in the thorough reorganization of the command machinery was to institute *fronty*, groups of armies deployed in sectors subject to pressure from numerous and seasoned enemy forces.[28] General Sytin, a former high-ranking officer in the Tsarist Army, who had held command posts with the Red forces on the northern front, was now sent to the southern front as commander of all the armies in the area. He established his headquarters in the town of Kozlov.[29] This marked the beginning of an attempt by the centre to organize the scattered Soviet armed forces along the lines that had brought them success at Kazan'. Here, on the eastern front, the new approach immediately found a terrain on which it could take root. This is not to say that there was any shortage in this area of armed formations whose members bowed to no authority other than their own view of short-term military and political expediency.[30] Yet at the same time the eastern front showed promising signs of a development of a diametrically opposed kind. From June onwards, for example, the 1st Army Command had resolutely carried into effect the instructions of the centre, mobilizing ex-officers in the provinces of Penza and Simbirsk. In this undertaking they were supported by the local Soviet, under the leadership of I. M. Vareikis. V. V. Kuibyshev, a former 'left communist' and the party leader in Samara, was a member of the Army Command, together with Tukhachevskii.[31] The situation was not everywhere quite so favourable. Indeed, it was the southern armies that later proved far from eager to accept without a struggle the arrangements recommended by the Supreme Command.

At the time RVSR was engaged in drawing up Sytin's commission, Red formations in the area were still under the command of the 'Council of the military district (*okrug*) of the northern Caucasus', of which Stalin had had himself appointed leader.[32] Dispatched to the south at the end of May as a plenipotentiary agent for supplies to central Russia, on 10 July Stalin had assumed full military and civilian powers. He established his headquarters in the town of Tsaritsyn, an important centre of communications, hard-pressed on several sides by the White forces led by General Krasnov.[33] By taking this action, Stalin had merely given a broad interpretation to the commission that he had received from the government (signed by V. D. Bonch-Bruevich and by Lenin). This stated that not only railways and communications lines but also 'general staffs and detachment commanders' should deem themselves subject to his orders.[34]

The centre sanctioned this *fait accompli*. According to letters sent by Stalin to Lenin, military difficulties in the south were mainly the result of the incompetence of the local professional soldiers. He had presented his self-appointment as a step that the civilian authority had been obliged to take.[35] As we shall see, many of the arguments that Stalin later employed in his polemic with the central military authorities were founded on the conviction that civilian and political power had to be pre-eminent. These assertions have the ring of a persistent and mulish defence of the legitimacy of his original assumption of military responsibilities.

On 22 July, the Red military leaders of Tsaritsyn joined forces to form the 'Military Council of the Northern Caucasus'.[36] In the text they produced, no mention was made of any command body other than the Council, considered as a college, consisting of Stalin, Minin, and Voroshilov. A certain Kovalevskii, an officer whose membership gave this body a semblance of conformity to the instructions of the centre, also signed the document.[37] On 17 September, however, RVSR issued its own instructions regarding the composition of leading front-line organs, which were named 'RVSs', after their counterpart at the centre.[38] The appointed members were Sytin, in his capacity as front commander, Stalin, Minin, and, in the role of Sytin's 'assistant', Voroshilov. On 23 September, after discussing this order, the three members of the previous Council decided to designate themselves the 'RVS of the southern front', even before the new commander had arrived.[39] Stalin, Minin, and Voroshilov thus presented Sytin and the centre with a ready-made command apparatus, through which they would continue to exercise full power over operations in the south.[40]

Sytin arrived at Tsaritsyn on 29 September and immediately had a meeting with the self-appointed RVS. It was on this occasion that the clash that marked the start of the famous episode occurred. The following day, Sytin sent RVSR an account of the interview, in which he set out the reasons for the conflict.[41] An agreement had rapidly been reached on the division of the front into various sectors and on the assignment to them of the various armies operating in the area. They had then moved on to an examination of 'the way the front and the armies should be run'. Stalin and his comrades declared that the 'selection and appointment' of army commanders, as well as 'the conduct of large-scale military operations' was up to the RVS, meaning that such decisions should be taken collectively. Sytin replied that he had a commission from RVSR stating that the appointment of army commanders was his own exclusive responsibility, and that the RVS, meeting as a college, could do no more than reject the names that he put forward. He had also been given 'full powers' (*polnaia vlast'*) over military operations. Mekhonoshin, who attended the meeting, spoke in support of Sytin, insisting that the commission that Sytin had received be 'approved and executed without objections'. At this juncture, the other three members declared that they were:

> 1 – Unable to yield to the conferment of full powers over the conduct of operations to the commander of the southern front.
> 2 – Not of the opinion that the commission presented was an official order that had to be executed by them.

Sytin thus insisted on the adoption of measures similar to those that VTsIK was poised to approve formally in Moscow the following day, and which were designed to strengthen the hand of the Commander-in-Chief. However, Stalin, Minin, and Voroshilov decided to reject not only the appointment of Sytin as commander of the front, but even the very policy that was being hammered out in the leading military and legislative organs of the Republic.

· In these awkward circumstances, exacerbated by the further refusal of the *tsaritsyntsy* to transfer their headquarters to Kozlov, Sytin decided to divide the operational zones in such a way that the defence of the Tsaritsyn sector would remain the responsibility of his adversaries. But the issue of command remained dramatically unresolved.

On 2 October, Stalin, Minin, and Voroshilov sent RVSR a report in which no mention was made of the disagreement that had arisen only a few days earlier.[42] Nonetheless, its contemptuous and accusatory tone (they complained that they had still not received the supplies and arms insistently requested) revealed that by this point they considered themselves to be in open polemic with the Supreme Command. The previous day, 1 October, Mekhonoshin too had sent RVSR a report in which he fully corroborated the version that Sytin had presented. The position assumed by his interlocutors was described in a somewhat muffled form: 'Comrades Stalin, Minin, and Voroshilov advocate the collegial form of front-line leadership as the most opportune at this moment, and collegial decision-taking on all operational questions.'[43]

Thus, in Mekhonoshin's account, the southern RVS made the problem of command more a question of short-term expediency than of principle. Displaying a remarkable faculty for fence-sitting, which may have reflected his uncertainty about the position that his superiors would assume, he pressed for an 'energetic' decision, 'one way or another'.

Perhaps even for the sake of diplomacy, the three men may – judging by this last document – have attempted to give their standpoint a less rigid appearance than that which emerged from Sytin's exposition. As Erickson has noted, the conflict was also presumably affected by the protagonists' differing assessments of the strategic objectives needing to be pursued on the southern front. However, from the evidence of these and subsequent documents, the Tsaritsyn dispute does not, it seems to me, emerge as a chance occurrence. Rather, it was a conscious attempt to resist the re-establishment of an orthodox line of command, a trend that had begun, as we have seen, on the eastern front.

On 2 October, the day on which the southern RVS' complaints and further requests for munitions reached RVSR, the Central Committee approved a resolution calling upon the southern RVS to 'submit unconditionally' to the decisions of RVSR. The resolution noted that the general official position that had to be observed was set out in the *polozhenie*, passed by VTsIK on 30 September. Informing the *tsaritsyntsy* of the Central Committee position, Sverdlov conceded that the party would be willing to rediscuss Sytin's appointment, if Stalin and the others really regarded it as 'damaging'. But he also roundly condemned their insubordination to the orders of the centre.[44] The southern RVS, however, appeared unwilling to change course. On 3 October they wrote to Lenin. Not only did they restate their lack of confidence in Sytin and in his military abilities, they also rejected the compromise that had been offered them. Unleashing a full-scale attack on Trotskii, they outlined what had by this time become an alternative platform to official military policy. However it had all started, a question of principle was now involved:

> To Lenin, 3 October 1918.
> We have received a telegraphed order from Trotskii, a copy of which you should have received along with [our] reply. In our view, this order was written by a man who knows nothing about the southern front, who threatens to place all the affairs of the front and of the revolution in the hands of General Sytin, a man who not only is unneeded at the front, but who does not even merit confidence and is therefore damaging. We certainly cannot approve of the front going to ruin as a result of an untrustworthy general. Trotskii may hide behind talk of discipline, but everyone realizes that Trotskii is not RVSR and that an order from Trotskii is not an order from RVSR.
> Orders are meaningful only if based on a calculation of forces and on a thorough knowledge of the issues. To hand the front over, as Trotskii has done, to a man who does not merit confidence, is

tantamount to trampling on the most elementary image of proletarian discipline and of the interests of the revolution, and of the
front. Accordingly we, as members of the party, categorically declare
that we consider the execution of Trotskii's orders to be criminal, and
his threats unworthy.

The party Central Committee needs to discuss the behaviour of
Trotskii, who abuses very eminent [!] party members to the advantage of traitors among the military specialists and to the detriment of
the interests of the front and of the revolution. It needs to examine
the intolerable fact that Trotskii issues orders on his own (*edinolichnie
prikazy*), which bear absolutely no relation to the conditions of the
place and time, and which threaten the front with disaster. It needs
to review the question of specialist officers who belong to the camp
of non-party counter-revolutionaries.

We therefore propose that the party Central Committee discuss all
these problems at its next sitting, to which, in the case of special
need, we shall send a spokesman.

Central Committee member Stalin
Party member Voroshilov.[45]

RVSR reacted swiftly. From Voronezh, that very same day, Mekhonoshin issued an order regarding the command structure, which
faithfully repeated the passage in the *polozhenie* of 30 September
that had referred to the military commander's 'full independence in
matters of strategy'.[46] Danishevskii, from the eastern front, complained that the southern RVS was refusing to transfer to Kozlov and
that it was concentrating its work on the Tsaritsyn sector at the
expense of others.[47] On 4 October, Trotskii telegraphed Lenin
demanding 'categorically' that Stalin be recalled.[48] He poured scorn
on Voroshilov's military abilities and threatened to have him and
Minin arraigned, arguing that apart from anything else they were
guilty of not keeping him sufficiently well-informed of the course of
military operations. Ignoring the self-appointment of the *tsaritsyntsy*,
RVSR decided to appoint a southern front RVS different from that
previously indicated, the formal constitution of which had been defer-
red owing to the dissension that had erupted on 29 September.[49]
Under an order issued by Trotskii on 5 October, the new command
organ consisted of Sytin, Mekhonoshin, Shliapnikov, and Lazimir.[50]
In an appeal to front-line soldiers on the same day, Trotskii restated
his own confidence in Sytin, 'an expert military leader, who has
proved through his own actions his loyalty to the workers' and
peasants' revolution'.[51] Subsequently, Okulov, one of Trotskii's right-
hand men, was also appointed to the body, with the task of keeping a
close watch above all on the behaviour of Voroshilov.[52] Minin and

Voroshilov were for the time being left at the head of the 10th army, which was defending Tsaritsyn.[53]

Stalin was recalled to Moscow on 6 October and conferred with the party centre. On the 8th he had an interview with Lenin.[54] What was said on that occasion clearly seemed sufficiently reassuring to prompt him that same day to telegraph Minin and Voroshilov informing them of his personal conviction that the matter could be settled 'noiselessly, within the compass of existing formalities'.[55] Accompanied by Sverdlov, he therefore went first to Kozlov and then back to Tsaritsyn. Nonetheless, between the 9th and the 11th, he either resigned or was dismissed from his post on the southern front RVS.[56] On the 19th, he left once again for Moscow, where he arrived on the 22nd.[57] He had an interview on the 23 October with Lenin, who on the same day sent Trotskii a telegram in which he outlined what appeared to be a draft compromise.[58] According to this telegram, Stalin had succeeded in 'persuading' Voroshilov and Minin to 'show the centre full obedience'; indeed, Stalin had even said he would be prepared 'not to impose an ultimatum on the removal of Sytin and Mekhonoshin' from the front and to work alongside them. Stalin also wished to be appointed to RVSR. Lenin asked Trotskii to 'think it over' and to meet Stalin, and he urged him to consider whether it might not be a good idea to 'set aside previous tensions and to work together'. This, he added, was 'something that Stalin greatly desires'. In Lenin's view, it was necessary 'to create all the conditions for undertaking work in cooperation with Stalin'.

But Stalin was not restored to his previous functions at Tsaritsyn. Something in the attempt at mediation that the party centre and Lenin in person had made failed to work. A meeting between Trotskii and Voroshilov at Tsaritsyn, according to reports from both parties, led to a new clash,[59] and the one between Stalin and Trotskii, apart from a fleeting reference that Trotskii made to it many years later,[60] remains shrouded in the most impenetrable obscurity. It appears nonetheless that Stalin became a member of RVSR, an appointment which, considering his removal from the theatre of operations, smacks of a concession made to console him.[61] Trotskii later asserted that he had been in favour of Stalin's appointment to the highest military organ, on the grounds that it would give him the chance to express 'in an open manner' his opposition to the military policy, if that was what was really entailed.[62]

What Trotskii apparently considered to be damaging was not so much the launching of a debate at top party level, as the possibility that it might take on a broad public dimension. On this point the Central Committee was in agreement with him.[63] On 20 October, he wrote to Sverdlov of his fears that the Tsaritsyn delegation might want 'to raise the question of reviewing military policy' at the imminent Congress of Soviets, and cautiously sounded out Sverdlov to discover whether or not the party leadership would allow them to do so.[64] On 1 November, he again asked Lenin whether it was really necessary that he attend the Congress.[65] In the same message, he informed Lenin of his intention to keep Voroshilov at the southern front, but to prise him away from Minin. Minin he termed 'a serious obstacle', who would in any case have to be sent to work elsewhere. On the 3rd, Lenin wrote back with an assurance that 'military policy is not down and will not be put down on the agenda of the Congress', while at the same time dispensing with Trotskii's obligation to attend.[66] Trotskii did, however, address the Congress of Soviets on 9 November, but as far as the southern front was concerned, he confined himself to noting that 'the centralization of all military functions continues to encounter difficulties'.[67]

The last days of October thus witnessed a certain relaxation in tension, a prelude to the final solution to the conflict. Voroshilov, who, as Trotskii now acknowledged, possessed 'a pretty firm hand',[68] was left for a while longer at Tsaritsyn. Sytin was recalled to the central offices of RVSR in mid-November,[69] and Minin was transferred to the Commissariat of the Interior, the following month.[70] Even if the compromise that Lenin had suggested to Trotskii was not reached, the settlement of the dispute appeared even-handed. Trotskii had won, but he had either not wished, or not been allowed, to win hands down: the careers of his adversaries remained virtually unharmed. Probably too, Trotskii had to employ considerable energies to moderate the reactions of the Supreme Command, especially Vatsetis. Indeed, as late as mid-October Vatsetis addressed Voroshilov in the severest of terms, accusing him, with his acts of indiscipline, of bringing about the 'catastrophic situation' at Tsaritsyn.[71] But the significance of what had occurred went far beyond the fate of those individuals who had been directly involved. The Tsaritsyn dispute was the first signal that an opposition to official military policy could be set in motion and that it might find benevolent and authoritative listeners at the party centre. Moreover, a precedent for raising the thorny issue of employing 'military specialists' had now been clearly set.

It still remains hard to understand why the leaders of the southern front decided to risk a head-on clash with the centre. This is especially true in Stalin's case. Reconsidering the Tsaritsyn affair many years later, Trotskii recognized with bitterness that Stalin had conducted himself 'in a way that enabled him to withdraw at any moment', implying that there were no reasons of principle underlying the disagreement between himself and his great future antagonist.[72] The way was thus thrown open to interpretations of the Tsaritsyn conflict in terms of personal rivalry.[73]

However, some of Stalin's writings of summer and autumn 1918 provide interesting evidence of his view of the issue of 'military specialists'. In a message to Lenin, sent on 7 July, he accused them of superficiality and inertia ('bunglers!').[74] Yet, in an interview in *Izvestiia*, he stressed enthusiastically that they were witnessing 'the appearance of a new corps of commanders consisting of officers promoted from the ranks who have practical experience in the imperialist war, and also enjoy the full confidence of the Red Army men'.[75] Similar statements appeared in the two interviews, published on 30 October, that Stalin gave at the end of the Tsaritsyn affair.[76] In the first of these, he did not hesitate to assert that this type of 'Red officer', after undergoing an initial 'baptism at the front', 'was now well-versed in the art of warfare'. As is well-known, Voroshilov belonged to this category. From this viewpoint, the Tsaritsyn dispute takes on the appearance of a clash between the psychology and methods of self-taught soldiers and the psychology and methods of academically trained high-ranking officers. The reorganization of the Supreme Command at the same time evidently brought with it a restoration of values and of a hierarchy that the novices in the art of warfare could not but view with suspicion and apprehension. Stalin had no doubts as to which side he should take. He presented himself as the intransigent supporter of the cadres that the revolution had promoted from the ranks and of the revolutionary principle of collegial command (which gave them the room for action that they required). Yet he avoided displaying any excessive propensity for patterns of military organization different from those officially advocated.

The cases of Voroshilov and Minin were somewhat different. During this period, Voroshilov appears in fact to have favoured a military system that would 'change the army from its roots up',[77] and a few years later he rushed to join the ranks of those who supported innovatory military 'doctrines'. The case of Minin was even more significant. From mid-1918 on, he led the Tsaritsyn Soviet as its

president, and it was the political features of the Bolshevik party in
that city that accounted for his membership of the trio.[78] In February
1918, Tsaritsyn had been a centre of lively opposition to the signing of
the Brest–Litovsk treaty: the close link between opposition to the
treaty and opposition to 'military specialists' is demonstrated both by
the case of the 'left communists', and by that of the Social Revolutionaries.[79] The Tsaritsyn party did not fail to support the rebel group
when it found itself at loggerheads with Moscow. On 7 October, after
Stalin's departure from the town, a meeting of responsible Bolsheviks
decided to propose to the Central Committee 'a review of the expediency of tolerating generals in our ranks, and the convening of a
congress to reexamine and assess the policy of the centre', adding,
with characteristic democratic concern: 'especially since, at a time of
revolution, we consider such a long interval between one congress
and another to be wholly absurd'.[80]

For his part, Trotskii was not in the least degree willing to make
allowances for extenuating circumstances. Throughout the entire
Civil War period, the behaviour of the troops in that vast area stretch-
ing from the Ukraine to the northern Caucasus constituted for him the
clearest and most eloquent example of the difficulties that the construction of a centralized and disciplined army had to face in revolutionary Russia. For a long time, he continued to refer to the apparently chaotic situation on this front as to a phenomenon that
amounted to much more than just a series of local episodes. In
organizational terms, the southern front had lived through 'exactly
the same stages as the eastern front, but on a broader scale'. It was
only much later that the southern front would overcome endemic
resistance to order, to discipline, and to cohesion.[81] In December
1918, dismissing the first public attacks on official military policy,
Trotskii denounced his adversaries' attempt to portray the clash
between the military authorities and their critics in terms of principles, as if the dispute were between those who supported the
supremacy of the party over the 'specialists' and those who advocated
the reverse.[82] He also pointed out that it was not only regular officers
who were unpopular with the southern troops, so too were the
'political specialists', the commissars. Contrary to what the local Bolsheviks would have people believe, local party work was in fact in an
appalling mess. They were simply trying to use the professional
soldiers as scapegoats, to make them take the blame for setbacks that
had really resulted from their own ignorance. In general, Trotskii
viewed the south and the Ukraine as areas where 'centrifugal ten-

dencies' assumed the most extreme forms. Traditional local autono-
mist feeling, coupled with the anarchism characteristic of Red Ukrainian soldiers (as also of the formations of the famous Makhno) made
common cause, in Trotskii's view, with a more general resistance to
centralized military authority, widespread in the Red Army.[83] The
results of this could be seen in the 'arbitrary actions' of the commanders and commissars, in the custom of consulting with soldiers before
issuing orders, and in the adoption of the disorderly methods of
'partisan' warfare.[84]

The reorganization of the party

Once opposition on the southern front had been temporarily
overcome, the central military authorities set to work to complete and
perfect the command structure at its various levels. Towards mid-
December 1918, the *polozheniia*, setting out the functions of the
Supreme Commander of the armed forces of the Republic, and those
of the front and army commanders, were published.[85] The power that
the document of 30 September vested in the highest-ranking leader of
the operational army was confirmed and specified. He had the right to
'appoint, transfer, and remove from the offices they occupy' any
member of the command corps. RVSR, meeting as a college, could,
however, modify appointments, if it felt this to be necessary. In the
case of the appointment of front and army commanders, the Supreme
Commander submitted his own candidates to the approval of the
president of RVSR. All the other appointments and orders of the
Supreme Commander had to be validated by a member of RVSR, to
whom that body would confer this specific function. He might refuse
to sign, in which case the orders would not be valid.

The powers of the front commander were more limited. Like the
other members of the front RVS, he too was appointed by RVSR. The
civilian members of the RVS (the commissars) had the right to 'limit
[his] powers' providing this did not undermine his authority in the
sphere of operations or in that of the 'composition of the entire staff in
service at the front'. The commission given to Sytin at the end of
September thus received statutory confirmation. The commander
could be removed from his post only on the order of the Supreme
Commander or of RVSR, although, 'in exceptional cases, not allowing
of delay', the decision might be taken by the commissars of the front
RVS. The powers of front army commanders were similarly defined.
It was, however, stipulated that every measure regarding the

economic life, public order, civilian institutions, or which concerned in any way the population in the area in which the army was quartered, was the responsibility of the RVS as a college.

At the same time as these important regulations were issued, an impressive plan was launched to replace the party organization network in the units with a radically new type of apparatus, thought to be better-suited to the centralized and unified structure that the Red Army was by this time clearly assuming.

In the late summer and autumn of 1918, huge groups of Bolsheviks were dispatched to the front-line and to the immediate rear to form the backbone of the first rather shapeless regular units. In its resolution of 29 July, the Central Committee emphasized that the formation of party cells in every detachment was one of the measures most urgently needed to strengthen the front. A great many of the communists from the Urals were incorporated into the Red Army, while compulsorily conscripted soldiers began to be enrolled in the party. Soon there arose the issue, until then evaded, of the organizational form that the party should assume. At first, party structure within the army took shape in accordance with two distinct but often co-existing principles: from below, faithfully copying the 'democratic centralist' pattern, as it applied to civilian and territorial party organizations; and from above, with the introduction of original patterns of organization, created by the political commissars attached to the higher command staffs.[86]

In the first case, a pyramid of bodies sprang into being. These included company, or more often, regimental committees (elected by the cells), and divisional and army committees (elected by party-member conferences at higher unit level). In July, a largely elective front party committee had been created on the eastern front. It had informed the Central Committee of its existence and requested formal recognition and the establishment of regular relations.[87] A few weeks later, the party committee of the 4th army of the same front was also able to inform the Central Committee of work that it had already carried out.[88] This particular committee was elective and deemed itself the unit's highest organ of power. It had created links with the territorial party organization (in Saratov) and had even appointed someone to take charge of the organization of 'poor peasants' committees' in the area where the army was quartered. The report also spoke of a strong tendency among the troops to found party cells, and to dismantle committees of the old type (those, the document specified, 'that are non-party, elective, the kind of military committees that existed under Kerenskii'). One military unit, which later drafted regulations regarding its own internal life, possessed a similar network of party cells and committees. Its supreme organ, the army committee, 'direct[ed] all the political and organizational work of all the party organizations in the detachments, and of all the communist groups attached to the various army commands'.[89] Where specifically named in these statutes, the office of commissar appeared to be subordinated to decisions taken by the collective and elective organs. And it was these organs that assumed the task of carrying out checks on the officers. They regarded the commissars as their own executive organs.[90] Nor was this type of political structure confined to recently constituted or hastily mustered formations. The Latvian division (of which Vatsetis had remained colonel until July 1918), having gone over *en masse* to the Red Army, was sustained by a rigid hierarchy of party committees.[91] Party life in the detachments of the military *okrug* of the northern Caucasus was governed by an *instruktsiia*. This provided for a structure intended to work closely with territorial bodies, and which bore a strong resemblance to the Central Committee *voenka*, that had been active both before and immediately after the October revolution.[92] Commissars were selected according to a system that gave party members, even civilian ones, a considerable opportunity to influence the outcome. Party cells selected their 'best comrades' to stand alongside existing commissars, and it was from among these candidates that the supreme military committee and the local town committee agreed to pick the new commissars.

With or without a party structure modelled on the territorial civilian pattern, the first 'political departments' (*politotdely*) began to appear. These were created on the initiative of communists attached to superior unit command staffs. There still remains some doubt as to their precise origin. One encounters them for the first time at the eastern front military commands and at the front RVSs.[93] The name was presumably borrowed from the political offices that the Provisional Government had attached to the central military organs, and which had been maintained after the October revolution. To begin with, their duties must have been complementary to those of the higher-ranking commissars, members of the RVSs, of which they were an emanation. Even though they were able to avail themselves of a special apparatus of agitators and propagandists, their work was at the outset mainly of an administrative and clerical kind: the assignment of lower-ranking commissars to the various detachments, the circulation of newspapers, the drafting of background reports on officers. Even more than the commissars themselves, they lacked in their early days the character of party organs: this they only acquired later on. As their very title suggests, the political departments came into being as one of various branches or offices into which the general staffs of the units were divided. In September, a political department, defining itself as 'an organic part of the general staff', was already in existence in the 3rd army on the eastern front, and already had under its command other bodies of the same name in the divisions and brigades of the unit.[94]

Often a political department evolved in competition with an elective party organization. But in other cases it was the only organ of agitation and political organization active among the soldiers, and it would then turn to the Central Committee for instructions on how to set about building the party in the detachments.[95] Once a political department was solidly established and had begun to extend its control over the regimental commissars and party collectives, its work tended in its turn to follow the directives of its superior organ. It would show resentment and impatience with the territorial organizations' continual insistence that they were entitled to interfere and to have a say in political work among the troops.[96]

Organization and leadership of the party from above had the obvious advantage of eliminating the various different sources of authority in the detachments and units, by centralizing them and restricting opportunities for abuse. Moreover, all the different elements of the army's own structure met in the political department. The commissars, party organs, tribunals, organs of repression and information, command staffs, were all subordinated to the requirements of the higher collegial commands. Through the political departments, higher-ranking commanders could at any moment obtain both an overall picture of troop morale and any information they required relating to service personnel. Through the same channel, directives could be rapidly and efficiently issued for the preparation of operations complementary to those of a purely operational character.

The political leaders of the eastern front – the front that was the best organized and the best staffed with party members – soon took note of these possibilities. From 21 to 24 October 1918, a 'meeting of those in charge of front political departments' was held in Simbirsk. Although there is no clear evidence of this, it is likely that the diffusion of these new organs had at this date already received a strong boost from the reorganization carried out in Kazan'. But it was in the decisions taken at Simbirsk that the political departments were designated as the organs that were to take control of party organization in the field army.[97] The creation of new cells was made conditional on the 'approval' of the political departments, and the relationship with the territorial organizations in the front-line was thus overturned: the political departments were now empowered to 'utilize [them]' for military purposes.[98] In areas liberated from the Whites, the political departments were to 'cooperate' with the local Bolsheviks on the construction of the new organs of Soviet power.

As for elective party committees, the Simbirsk meeting came out clearly against the 'parallel existence' of two sources of political authority, and recommended the 'merger' of the committees with the political departments (from the divisional level up). Affirming their own direct subordination to the party's Central Committee, the political leaders of the eastern front called for the creation of a 'specific central political organization' from which they could take orders. The main speech, delivered by I. N. Smirnov, proposed that the commissars' *biuro* be merged with the RVSR political department.[99]

The other speeches to the meeting demonstrated that the political departments already possessed a very complex internal structure. At divisional level, for example, there existed numerous subsections: 'for agitation-organization, publishing, information, press, agitation, transportation, and theatre work'.[100] Certain types of military work, such as counter-espionage, infiltration of the enemy rear, and military court hearings, were not yet under the control of the political department: for the time being, these tasks were left up to the organs of the 'military control' (*voennyi kontrol*). The meeting, however, voted in favour of the front and army political departments assuming responsibility for establishing relations with party organizations in the enemy rear.

On 25 October 1918, the day following the conclusion of the Simbirsk conference, the Central Committee of the RKP(b) reached a decision which, in institutional terms, seemed distinctly subversive. Kept secret for a long time, it has only recently been published:

> Organizations, committees, party groups, and party institutions with full rights (*polnopravye*) must not be formed within the army.
>
> The job of party militants is confined to: the formation of cells of party members, which must register their current members; agitation, and the distribution of printed material; raising the general level of the Red Army to communist consciousness; activity designed to heighten the spirit of discipline; contributions to the concrete realization of all directives issued by the various central institutions.[101]

Despite its terseness, the significance of this document is apparent. The leading elective organs of the party in the units and detachments were deprived of their authority, and were prohibited from reforming. In their turn, the party cells underwent a radical change in character: they were turned from decision-making political bodies into organs devoted to propaganda and to the execution of central instructions and commands. In importance, the task of reinforcing discipline was placed alongside that of spreading political awareness. On 22 October, Lenin had announced to VTsIK that a 'turn in the tide' had been reached in the determination of workers mobilized for front-line service to stand and fight.[102] In the Red Army, 'a new discipline' was being created, 'not the discipline of the rod and of the landowner, but the discipline of the Soviets', established by the cells, the workers, and the commissars. These words were not intended to provide an exact account of what was happening among the troops at the front. But they signalled nonetheless the beginning of a new stage in the military commitment of the party both at the centre and at the periphery.

The connection between the Central Committee resolution and the decisions reached at Simbirsk is immediately striking, even if one considers their timing alone. The Central Committee, however, remained deliberately silent on one essential question: which organs would from that moment on direct party work in the army, in the place of the committees. The embarrassment that Soviet military historians have demonstrated on this point is at least on a par with that displayed by the Central Committee itself in its elliptical resolution.[103] Over a month was to pass before RVSR officially declared that the political departments were the new organs of party leadership in the army, and over two before the Central Committee notified the party's military cells of the same decision.

In the meantime, at the highest levels of the military and political hierarchy, enveloped in the strictest confidentiality, there began a period of discussion and experimentation. A Central Committee *Instruktsiia* of 27 November requested information from the territorial party committees regarding the whole set of questions that the resolution of 25 October had failed to regularize: 'relations between the political departments, the communist cells, and the command staffs'.[104] A report drafted for the party centre by the eastern front political department painted a plausible picture of the transition period.[105] It proudly proclaimed that, with the birth of the political departments, the first step had been taken to 'put an end to "handicraft'' (*kustar'nichestvo*) practices in the field of political activity'. Political departments had by this time been set up in all the eastern front armies. Consisting of '12 to 15 comrades', they were divided into subsections. In the path of the complete centralization of political work there stood, however, considerable difficulties, which were created by 'detachments which turn directly to the president of the Central Committee or to that of SNK on military issues or for supplies'. 'In political work', furthermore, this 'happen[ed] constantly'. This attitude of 'separatism' (as the report put it), which certain armies displayed, obviously reflected the federative structure that had existed until a short time before, and which recalled various features of *komitetchina*.

At the beginning of December 1918, the reorganization of the party got under way on the southern front. On 3 December, a 'meeting of those in charge of the political departments' of all the southern front armies was opened.[106] Also taking part in the meeting were 'representatives of the VBVK', including its leader, Iurenev, and I. N. Smirnov, who, as we have seen, had been one of the promoters of the new system on the eastern front.[107] The meeting approved an *instruktsiia* to the political departments, which constituted the first wide-ranging and detailed set of regulations of the new army regime.[108]

It was laid down that commissars (though not those of the army and front RVSs) would be 'subordinate' to the political department at the corresponding level, which would 'unify' their activity, 'direct' their work, and keep a 'check' on them. The political department also had to 'keep relations between commissars and commanders under close surveillance', making sure that commissars did not meddle in 'operational matters'. Political departments were to direct the cells, arrange 'educational' activities among the troops, keep a watch over the soldiers' morale and their state of discipline, and make sure that there was a general respect for discipline among soldiers, commissars, and commanders. An entire chapter was devoted to the 'regulation of the army's relations with the local population': in this area, the new organs were entrusted a prominent role.

The differences that may be noted between what we know of the political departments on the eastern front and those of the southern front during this initial phase seem to reflect the different problems facing the two fronts. In the east, the political department seems above all to have been keen to eliminate competition from the strong and prestigious committees. In the south, stress appears to have been placed first and foremost on the need to create 'out of nothing' both party cells and commissars' corps. According to the most complete Soviet study available, no genuine party structure had previously existed among the armies of the southern front: it began to emerge at the end of 1918, thanks mainly to the initiative of the new organs.[109]

From a report to the Central Committee written by Efremov, the head of the southern front political department, we know that at the meeting of 3 December he presented for discussion a draft *instruktsiia* for the cells. To this, the participants at the meeting made a number of alterations.[110] The most important of these had to do with the principle of the election of the party's leading bodies. Efremov, rather sceptical about the political departments' ability to assert themselves as anything more than the 'commissars' technical executives', had envisaged the institution at divisional level of a party *biuro* (a representative organ with powers narrower than those of the committees). Only at a later stage would these *biuro* be able to 'turn themselves into' political departments. The scheme was rejected. And, against Efremov's advice, a move was accepted which introduced party conferences at divisional, brigade, and army level. (Efremov feared that this might give 'party demagogues' too much space.) Responsibility for approving admissions and expulsions was completely removed from territorial organizations and cells, and was entrusted to the divisional political departments. Lastly, it was laid down that the cells, the executive role of which was again emphasized, would no longer be entitled to manage their own organs of press, except through the commissar.

For the southern front, these regulations marked a sharp change of course. Writing to the centre in mid-January, the leader of the 8th army political department, for example, stated that the start of serious organizational work had led at first to the proposal to 'create an agile party organization, with elected centres led by an army committee'.[111] But then the wind had shifted, especially after the meeting of 3 December, and support had grown for the formation of political departments instead of committees. Needless to say, this zealous official declared that he himself had been 'a resolute supporter of this standpoint' from the start, averring that 'in our army, there have never been any *biuro* or elected committees'. Informing the Central Committee that a new division from Moscow had recently joined the army, he expressed the conviction that it would be expedient 'to reorganize' its party structure which was, naturally, of the elective kind.

On 5 December, RVSR sanctioned for the first time the existence of

the political departments, entrusting them with 'political and edu-
cational-cultural (*kul'turno-prosvetitel'nyi*) work' in the field army and
in the front-line area.[112] The system of political departments was to be
managed by the VBVK, which had to operate 'in the closest possible
contact with, and in accordance with the directives of, the Central
Committee of the RKP(b)'. An RVSR order of 25 December also
sanctioned the existence of divisional political departments, which
had not been covered by the previous order.[113]

On 19 December, the Central Committee decided to set up a commission to 'examine immediately and to ratify' the southern front
instruktsiia, and to draft a text valid for the entire Red Army.[114] The
commission consisted of Sverdlov, I. N. Smirnov, Iurenev, and
Stalin. On 10 January 1919, in response to urgent appeals from the
VBVK leaders,[115] *Pravda* at last published the '*Instruktsiia* to the party
cells of the Red Army forces and of the rear', which the Central
Committee had approved on 5 January.[116] This was the first communist soldiers' statute that the Central Committee had passed since the
one in July 1917 regarding its own 'military organization'. In its
essentials, the document of 5 January remained valid throughout the
entire course of the Civil War and beyond.

The commission confirmed most of the articles of the *instruktsiia* of 3
December. The new text also included a series of norms relating to
party cells in rear units, which had not been considered in previous
similar documents. It was now stipulated that the admission and
expulsion of new members could be left up to the territorial committees. Furthermore, while it was specified that cells at the front were
linked to the Central Committee only by way of the political departments' hierarchy, in the rear it was the ordinary party organizations
that provided the link. One important difference, however, was that
the document of 5 January no longer made any mention of party
'sympathizers'. This probably signalled the gradual abandonment of
this institution not only in the army but in general recruiting policy
also.[117] Moreover, in the new regulations, the cells lost their right to
complain to the command staff about commissars if they proved to be
'incompetent or unable to perform their job', an eventuality which
was simply no longer contemplated. Providing the army political
department agreed, 'divisional *biuro*, consisting of representatives of
regimental cells', could be formed. As a rule, however, elected bodies
of limited power but of markedly executive character could only be set
up by regimental cells (company cells as yet not having been instituted). The rule whereby 'no party member, regardless of his rank,

may lay claim to any superiority' over his comrades was the only concession to party ethics, by virtue of which all members automatically possessed equal rights. But the commissar retained the power to grant or withhold approval from 'any resolutions passed by the general meeting that have any relation whatsoever to life at the front'. Significantly, no formal definition was provided of the political department as a party organ, even if the description of its relations with the party cells left little doubt on this score. The commissar, on the other hand, acquired a clearer status than previously: 'the plenipotentiary appointed by the superior party institution, in charge of party activity at the front'. The Central Committee hesitated to give even this office a fully political character, but nonetheless contradicted the non-party definition that had previously been given by Trotskii.

In December, the command structure that had been outlined in March was finally sanctioned. Each RVS was to consist of at least one commander and two commissars. The number of commissars could be increased according to need. The command staff, the revolutionary military tribunal, the military control, and the unit political department were all subordinated to the RVSs. Furthermore, the revolutionary military tribunal, the military control, and the unit political department all fell under the direct control not of the commander but of one of the RVS (army or front) commissars.[118]

It was therefore in December 1918 that the essential features of Red Army structure took shape. The Central Committee resolution of 26 November, 'On the strengthening of the southern front', gives an idea of the climate under which the organizational shake-up was planned and carried out. The soldiers were enjoined to follow the lead given by 'the military successes of December on the eastern front'. The beginning of 'Red terror' between the troops and their leaders was proclaimed: 'The Central Committee categorically commands all party members – commissars, commanders, and soldiers – to make every possible effort to bring about a much-needed and swift upturn in the morale and conduct of the detachments ... no violation of discipline or of the revolutionary military spirit may remain unpunished.'[119]

The *instruktsiia* of 5 January to the cells marked the start of a process that Trotskii later labelled (in a way that was only apparently paradoxical) 'the militarization of the Red Army'.[120] As far as the party in particular was concerned, this process comprised two logically distinct but in fact inseparable stages.

First, the internal democracy of the party was drastically curtailed, inasmuch as it could no longer elect its own leading organs, nor schedule or plan the forms that its activity was to take. Secondly, the party's grassroots organs, the party cells, were barred from taking operational and administrative decisions. The right to intervene, in certain circumstances and within certain limits, in the directives of the command staff hierarchy was rigidly confined to a parallel party hierarchy (commissars, political departments), which was coming to replace the elected organs of leadership. At the same time, this party hierarchy was beginning to occupy a position, however hard it may be to find a precise label for it, within the service structure of the Red Army. Incorporated in this new machinery, party cells, in the last instance, came under the control of the units' general staff and RVSs. Political work inevitably turned into 'a weapon of a particular kind';[121] party discipline, into 'an auxiliary means of military discipline';[122] the allocation of communists to particular detachments in order to stiffen their fighting spirit, an organizational factor of interest above all to 'military specialists'. In these circumstances, it became hard to distinguish between party organs (especially those that were not subject to election) and state military administrative bodies, especially within the collegial command organs. Nonetheless, the most striking aspect of party reorganization during this initial period was the way in which the party increasingly acquired the characteristics of a state apparatus.

The spirit of the document of 5 January and some of the reasons for its publication were soberly expounded in the press by Gusev, an important political leader on the eastern front, and a man who had been a staunch supporter of party reorganization in the army ever since the Central Committee resolution of 25 October.[123] In Gusev's view, wartime conditions made it necessary to adopt uncustomary organizational methods in an operating army, different from those applicable to the normal life of civilian party organizations. Arrival at the front was always a traumatic experience for communists:

> They arrive with a ready-made pattern of party organization in the rear and take some time to familiarize themselves with conditions peculiar to the front. All the more since the 'normal' organization in the rear – committees, *raiony*, *podraiony*, cells – has been set up with a considerable degree of harmony and naturalness in the division, regiment, battalion, and company.

Combat technique, however, was incompatible with the ordinary structure of the party. It presupposed the dual criterion of the 'greatest possible centralization at an operational level' and the 'greatest possible free creativity of each tactical unit (and also of individual fighters)':

> These 'laws' make themselves felt even in party organizations at the front. Here, the question of a centralized . . . democratic organization does not even arise. The centralized leadership in the army committee of the work of the regiment and company organizations, the principle of election, the congresses, the sending of delegates: all that turns into pure sham, remains on paper but is not carried out in practice.

The fact that combat activity centred on the smallest military unit, the company, would by itself have led to a rebirth of the 'craft approach' to political work, if the company had not been under the rigid control of its commanding units, a control enforced by the commissar hierarchy. 'Communism is communism', pronounced Gusev, 'but *à la guerre comme à la guerre*':

> Once again the division of duties needs to be structured according to the military pattern: directives, instructions, orders that must be carried out 'infalliby' and 'immediately'. The political department, appointed from above (and not the army committee, which is elected) issues orders through the political commissars of the division, brigade, regiment, whom it appoints, to the company cells . . .
>
> In a word, party organization in the army remodels itself along military lines and, as with the army, democratic centralism is replaced by military centralism; instead of elections, appointment; in the place of resolutions, orders and reports. Party organizations lose all their 'political rights'. They retain one right alone, the right to work, to carry out 'without exception' the orders and instructions of the political department . . . Our army suffers not from an excess but from a lack of discipline. It is in this direction that we shall have to turn our energies for a long time to come.

Another document, *The front-line communist's vademecum*, which circulated widely on all the fronts, also came out at the end of December. Originally written by the southern front political departments for the armies under their command, it received Lenin's personal approval on 29 December. The principles that should inspire the behaviour of the party member in the combat army were illustrated in a direct and exhortative manner. The *vademecum* therefore provided a reasonable example of how the new organizational system should work at the party grassroots.

The text began with an appeal to the communist soldier to resign himself to an 'obscure task', and not to expect 'commissar-type' responsibility merely because he was a party member. It went on:

The communist must be a model of discipline, submission, and the ability to execute orders. If your commander gives an order, validated by the commissar, your duty is to submit to it without question, however senseless it may seem to you. You occupy a small sector, you don't know what is happening on the whole of the front; to you, as to any other single individual, any order may seem senseless. Don't let yourself be taken in by such a state of mind: it could ruin both yourself and the cause you serve. Don't question an order, don't discuss whether it is good or bad, because that will set others discussing it too, and so, instead of carrying out an action, all you will have is disputes and disorders, while the enemy is doing his perfidious deeds. Your duty is to be the first to execute each order and to call on all the soldiers of your detachment to do the same.

Therefore, should 'irregularities and omissions' appear in the life of the detachment, the communist should act with a sense of responsibility and take the appropriate precautions:

If, in your opinion, the commissar is guilty of some omission, write to the political department at divisional, army, or front level. Your communist party comrades perform a responsible job in the political department. If you make a timely statement, it will be followed up at once. But don't interfere personally with orders. If everybody starts handing out orders, even greater disorder will result...

Remember that no meeting may be convened at the front on your own initiative. The detachment commissar alone is empowered to convene a meeting, even that of the party cell. If in your opinion the commissar has banned a meeting without sufficient justification, lodge a complaint to the political department: an enquiry will be set up forthwith...

Communist comrade! Wherever you are, whatever job of responsibility you are doing, you must be in the most conspicuous position. You must enter battle first, and emerge last.[124]

It was a new ethics, in part a spontaneous creation and in part imposed on the firing-line, founded on discipline, anonymity, and the undisputed recognition of all higher authority. At the end of January, Lenin stated that the Red Army was being formed 'by working in a new way, by political propaganda at the front, by organizing the communists of our army, by the self-sacrificing organization and struggle of the best of the workers'.[125] But ever since the beginning of November, the discontent of party cadres, at the front as in the rear, had begun to become apparent.

4   Opposition within the party

The birth of mass opposition

The determination to expand substantially the ranks of the armed forces was solemnly declared during the very days in which the Central Committee was deciding how to settle the Tsaritsyn conflict, and at a time when crucial steps were being taken to reorganize the army's command structure. On 3 October 1918, in a famous letter to VTsIK, Lenin set the target of creating an army of three million men.[1] Following the Central Committee session of 25 October, party and Soviet newspapers opened their pages to documents, declarations, and letters relating to military life, both in the rear and at the front. An editorial note that appeared in *Pravda* on 10 November invited readers to send in articles and other material on the topic: 'What needs to be done to create a large Soviet army?' Information was also requested about what was happening at a local level and about any 'defects' that might have come to people's notice. Soon afterwards, the newspapers *Bednota* and *Kommunar* made a similar appeal to their readers to send in news about life in the units, including accounts of any 'abuse of power committed by responsible officials'.[2] Letters and news poured in. By the first few weeks of 1919, this issue had become a topic for general debate in the lead-up to the 8th Party Congress.

Despite the constructive slant that *Pravda* had intended to give to public discussion of the issue, many of the articles and resolutions submitted by local party organs on military questions were outspoken in their criticism. Often, after a declaration of 'overall' support for official policy, there followed an attack on certain of its essential features. Criticisms tended to follow a number of easily identifiable lines.

First of all, the existence of widespread opposition to the creation of a 'regular' army was confirmed, and the conviction that a 'militia' system should be adopted as early as possible was emphasized. This issue was raised with even greater frequency in the second half of February, just before the Congress opened. The precongressional Serpukhov town Party Conference endorsed a form of 'out-of-barracks' training, even if it accepted the arguments that the main speaker Okulov marshalled to justify steps taken in the opposite direction.[3] In the view of the meeting, a territorial militia would act as a guarantee of the 'proletarian class' character of the armed forces, inasmuch as it would be based prevalently in the factories. The Viatka *guberniia* Party Conference devoted closer attention to this particular point. It proposed that detachments trained in barracks at the rear should no longer be sent to the front, and that they should be replaced by formations trained locally under the Vsevobuch system.[4] Conference expressed its concern over the strain under which the 'class character' of the army was being put, owing to the influx of 'broad strata of the non-revolutionary peasant element', brought about by compulsory generalized mobilization. No attempt was made to conceal the fear that the existing military regime might lead to the formation of a dangerous separate body, of an army 'state within a state'. The party was accordingly put on its guard against 'copying the military mechanism of the bourgeois state in the construction of the Red Army'. It was in this spirit that a rapprochement and a 'genuine collaboration' between 'civilian and military organizations' was proposed. Perhaps with one eye on such a mood, *Pravda* on 1 March reported the creation of a 'Workers' Military Inspection' within the existing Supreme Military Inspection, which had been functioning since spring 1918 under the leadership of Podvoiskii.

The prospect of a regular army also worried party militants for various more tangible reasons. Many of the articles and resolutions aimed their critical comments at the system of pay differentials based on rank. At the beginning of December, one particularly dramatic letter from the front, which then led to a spate of others, read:

> why do brigade, division, and regimental commanders receive a high and undemocratic salary, and then come preaching equality and brotherhood to us? Why are the superior commanders well-clothed, washed, and kept nice and warm, while we freeze? Why doesn't the Supreme Command come and visit us and see for itself what our needs are?[5]

Preobrazhenskii called for the suppression of money privileges – not only those enjoyed by military commanders but in general those of all specialists and employees of the Soviet state. He linked hostility to this aspect of military policy with his broader battle against salary differentials in the industrial and administrative fields.[6] In his view, the disparity in the treatment that soldiers and their commanders received did so much harm to relations between them that many commanders would willingly forego their salaries just to be able to 'maintain old comradely relations' with the men. The Ufa conference, in March, called for 'the elimination of the privileges that make commanders a special caste', the abolition of compulsory saluting, of badges, and of ranks.[7] The communists of one front-line army pointed to the high salaries that officers received as evidence of a rebirth of 'militarism' in Soviet Russia.[8] 'The infiltration of the old militarist spirit' among the troops was also sometimes highlighted in relation to phenomena of a different kind. 'Frequent cases of provocative conduct by soldiers, – involving in particular people holding responsible positions within the Red Army – directed both at the civilian population and at their subordinates within the army's own institutions', were, for instance, denounced in November by the military commissar of the *guberniia* of Saratov.[9] Episodes of this kind, prompting the bitter comment that 'a great many members of the Red Army have forgotten or have never wished to grasp the fact that the Red Army merely represents the organization of the proletariat in its rebellion against capital and in favour of communism', seemed to confirm the fears of those who worried that the regular army would set itself up as a body distinct from Soviet power.

In a very hard-hitting article at the beginning of January, Iaroslavskii portrayed the phenomenon of mass desertions from the Red Army as irrefutable proof that its structure was at fault: 'We must acknowledge that the desertions from the Red Army put us to shame.'[10] They were attributed to a number of different causes. The most important was the socially spurious character of the army, the lack of strictly working-class recruiting. The soldiers' 'education' also revealed considerable weaknesses: the workers and peasants who had been mobilized did not in fact know 'why there is a war, why we are fighting, why the problems that history has posed cannot be settled peacefully'. But, facing his adversaries on their own ground, Iaroslavskii asserted that the 'military training' the troops received was inadequate, and the organizational shortcomings affecting supplies were conspicuous. The composition of the officers' corps, with its inclusion of former Tsarist personnel, further demoralized the soldiers: 'those who commit treason damage the cause of the Red

Army among the mass of the soldiers'. These points had been carefully selected to suggest that there was a basic continuity between the structure of the Imperial Army and that of the Red Army. Then as now, soldiers deserted because the military apparatus seemed alien and oppressive to them.

A lot of articles and letters focussed on the relationship that was evolving at the front between the commanders and the commissars. The Moscow party committee showed particular interest by deciding in November to create a regular network of its own correspondents in front-line units. By maintaining close contact with the political organs of the city *raiony*, they would be able to file reports on everything that occurred.[11] In many cases, they had joined nuclei of communists who had been mobilized in their town organizations. One of these sent *Pravda* an interview with a commissar who reassured readers as to the vast extent of the powers and authority that communists possessed in their capacity as commissars: their job was by no means 'simply negative . . . , a matter of standing guard over the officers'.[12] But the party meeting of the Basmennyi *raion*, after listening to the speech made by its own front-line correspondent, passed a more pessimistic resolution. The position of political commissars was judged to be 'extremely abnormal', inasmuch as they had been prevented from 'exercising their influence' among the troops. More generally, 'the experience of collaboration between communists and military specialists in the form in which it has so far been practised has turned out to be a total failure, because the behaviour of most military specialists clearly and consistently amounts to sabotage, treason, and counter-revolution'.[13]

It was accordingly necessary 'to limit' the rights of the specialists, and, conversely, 'to define precisely the area of activity of the political commissars, giving them broad rights to supervise the military specialists'. A few days later, even the meeting of the Bolsheviks of the Gorodskii *raion* of Moscow requested 'a reexamination of the *polozhenie* of the political commissars and the commanders in such a way as to give the political commissars more sweeping rights'.[14] On the eve of Congress, the Penza Party Conference accepted the principle of employing former Tsarist officers, but expressed its uneasiness by warning explicitly that 'military specialists must be used in our class interests and we must make sure that it is not they who use us'.[15] These worries did not bedevil communists in the rear alone, they were also clearly voiced in confidential reports compiled by front-line political organs. A member of the southern front RVS, for example, informed the front political department of the 'humiliating position of political commissars, and the command's contemptuous, negligent attitude towards them' in the 13th army. This denunciation was accompanied by the familiar request for the 'publication of a specific order confirming and requiring the recognition of political commissars by all commanders, with an indication of their rights and duties and, in particular, the regulation that the order of the commander is not by itself legally binding without the signature of the commissar'.[16]

There was also considerable dissatisfaction about the way in which those aspirants to the post of 'Red officer', who did not issue from the old command corps, were apparently being educated. This feeling was very significant, as it called into question the political will of the top military authorities. For example, it was reported with great alarm that at the end of 1918 three-quarters of those taking part in training courses for commanders had never been active in a political or social organization (a Soviet, trade-union, or soldiers' committee).[17] More stress, it was felt, should be laid on pupils' 'political literacy lessons', rather than on exclusively technical and military training: 'It is not to be tolerated that the centre of gravity of the political catechism of the majority of those taking part in the course is situated in the realm of apolitical considerations or of a vague sympathy for the Bolshevik-communists.'

In the 24 December issue of *Pravda*, a certain 'S. L-ii' championed a method of training new commanders based not only on 'outward bearing' and on combat preparation (features which, in the writer's view, were proper to Imperial *junkers*), but above all on 'the revolutionary communist spirit'. 'Our Soviet authorities' paid this aspect far too little heed. Distinguishing between the two groups that staffed the Soviet High Commands – the cadres of the Imperial Army, and the party militants and leaders attached to the Commissariat of War – the writer of the article commented with delicate irony:

> Evidently 'military specialists' consider 'the political literacy course' a question of secondary importance. But to this point I should like to draw the attention not of those members of the administration who are 'young communists' but 'old specialists' but rather to those who show themselves to be 'old communists' but 'young specialists'. They must now take the political education of the Red officers in hand.
>
> If, comrades, the old-communists-but-young-specialists of military matters are so busy in their new field of specialization that they cannot devote themselves to the political education of our officers' corps, then they must appeal to the highest Soviet institutions to

create some commission or other for this purpose. With a war under way, unleashed upon us by world imperialism, there is no time to be lost in drawing up an ideal course of training for Red officers.

At the beginning of January, Mgeladze, a member of the editorial committee of *Kommunar*, expressed similar misgivings: 'Our fighters must not be simply courageous. They must also be good communists'.[18] Distrust in the old officers turned into a kind of fundamentalism the moment the issue of new cadres was raised. To the authorities all that mattered was that they were men 'taken from the ranks of the workers and peasants'.[19]

The consolidation of the system of political departments at the front made communists – especially those in combat detachments – very uneasy. The party cell attached to the eastern front High Command questioned the subordination of the party cells to the new bodies. It affected reluctance to turn the issue into a question 'of principle', and stressed that it did not wish to rediscuss 'the essentials' of the Central Committee's decisions.[20] They confined themselves to complaining about the lack of guidelines on relations between cells and political departments, apart from purely restrictive ones that laid down the tasks and rights of the cells. The cell proposed a solution 'from a wholly practical viewpoint', whereby the political department would organize 'joint meetings' with the 'party collective', so that every communist 'can be informed about the problems and can make his/her own contribution to their resolution'. Under the guise of desiring to 'facilitate' the work of the new leading bodies, these party members in fact expressed the determination to play their part in the management of political work and to have a say in other important decisions.

The increasing rigidity of vertical party structures did not fuel a mood of demoralization among communists alone. At the end of December, the Party Conference of a southern front unit observed 'a sad phenomenon: communists are regarded not as comrades but as representatives of the powers that be (*ne kak na tovarishchi a na vlast'*)'.[21] The Conference significantly declared that the divisional political department should be simply 'the party committee of the entire division', or 'the central committee of the cells of the detachments of the division'. Phenomena of the type reported here must by this time have become very frequent if the Central Committee considered it expedient to explain to the southern front communists that 'belonging to the party does not bring with it any privileges'.[22] In that specific instance, the Central Committee condemned the special rules which the communists of a particular unit had arbitrarily laid down, designed to shield them from liability to arrest by the military authorities: a kind of impunity for party members.

There is no doubt that behind some of the demands for a restoration of broad internal democracy and of the independent initiative of party cells there lay a regret that communist soldiers had lost their position of pre-eminence over their fellow-soldiers. The setting up of rigid machinery did not of course give everyone the chance to reacquire a position of prestige and authority. Faced with the real possibility of being deprived of their power, ordinary party members would sometimes react by identifying psychologically with the mass of soldiers, and at other times simply by calling for a return to previous conditions. For example, the explicit instruction contained in the statute written by the Petrograd party committee for detachments stationed in the region, whereby 'the party collective is not an organ of state power',[23] was extremely ambiguous. It could be interpreted as a proud assertion of autonomy and of non-submission to the powers of the state, or alternatively as an acknowledgement that, in the new mass army, members of cells were, in the eyes of the military authorities, ordinary citizens just like non-members. The non-state and non-administrative nature of the party could be invoked both by those who supported the party's subordination to military organs, and by those who opposed it. This, as we shall see, is what actually happened quite frequently. Here, for example, is how a military policy-maker like Smilga interpreted this state of mind among the rank-and-file in January 1919. The revolt was regarded above all as the work of members who had joined the party after the February and October revolutions: 'To them, our party is not first and foremost the party of the proletariat that has carried out the social revolution, but the party of government: "we did not shed our blood in October to submit now to people who have no party".'[24]

In other ways, however, the reinforcement and the rigid codification of political work in the detachments no doubt made it more important to belong to the party. Even within the new framework laid down in the autumn, rank-and-file communists continued to play a vital role, however limited and subordinate. The new disciplinary course marked in fact a break with the vaguely revolutionary spirit which until then had prevailed in the detachments. It was also a consequence of the deep rifts and intense struggle which, with the spread of the Civil War, increasingly divided the parties and the socialist currents. At the beginning of March 1919, a northern front agitator informed the press on how reorganization was progressing. The party strongly encouraged the formation of cells, the circulation of 'scientific and political literature', and was committed to 'working hard' to provide the mass of soldiers with elementary education and indoctrination.[25] However, certain extremely cohesive sailors' contingents, permeated with an *esprit de corps* that was peculiar to them, viewed all this with little sympathy. As our source complained:

> They have their collectives, and convene their own meetings. But how they carry out their work, and how thorough this is, it is hard to say. It is as if they were armour-plated against the rest of the world: 'We are the most revolutionary: what is it they want to teach us?!' But how many communists are there in the battalion? Four, and a hundred sympathizers.

Following the publication on 10 January of the *instruktsiia* to the Red Army cells, the party organizations' misgivings grew both in number and in strength. We shall limit ourselves to examining the positions assumed by two important territorial organizations, in Nizhnyi Novgorod and in Moscow. At the beginning of March, a survey in *Pravda* gave an account of an article by 'Comrade L. M. K-ch' (very probably, Lazar Moseevich Kaganovich, then at the beginning of his career at the head of the Nizhnyi party), published by the newspaper *Nizhegorodskaia Kommuna*.[26] Kaganovich defended both the decision to build a regular army and the policy of employing military specialists. He reproached critics of the official line with having a 'craft' conception of the problems involved in the construction of the armed forces. Yet Kaganovich too had several serious objections to make. The impending Congress should, he thought, clearly state that 'excessive rights, an excessive faith' in military specialists was harmful. The way to ensure control over former officers and prevent treason was not through 'criticism', through 'words'. Having distanced himself from the most extreme opposition wing in the party, Kaganovich stated that 'the creation of the uniform conditions in which treason cannot possibly occur' necessitated 'some alteration to the *instruktsiia* that [had] been approved by the Central Committee regarding the party's military cells':

> In compliance with these regulations, the autonomy of these cells is reduced and they come under the commissar's power. Of course, these cells must not direct operations, they must not interfere in the technical side of the specialists' or military authorities' orders. Yet it is necessary to allow them to undertake political supervision, to exercise a political influence, of which at present they are often

deprived. There is no need to condemn the firmness and determination of the policy of the military administration, which does not even shrink from sending party members to the firing squad.[27] Only those who fail to appreciate the nature of wartime circumstances can criticize this. Of course, excesses do occur. Much is decided on personal grounds, there are distortions, and the Party Congress must put a stop to these things.

This position was hard to label. The question of the rights of party cells was seemingly the only major and explicit point of disagreement with a policy that was otherwise accepted in even its most ruthless aspects. One of the essential prerequisites for 'control' over 'military specialists' was thought to be a greater freedom of action for grass roots organizations. Kaganovich appeared to be denouncing the contradiction inherent in a line which, by restricting internal democracy and the ability of military cells to take action, risked making counter-revolutionary coup attempts that much easier. Hence the need for a broader sharing-out of supervisory duties beyond the commissars' corps. But this passage was of interest in other ways too. It foreshadowed the way in which Stalin and his supporters, at a later period, presented the line adopted by the 8th Congress on the military question, distinguishing between a line that was essentially just, and the 'personal' slants to which it was nonetheless subjected – those that is of Trotskii and of his closest collaborators.[28] But did Kaganovich's article in fact express personal and original views or should it be seen instead as an attempt to mediate between conflicting political tendencies within the Nizhnyi party? I would favour the first view, above all since Kaganovich had gained first-hand experience of military organization during the first stage of Red Army construction.[29] He may, however, have yielded to local pressure to criticize military policy from a more radical standpoint. A few days before the article was published in the central party organ, a meeting of party activists had been held in Nizhnyi, during which the majority of speakers had denounced the 'bureaucratization' and 'separateness' of the general staffs: the danger, in other words, that the commands might take the law into their own hands, ceasing to take orders from the party.[30]

The Nizhnyi Party Conference adopted the line that its secretary had proclaimed. The instruction 'not to go too far' in granting powers to officers was repeated word for word in the theses approved.[31] Point 10 of these theses echoed the criticism voiced by Kaganovich. Although it reinforced the cautious tone in which the criticism had originally been expressed, it finished by formulating a request in more precise terms:

> It is necessary to broaden the frontiers of the independent activity of party cells in the field of political work, in the detachments in the rear and in situations where there is no fighting. The cells need to be given more space and independence. In view of this it has to be recognized that the Central Committee *instruktsiia* to the military cells stands in need of correction.

In Moscow, the evolution of the platform that the party organization presented to Congress can be followed in greater detail. In the first half of December the Moscow committee passed a resolution regarding the problems of 'the deployment of *rabotniki* at the front'.[32] The principal concern of the resolution was that the said field of work had been taken away from the party and entrusted to chance or to the arbitrary power of exclusively military authorities. The committee demanded that the apparatus for deploying cadres be 'concentrated in the Central Committee', that every communist in a position of responsibility at the front be 'fully subject to the party', and that every appointment of a communist military leader be 'brought to the knowledge of the local party organizer'. The resolution went on:

> Owing to the friction that has been observed, on the one hand, between the commissars and the commanders and, on the other, between the political departments and the party cells, the Moscow committee of the RKP(b) feels it necessary to call on the Central Committee to draw up appropriate regulations to fix relations between the said institutions.

As is now clear, the call to provide a formal definition of their respective spheres of authority cloaked a reservation in principle regarding the position of the party's various organs and representatives vis-à-vis the military organs. This call went hand in hand with the claim that collective and statutory requirements should take precedence over those of individual leaders.

In the second half of December, the conference of the *raion* organizations confirmed that control over the officers, 'divested of its clerical character and concentrated in the hands of the commissars', should be 'rigidly' specified.[33] The reference to clerical work has to be interpreted, I believe, as a declaration of hostility towards the political departments. In March there appeared at last the Moscow *guberniia* Congress resolution on military policy. It is not hard to hear in this the echo of the positions of former 'left communists', many of whom belonged to the Moscow organization. The aim that obsessed the Muscovite militants was 'the planned and systematic conquest of the command apparatus' of the Red Army:

> 1 – The creation of a cadre of communist officers trained in military-political schools.
>
> 2 – The broadest possible representation in the command corps of communist soldiers who have assimilated practical military technique.
>
> 3 – The limitation and restriction of the rights of so-called 'military specialists', by means of a precise indication of their sphere of activity, and the subordination of this activity to diligent and many-sided supervision by communist soldiers.
>
> 4 – The annulment of all decisions and directives containing threats of repression that destroy independent revolutionary activity undertaken by communist soldiers in the interests of the proletariat.[34]
>
> 5 – The maintenance of normal party rights for party organizations in the army.[35]

The only point that the Muscovites did not consider it necessary formally to contest was the 'regular' form that the armed forces were gradually assuming. But another point in the resolution revealed the fear that the local civilian authorities might be crushed by the arbitrary directives from military commands present in the same area. The power to proclaim a state of war in a given area therefore had to be removed from 'RVSs, individual general staffs, and individual commissars' and vested solely in the executive committees of the Soviets and VTsIK. In this case too, the promulgation of a specific set of regulations was requested.

Obviously, not all of the articles and materials published in *Pravda* during this period contained criticisms and complaints. Other than the article by Gusev, which we have already examined, one could point to that of Khodorovskii, in which the author rejoiced that the 'craft stage, of partisan methods, of voluntary service' had been superseded, acknowledging with satisfaction that by that time the Red Army was 'hard to distinguish from the other European armies'.[36] The employment of 'military specialists' was warmly defended, all the more since the success of the mobilization of former officers revealed a general shift to the left of the country's 'petty bourgeoisie'. Khodorovskii – without, of course, naming any names – held up for the approbation of the forthcoming Congress the progress of reorganization on the southern front arguing that it provided a valid model for all the armed forces of the Republic. And yet even this staunch supporter of the official line questioned several negative aspects of military construction. Compulsory conscription had induced local commissars to allow themselves to be guided by the 'desire to provide more men' and consequently to disregard the 'class character' of the contingents, letting in peasants and kulaks indiscriminately. Secondly, the commissars and the party organizations in the army had given frequent signs of weakness and had allegedly displayed their inability to keep the officers under control. Both criticisms were compatible with the strenuous defence of official policy, since they seemed to lay all the blame on individual leaders for whatever went wrong. The conclusion that Khodorovskii drew from the second criticism in particular was not that relations between the party and military organs should be altered but that the party should be enabled to carry out its work more effectively, by enhancing the quality of its cadres. Of the interventions in favour of the official line, the Riazan' Party Conference was probably the only one that resolutely declared that it was 'in unanimous agreement with the theses that Comrade Trotskii expounded'[37] for discussion at the 8th Congress.[38] The Simbirsk Party Conference, even though numerous criticisms had been expressed during the course of the debate, was guided by Gusev towards a more lukewarm resolution 'to adopt and support the policy of the centre'.[39]

The long discussion of winter 1918–19 thus highlighted the contrasting moods and sharply differing political positions existing within the party.[40] These positions varied not only in their degree of radicalism, but also in the ways in which they were formulated: sometimes expressed in cautious and measured resolutions, at other times voiced in a dramatic and spontaneous form. Was there a common pattern? The preceding sections have perhaps already suggested one answer. To the points that have already been mentioned, one obviously needs to add the deep and widespread popular feeling of instinctive opposition to the constriction and inequality that was becoming increasingly pronounced with the formation of a solid military structure. I would suggest, however, that the decisive factor in arousing broad opposition within the party to military policy was the reaction of those militants recruited just before and during the October revolution to the radical changes that the Bolshevik military organization underwent on the front over the decisive months of autumn–winter 1918. On the eve of Congress, the mood of communist soldiers was solemnly expressed in the resolution of an army conference, the serial number of which *Pravda*, as was usual, for

reasons of security did not give.[41] This resolution listed almost all the
reasons for discontent so far recorded: support for the 'militia' as
against resurgent 'militarism'; the demand for the abolition of material
privileges reserved for commanders; the intransigent defence of the
'class-based' army; even a reference to the peculiarities of 'revolutionary warfare', which the centre was allegedly incapable of grasping.
But the most significant passage came when the cadres of the underground and revolutionary periods recalled with pride their own
tradition of revolutionary organization:

> Conference expresses even greater disagreement over the problem
> of the attitude to be adopted towards mobilized communists within
> the army, and on this point is inclined to regard the position of the
> Central Committee as mistaken even from the point of view of
> principle.
> Conference considers it to be its duty to state that on this issue it
> has noted a radical retreat by our party from the old line of Bol-
> shevism, as it had taken shape over years of revolutionary struggle.
> We, Bolshevik communists, have always been happy in every situ-
> ation to consider our party as something completely self-sufficient
> (*samodovleiushchee*). But today, members of our party, called upon to
> serve in the army, are deemed to be at the exclusive disposal of the
> military organizations. There is no sense in this whatsoever, because
> there is nothing more binding and nothing of which one may be
> more certain, than the spirit of discipline of a true communist –
> inasmuch as it is party discipline – and every other type of order has
> less effect on party members than a couple of bare lines of a rec-
> ommendation from the party Central Committee.
> Hence, for RKP members in the army, conditions must be created
> that ensure their independence in political and social work, and in
> these fields there must be no subordination to military authorities. In
> their work, RKP members take orders from a purely party organi-
> zation only and not from institutions such as the *biuro* of commissars
> or the RVS.

In line with the convictions expressed here, the resolution concluded with the commitment to 'do their work as before', and the
statement that 'there must be no violation of established discipline'.
But military discipline, external and mechanical, was still contrasted
with party discipline, which sprang from a profound adherence to the
value of the voluntary organization and its programme.
The markedly elitist tradition of the Bolshevik party provided
further psychological and emotive strength to an element, characteristic of moments of great and violent social transformation, which has
been pinpointed and studied, for example, in the Jacobin *armées*

révolutionnaires: 'The revolutionary does not respect hierarchy, but if his officer appears to behave in the manner of a "revolutionary patriot" he obeys his orders spontaneously. But at no time does the revolutionary renounce his rights as a *sectionnaire*'.[42]

Even when those who belonged to the Moscow or Petrograd parties were sent to the front, this peculiar concept of discipline would click into action, leading above all to the rejection of a body, the regular army, which they felt to be at loggerheads with their own revolutionary experience. Communists in the Red Army still laid the greatest stress on the assertion of their own 'rights', mixed with a feeling that they constituted 'a privileged political elite',[43] 'une armée des purs':[44] each individual cadre seemed to form an image of the armed revolution as an army for 'a minority of militants'.[45] The Bolsheviks of the first regular formations within the Red Army typically displayed an intransigent class-based attitude, a desire for freedom of action and the tendency to intrude in technical and military matters. And these positions amounted to open struggle against the notion of a mass army, the hierarchical organization of functions, and the militarization of the party. In the background, less articulate politically but certainly more violent and menacing, stood a human mass, tired and impatient, which its leaders were attempting to mould into the form of an army.

The military administration on trial

From the picture of scrappy discontent portrayed in the pages of *Pravda*, there emerged the somewhat clearer outline of a number of interventions. These set out not only to criticize official policy in terms more or less 'of principle' but to place in difficulty one part of the leading group within the party, the men at the head of the military administration, and their 'specialist' collaborators. It was not therefore merely a matter of rumours of discontent or of an attempt to promote a frank internal debate: an orchestrated initiative was being launched by one section of party cadres against another. The people behind this offensive had their own sources of information, and friends in high places who could protect them. The Central Committee had chosen not to muffle the criticisms that had emerged in public discussions. It reacted firmly, however, when it became clear that an attempt was being made to mount a campaign designed first to discredit the highest military leaders and then to reverse major aspects of official policy.

On 29 November 1918, *Pravda* carried an article by Sorin – a member of the Moscow party committee – with the seemingly inoffensive title 'Commanders and Commissars in the Field Army'. The editors introduced the article with a note which, having left to the author full 'responsibility for the accuracy of the facts he reports', called upon readers to 'express their views on the issues raised'. Given the content of the article, however, this declaration lost all its studied candour.

Sorin referred to a 'scheme regarding the relations between the RVSs and army commanders' which the press had not published and which, judging by the account he gave of it, must have been very different from the set of regulations later approved by SNK on 5 December and published on the 12th.[46] According to Sorin, the scheme resolved the problem posed by these relations 'in a form absolutely unacceptable to proletarian communism'. He therefore denounced the attempt by the authors of the scheme (unidentified but presumably high-ranking 'military specialists') to have it implemented 'without any debate whatever'. Sorin, on the other hand, proposed that it be publicly discussed without any attempt being made to silence the disagreements 'of principle' that it might occasion. The idea that Sorin cherished of the RVSs was that of 'plenipotentiary' bodies which enjoyed full military powers only when they met together as a college. This clashed with several sections of the 'scheme', whereby military commanders were to be granted extraordinary powers beyond anything that the commissars could possibly supervise. The first 'extremely hazardous' provision involved the adoption by army commanders, 'on their own authority', of discretionary measures 'in exceptional circumstances', the only limitation being that the front command had to be informed. This raised the question: 'Won't people who have nothing in common with communism possess their own personal opinion as to what is exceptional, an opinion formed even prior to the revolution?'

Moreover, since orders in any case required the counter-signature of a commissar (as was confirmed elsewhere in the 'scheme'), this commissar would necessarily be turned into 'a figurehead obliged to sign even against his own will all the commanders' directives'. And yet, had not the powers that were vested in army commanders to inflict punishment been directly copied from some 'set of regulations from Tsar Nicholas' academy'? In Sorin's view, it was no accident that the War Commissariat's press organ featured at that very time an article by an old 'specialist' who called for the abolition of the RVSs. But the range of criticisms broadened still further: 'To the same order of ideas belong those methods, practised in the army, which, while designed to create "iron discipline", in fact undermine and weaken the revolutionary activity of communist soldiers.'

In particular, Sorin stated that the RVSR order making commissars 'answerable with their lives' for the performance by their men of superior orders had a demoralizing effect on those responsible for political matters within the Red Army: 'An order of this kind, alongside guidelines such as: "inquiries must not take too much time and disciplinary offences must be punished immediately", can at times literally strike terror into party comrades.'

At this juncture, Sorin dealt a decisive blow. He cited an episode that would often be referred to throughout the course of the polemic that followed, until the 8th Congress: the so-called 'Panteleev case'. Panteleev, a commissar, had had to face the firing squad because of the flight of his detachment before the enemy, during the fateful days of the battle for Kazan'.[47] Sorin presented this episode as evidence that 'the fear of being shot merely for formal reasons means that commissars are reduced to mere tools in the hands of the commander, instruments which he uses for addressing his subordinates'. Responsibility for the execution of Panteleev was laid squarely at Trotskii's door. The article concluded with a call to battle, an exhortation to 'struggle with determination against the attempt to enfeeble the dictatorship of the communist party in the army, to depersonalize communist soldiers, to tire out their revolutionary endeavour'.

At the time, Trotskii ignored the accusation and made no reply. But if one of Sorin's aims was to weaken the position of the orthodox military experts within the Commissariat for War by making sensational revelations, in the days that followed some measure of success was attained. If one compares the numbering of the sections in the 'scheme' referred to in the article with the text of the regulations that were actually approved, it is evident that the latter was perhaps a reworking of the former. In the regulations that were approved, the clause that dealt with the extraordinary powers to which army commanders might resort in situations of exceptional gravity did not appear. The section on punishments also demonstrated a certain formal affinity with that cited by Sorin, although the actual measures introduced were milder than those he gave as examples. It may be that Sorin had cunningly referred to one of the various schemes under discussion in November in the competent circles: perhaps to the strictest and most traditional one, counting on the fact that it would in any case be rejected and altered by SNK. However, on 12 December, when the final set of regulations was published, what the outside world saw was that the attempt made by certain leaders of the Commissariat for War to reimpose the old disciplinary rules and to vest excessive power in high-ranking former Tsarist officers had for the time being been foiled, thanks to the courageous intervention of a vigilant (and well-informed!) party militant.

This apparent success did nothing to allay the feeling of resentment for which Sorin had appointed himself spokesman. The scandal of communists 'executed by firing squad' at the front failed to explode, and the party centre gave no indication that it had noticed the allegations against Trotskii. But the communists of the Basmennyi *raion* of Moscow included in their resolution of 19 December a point that sounded like a conscious statement of support for the arguments put forward by Sorin:

> The meeting expresses its indignation at the hierarchical relations existing between party militants at the front. The acts of repression against eminent party militants that have recently taken place are considered absolutely unacceptable. The meeting insists that the issue of the situation at the front be discussed at the conference of the *raiony*.[48]

On 25 December, a further polemical broadside again raised several of the issues that Sorin had touched on. It also introduced a number of new points that had not before been broached in the columns of *Pravda*. The party paper published an article by A. Kamenskii, bearing the elliptical but significant title: 'The Time Has Now Come'. As became clearer in the article, the suggestion was that a certain type of military policy should now be scrapped. As Kamenskii explained, he had been personally involved in the legendary retreat effected in the previous summer by the Red troops fighting in the Ukraine between Lugansk and Tsaritsyn.[49] The withdrawal had been led by Voroshilov, and Kamenskii had become his commissar at the head of the 10th army. Kamenskii acknowledged Sorin's merit for having initiated an urgently needed discussion, and took his cue from the grave questions that Sorin had raised. His purpose was to defend the military policy that the defenders of Tsaritsyn had implemented and which had been censured (albeit not publicly) by RVSR and the Central Committee at the beginning of October.

Kamenskii's article centred on the axiom that there were 'tactical approaches and considerations of military strategy' that were typical of the 'policy of the revolutionaries', inasmuch as they were distinct from traditional military doctrine. Manifest even at the very beginning of the Civil War in the Ukraine, and later at Tsaritsyn, these aspects would, he thought, remain valid in the future, should there be an 'imperialist war ... on a world scale' against the Soviet Republic; a war that would inevitably be accompanied by the outbreak of civil wars throughout the entire world. In Kamenskii's view, it was the RVSs of the Red units – the collegial bodies (and here Kamenskii returned to one of the issues that Sorin had raised) that some people apparently wished to abolish, in order to re-establish the 'military specialist's' one-man command – that were to thank for the innovations that the Russian Civil War had made in military art. The RVSs had shown themselves to be valuable and original centres for the formulation of a political approach to military operations, that complemented the purely technical outlook. If power had been vested wholly in the commanders, this vital contribution could not have been made. But Kamenskii went much further than Sorin and attacked the section in the regulations relating to the powers of the army commander (a point which had in fact been retained in the version approved by SNK) where it was laid down that RVS members did not have the right to intervene in the commander's field of operations. A principle that had been asserted by the political and military authorities of the Republic ever since March 1918, and which even Sorin had taken care not to contest explicitly, had thus been called into question. According to Kamenskii: 'In our language this means that the commander is an autocrat and that the members of the military council, in this case, will be appending a purely decorative signature (to the commander's orders).'

There followed a passage that provided a good illustration of the viewpoint and leanings of the Tsaritsyn group at the time of its clash with RVSR:

> They have often pointed out to us that the conduct of a war is so very complicated that without military specialists we would not be able to cope. Military specialization certainly is complicated, but it is also an integral part of something more general and delicate, the running of the whole state machine; and we have already displayed the courage to run the state by carrying out the October revolution.
>
> There are a great many deformities but from the start we have refrained from appealing to 'princes from across the sea';[50] on the contrary, we have chased them away because they were carrying out sabotage.
>
> And, in one way or another, we have coped.

It was the kind of reasoning that would enrage a man of the cultural and political level-headedness of Trotskii, and yet it had both force and above all an irrefutable basis in truth. Kamenskii felt that the justice of this position had been given clear expression at Tsaritsyn:

> But even if we admit that the military specialists are the air without which the existence of a socialist army would be unthinkable ... What good have they done? None whatever. And what harm? A vast amount! They were on the point of giving up Tsaritsyn and they would have succeeded in doing so had we not removed them in the nick of time.

Up to this point, the article had merely alluded to Stalin, Minin, and Voroshilov's self-appointment, during the course of the summer, as the highest political and military authorities in the Northern Caucasus. But at this point there appeared a more precise reference to the events of September–October and to the clash with General Sytin. Bearing in mind that the episode had not yet been touched on in the press and that there had probably been a general agreement to keep it secret, Kamenskii's words were extremely audacious. What is more, the said events were set within an apocalyptic context of disintegration and repression:

> Without our agreement and against our protests they 'set up' in our area a group of gentlemen whom they had removed from another front and who carried on their damaging work here ... Comrade Okulov, a member of the southern front RVS, has declared that during the fighting near Orenburg twenty officers fled from his staff. Another seven fled from the eastern front, and, because of this, two of our best comrades, Zalutskii and Bekoi, were nearly sent before the firing squad, as happened to Panteleev, and only the firmness of comrade Smilga saved their lives.

The grave accusation that Sorin had made was not only confirmed, it was broadened to assume proportions that were the more threatening for being vague: 'About commissars. Having burnt our hands on more than one occasion with undeserved accusations and even with the shooting of our best comrades, we must be prudent. Commissars are our political representatives and it is intolerable that they be shot without trial'.[51]

In the space of a few blistering lines, the entire military policy that the party had followed over the previous few months was dramatically denounced, by re-evoking a number of telling cases: the decision of RVSR to appoint Sytin to the southern front, transferring him from the northern one; the Panteleev case; the risks that other commissars had run on the eastern front (further information made public thanks to the zeal of Kamenskii); and lastly, even Okulov, the man that Trotskii had appointed to work alongside Voroshilov, in order to prevent Voroshilov from creating too much havoc, recognized that a great many of the officers in fact had turned out to be traitors! Doubtless not everything can have appeared clear to the ordinary readers of the party press, but to the initiates nothing could have been more eloquent. It was a forceful and well-aimed blow. This time Trotskii could not ignore the attack.

On the same day that Kamenskii's article appeared, he sent a letter to the Central Committee demanding that they issue a public statement on the matter. He rejected the allegation that he had had Panteleev summarily executed and gave his own detailed version of the affair: responsibility was to be attributed to the military tribunal that had issued the sentence in accordance with perfectly regular procedure. Trotskii asked the Central Committee:

> To declare publicly as to whether the policy of the War Department is my personal policy, the policy of some group or other, or the policy of our party as a whole.
> To establish for the benefit of the public opinion of the entire party the grounds which Comrade Kamenskii had for his assertion about the shooting of the best comrades without trial.
> To point out to the editorial board of the central organ the total inadmissibility of printing articles which consist not of a criticism of the general policy of the department or even of the party, but of direct damning charges of actions of the most damning character (the shooting of the best comrades without trial) without making preliminary enquiries of party establishments as to the grounds for these charges, since it is clear that were there any sort of grounds for these charges, the matter could not rest at party polemic, but must become a subject for judicial investigation by the party.[52]

The way in which point (1) is formulated leads one to suppose that Trotskii was not totally sure of the attitude that the Central Committee would take. He was really asking not only for a statement censuring the behaviour of the Central Committee newspaper but also a vote of confidence in himself. What had started as a mere newspaper incident thus provided the cue for the highest political body to reconsider its approach to military policy. A resolution on behalf of the Central Committee was drafted that same day, 25 December, and published on the 26th.[53] This document has been almost totally ignored in reconstructions of these events, both in the USSR and in the West.[54] As far as I have been able to discover, no explicit reference was made to this resolution during the course of the political struggle over the military question during the months following its adoption. It therefore seems useful to quote the entire text here:

> In view of the fact that in some sectors of the party the opinion is widespread that the policy of the War Ministry is the product of the personal conceptions of individual comrades or of a single group, and given that statements to this effect manage to reach the pages of the party press, the Central Committee of the RKP deems it necessary to repeat in the most categorical form possible that the most responsible and expert militants in the party need not have the slightest doubt that the policy of the War Ministry, like that of every other administration or institution, is implemented in precise accordance with general directives issued by the party through its Central Committee and under its direct control.
>
> The fact that responsibility for the policy of the War Ministry is shared by the entire party as a body naturally does not remove the right of individual members to subject this policy to criticism, either of principle or of a purely practical nature. But in the opinion of the Central Committee, it is absolutely intolerable that some comrades, and indeed some organs of the press, attempt to mislead the public opinion within the party as well as that of broad social groups by presenting the policy of the War Ministry as the outcome of the improvisation of single individuals or groups. In particular, the Central Committee cannot but take notice of the article by A. Kamenskii in no. 281 of *Pravda*, which contains, perhaps without its author being fully aware of the fact, extremely serious accusations against comrades who hold positions at the head of the War Ministry. The article does not speak only of the granting of excessive rights to 'counter-revolutionaries of Nicholas' academy' but also of the 'shooting of our best comrades without a trial'. If any serious and responsible member of the party were in possession of information regarding rights of any type at all granted to 'counter-revolutionaries of Nicholas' academy' or of the 'shooting of our best comrades' without a trial, he would be duty-bound to inform the appropriate party institutions immediately, and to demand the most thorough enquiry into the matter. Comrade Kamenskii has never made declarations of this nature to party bodies. The references that his article contains rest on false rumours and on outright slanderous lies.
>
> The Central Committee hereby issues Comrade Kamenskii with a note of censure and warns that any future insinuations of this type, especially intolerable in view of the exceptionally difficult conditions under which the party has at present to work, will lead to the adoption by the Central Committee of more decisive administrative measures.

Differences may be observed between the requests that Trotskii formulated and the content of the resolution. The resolution, for example, reproaches the authors of the article with speaking of 'counter-revolutionaries of Nicholas' academy', a slogan whose thrust must have caused concern among those who drafted the Central Committee's text; yet Trotskii did not even mention it. Other differences reflect a milder response. However ambiguously, it was accepted that Kamenskii was in good faith ('perhaps without its author being fully aware of the fact'), and the editors of *Pravda* did not receive the clear and explicit warning that Trotskii had called for. The advantages of a relaxed approach to news policy must in this case have prevailed over the danger that it might invite gratuitous scandal-mongering. The change in the position of the inverted commas in the twice-repeated phrase, 'shooting of our best comrades without a trial' seems to hint at a slight hesitation as to the real foundation of the accusations in the form reported by Trotskii in his letter to the Central Committee. Only a few days later, on 11 January, Trotskii still felt obliged, in his defence, to send an account of the Panteleev case, provided by an eastern front military leader, direct to Sverdlov and to the editors of *Pravda* and *Izvestiia*.[55] The resolution, however, had exonerated Trotskii *a priori*. Most importantly, the Central Committee agreed to assume responsibility for the military policy that he had implemented. On the whole, the resolution displayed the resolve to prevent the recurrence of any such episodes in the future.

With the authoritative intervention of the Central Committee, the legitimacy of the line that RVSR had been pursuing received for the first time after many months an official and solemn sanction. There remained the fact that Kamenskii had been able to strike his blow with the support of the Central Committee newspaper. Further political backing was probably supplied by the Commissariat for Nationalities, headed by Stalin, to which Kamenskii had been appointed in November, as part of the transfers carried out by the central authorities on the southern front.[56] Those who had been defeated at Tsaritsyn showed that they had no intention whatever of laying down their arms. And the convergent attacks launched by the *tsaritsynets* Kamenskii and the former 'left communist' Sorin left little doubt that neither group would be too particular about where they sought their allies against the policies enforced by the War Ministry.

As we have seen, the attack on Trotskii was unleashed in December, when the process of reorganizing the Red Army was in full swing. But Kamenskii's move occurred within an even more precise context. On 14 December (nine days prior to the publication of his article in *Pravda*), Trotskii sent a message to Lenin, radically altering the hopeful opinion of Voroshilov that he had expressed at the time of the Tsaritsyn affair. Trotskii urged that Voroshilov be transferred to the Ukrainian front, and this request was in fact granted a few days later.[57] It is therefore likely that the *tsaritsyntsy* resolved to attempt a desperate defence manoeuvre. This, however, is not the only possible hypothesis. Judging by one particular passage in Kamenskii's article, it would seem that he was writing earlier than 12 December, perhaps even before the 5th.[58] Was the publication of his article deliberately postponed until 25 December? Did the editors of *Pravda* hesitate, and were they then won over by some authoritative external intervention, or was the date very carefully chosen? As we are about to see, on 25 December Soviet forces on the eastern front sustained a crushing defeat: Kamenskii's attack on Trotskii struck at a moment when the War Ministry was politically extremely weak.

The existence of a coordinated plan seems to be corroborated by a news item that appeared in *Pravda* on 29 December. This took the form of a message from the southern front RVS to VTsIK and it may be inferred from the text that it had been written several weeks earlier, not later than the beginning of October. Its delayed publication was probably intended to revive the faded public image of the Tsaritsyn group and to win for it the sympathy of the famished inhabitants of Moscow. Indeed, according to *Pravda*, the message accompanied a cargo of foodstuffs sent up to the capital from the south. The prose style of the southern front general staff official who actually composed the message provided a further taste of the political and personal characteristics of the Tsaritsyn group. He asked VTsIK to consider the load as a 'gift from the disinterested fighters of the southern front 10th army and from its leader, in the form of the RVS [*sic*], headed by the comrades Stalin, Voroshilov, and Minin, who have inspired the battle-hardened fighters in the defence of the southern fortress'. The portrayal of the food supplies as a 'gift' to Moscow from the south depicts the three men more as munificent *atamany* than as agents of the central power (which, after all, Stalin was – especially as far as supplies were concerned). But there is something even more striking than this unmistakable southern romantic aroma: the front RVS was held up as an example of collegial command, the collective 'chief' of the troops. And of course the note of self-adulation that appears in the text was not an innovation for the unscrupulous pressure-group that had operated in Tsaritsyn. Kamenskii himself, illustrating Voroshilov's qualities in his notorious article, had not hesitated to use terms such as 'glorious, undaunted, dedicated to the revolution . . ., old party militant, rich in merit': an impromptu attempt to launch a third-rate 'personality cult', perhaps a reflection of the climate that actually existed in the 10th army. This was then all rehearsed in the press in order to offset Voroshilov's loss of credit with those at the head of the armed forces.

In January a similar parallelism again became apparent between some of Trotskii's initiatives and the signs of a reaction by the *tsaritsyntsy*. While *Pravda* carried an article, this time written by Minin, in which the myth of the 'besieged fortress' and of its heroic defenders was created (the most important orders issued by Stalin and his colleagues were cited),[59] Trotskii, in his own confidential correspondence, continued to rail against 'the Tsaritsyn trend'. Following the transfer of Voroshilov to Khar'kov, Trotskii feared that the contagion might gain a hold in the Ukraine with a host of disastrous effects: 'Voroshilov plus the Ukrainian partisan movement, plus the backwardness of the population, plus demagogy'.[60] Complaining of the persistence of methods that made 'a fetish of ignorance', Trotskii invited Lenin to find out from Okulov 'what the Tsaritsyn-men are', and even went so far as to express his suspicion that Stalin was still providing Voroshilov with protection. And, with a startling sense of timing, Stalin himself now decided to enter the fray. This he did, not by seeking to gain credit for indefensible extremist positions on matters of military organization, but by presenting a platform which he hoped would qualify him as an up-and-coming military expert, and by confronting Trotskii and his colleagues on their own ground: the practical rules of warfare.

Military failure

On the same day that Kamenskii's article appeared, and the Central Committee issued its resolution in defence of Trotskii and RVSR policy, the city of Perm' on the eastern front fell into the hands of the White forces.[61] The Red troops fled westwards in total confusion, and the military commands melted away.

The catastrophe had been looming for several days. On 22 December, Stalin had proposed to the *Sovet oborony* that Vatsetis be called to account for a series of measures that he had taken in the area and to explain why certain operations had not been carried out.[62] Lenin had been given the task of conferring by telephone with the Supreme Commander. Meanwhile, it was left up to Stalin to ascertain the state of readiness of the Red troops that were defending the city, as well as the strength of the reinforcements that the Supreme Command were sending them. On 1 January, the Central Committee and SNK formally entrusted Stalin and Dzerzhinskii to conduct an on-the-spot enquiry into the causes of the reverse. They reached Viatka on the 5th,[63] and by the 13th they were already able to send Lenin and the Central Committee a 'preliminary report' on the situation. They wrote two further reports: one on 19 January (of little significance) and another on the 31st, which was presented to the Central Committee as the conclusions of the enquiry.[64] Only the second and third reports were included in Stalin's *Complete Works*: the first one has only recently been published.

The first report, on the 13th, listed the direct causes of the fall of Perm': the inadequacy of reserves, the lack of coordination between the 3rd army command (in charge of the city's defence) and the troops; and the incompetence of the army general staff. To these points, the second and third reports added a detailed account of the way in which the situation had developed, and the issues tackled were broadened to include the failure to deploy the troops correctly, the policy towards the civilian population, etc. But in the report of 13 January Stalin and Dzerzhinskii also formulated serious accusations against RVSR, which in the final report, delivered to the Central Committee on the 31st, were toned down. The 'counter-revolutionary spirit', allegedly displayed by Soviet troops dispatched as reinforcements to the beleaguered city, was due to 'the old pre-revolutionary methods of training contingents'. RVSR had demonstrated an 'intolerably criminal way of managing the front'; it had 'paralysed' the front with its own contradictory instructions and had deprived it 'of any chance of coming swiftly to the aid of the 3rd army'. In conclusion, it was necessary 'to transform RVSR so that it manages the armies effectively instead of disrupting them'.

This grave charge, levelled at the highest military leaders of the Republic, reappeared in the report of 31 January as a bland statement that 'RVSR did not maintain contacts with the front and ... the Commander-in-Chief issued ill-considered directives'.[65] In this way, most of the blame was laid on Vatsetis, while the responsibility of RVSR was played down. Although in the report of 31 January Stalin and Dzerzhinskii again advocated a reorganization of RVSR's mode of operation, there remained little of the verbal violence of the initial report.[66] In the third report, it was the VBVK that came in for the harshest criticism, with the investigators openly requesting an 'overhaul in the composition' of the body, a demand that had not been made in the report of the 13th.[67] In political terms, this meant that between 13 and 31 January Stalin and Dzerzhinskii shifted the target of their attack from Trotskii, the RVSR President, to Iurenev, in charge of the VBVK, and to Commander-in-Chief Vatsetis. At this date, however, Iurenev could be considered as one of Trotskii's men, having been a member, with Trotskii, of the *mezhraiontsy* group, which had gone over to the Bolshevik party at the 6th Congress (July 1917).[68] The report of the 31st restated, however, certain politically very sensitive criticisms made in that of the 13th, regarding the training received by detachments bound for the front. It was pointed out that, by taking over 'en bloc the training system of the Tsarist period', the general staff (*vseroglavshtab*) had enforced general mobilization without taking into account the 'economic situation' of the recruits. Also, they had failed to take the precaution of assigning the recruits to operational zones different from their recruitment areas.[69] Thus, not only had the class character of the formations often been violated, the ground had also been laid for a potentially disastrous link between anti-Soviet elements among the troops and their social and geographical background. The reserves sent to Perm', in particular, had 'all the hallmarks of a formation of White guards'.

In their third report, in any case, Stalin and Dzerzhinskii did not judge it expedient to press further those criticisms aimed implicitly at Trotskii, which they had felt able to voice in the more confidential report submitted on 13 January. When the Central Committee met, at the beginning of February, discussion was apparently confined to the way in which the *vseroglavshtab* prepared and trained the detachments in the rear.[70] Despite the advantage that the War Ministry had given them, Trotskii's adversaries evidently came up against a central authority that had only recently reaffirmed its full confidence in the leaders of the armed forces and personally in the Commissar for War.

Furthermore, the first and third reports seemed to reveal a clarification and perhaps a slight modification in Stalin's positions since the Tsaritsyn affair. On the complex issue of relations between 'specialists' and commissars, there remained the suggestion that the centre should not send people who were 'too young'[71] to act as custodians for the commanders at the front, and a (triumphant!) list of military and civilian 'specialists' who had gone over to the enemy during the course of the struggle for Perm'.[72] Moreover, the report of 13 January featured a determined plea that well-known left-wing sceptics such as Preobrazhenskii, Safarov, and Tolmachev be removed from the front-line area. In this regard, Stalin shared with the leading group within the army an antipathy for and distrust of 'party demagogues'.[73] To substitute the high-ranking leaders and commanders of the 3rd army, the report recommended men like Sokol'nikov and Smilga, who could certainly not be suspected of sympathizing with those who contested the existing machinery of the armed forces.[74] In general terms, although he continued to talk of the attitude of certain commanders and leaders as being that of 'feudal princes',[75] Stalin had clearly refined his initial form of opposition to 'military specialists'. Like the positions that Kaganovich later asserted, the reports written by Stalin and Dzerzhinskii in January provide a valuable key to understanding the complicated way in which the military question was settled at the 8th Congress.

5   Military policy at the 8th Congress

The debate

By 2 February 1919, when *Pravda* published the Central Committee decision to convene the 8th Party Congress, official military policy was under both frontal and indirect attack from sizable groups of militants and leaders. This broad front of opposition ranged from those (like Sorin) who backed 'left communist' positions, to supporters (e.g. Kamenskii)[1] of new and unorthodox 'revolutionary' military strategies, to those (like Stalin), who, even though they refrained from voicing broad political formulations of an alternative nature, nonetheless viewed official military policy as an unjustifiable means of reinstating men, ideas, and methods that had not been born of the revolution. But this was not all. Before Congress met in the first half of March, it was clear that, even at the party centre, there were considerable misgivings regarding the line that the War Ministry had been pursuing over the preceding months. Addressing the 3rd Congress of the Ukrainian party, Sverdlov declared, for example, that the Central Committee had passed the resolution of 25 December 'unanimously'. But although he stressed the lack of any real 'dissension' within the leading party organ, he had to admit that there were 'various shades of opinion'.[2] On 13 December, during a meeting in Petrograd, Lenin was no less ambiguous and evasive. In the middle of a forceful speech, calling for the employment of 'bourgeois specialists' in the army as elsewhere, he referred to the opposition in the most benevolent terms, recalling 'the controversy that has arisen over this question' within the party and even how 'some comrades, most devoted and convinced Bolshevik communists, expressed vehement protests' against this line.[3] These statements are significant, given the positions of authority held by those who made them, even if one cannot be sure that they were not dictated by the desire to maintain the utmost harmony and cohesion among party militants.

Trotskii, for his part, made a series of public statements designed to ward off the danger that Congress might seek to call into question the foundations of the line that he had so far been following.[4] The War Commissar declared that political work at the front, thanks both to the political departments and to the party cells – 'whose role in the task of educating the army [was] enormous' – had now, on the eve of Congress, been set on the right tracks.[5] Yet Trotskii admitted, 'truth to tell', that not everything was going exactly as it should, but he laid the blame for this on the front-line communists themselves. Their behaviour provided grounds for the widespread opinion among the men that 'privileges go hand-in-hand with the title of communist', and this was bound to disrupt the smooth working of the military machine. At times party cells violated discipline by attempting to 'take the place' of the commissars and commanders. 'Other' party members sought to 'shirk the fundamental duties of Red Army soldiers'.[6] Yet Trotskii considered that the problem of 'military specialists' had now been overcome by 'experience' at the front: no one could portray the current situation in less accurate terms than those who had claimed that there existed 'an anti-officer line and a pro-officer line'. He also felt it necessary to reassure his audience with regard to the supposed danger that 'Bonapartism might arise from the soil of revolutionary war'. It was of course possible that 'certain sublieutenants might stumble through the history of Napoleon', but the massive presence of the party in the armed forces and in the country as a whole constituted the best possible guarantee against such a threat.[7] As for the possibility that the impending Congress might witness an erup-tion of searing criticism, Trotskii declared that he was sceptical: he was quite sure that the debate would have a 'practical, let us say, technical' character.[8] Besides, the full-blown opposition to military policy that over the preceding months had raised its head had by this date ceased to exist within party ranks. In stark contrast to Sverdlov and Lenin, Trotskii played down the extent of disagreement, claiming that only a few peripheral organizations dissented (he made a passing reference to the Urals party committee), and arguing that one should see these manifestations more as a sort of ill-articulated 'grumbling' than as the expression of an alternative line. These 'left' criticisms, obsessed with the question of the 'specialists', were 'vague and formless', and lacking in any real substance.[9]

In this particular interview Trotskii also stated that he was on the point of leaving for the front, and that he felt not the slightest 'disquiet' regarding the conclusions that Congress might reach.[10] But the history of his decision not to attend Congress – a decision which as Trotskii himself stressed was reached 'with the consent of the Central Committee' – belies the optimism of such declarations. Authorization for his departure was given on March 16 at a Central Committee meeting which he too attended.[11] The way in which the military question was to be addressed at Congress was one of the issues raised. The Central Committee reversed a previous decision whereby Congress delegates from the front were commanded to return to their combat units at once, owing to the deterioration of the military situation. A number of *frontoviki* had raised

> the question of the correctness of this decision, which might be interpreted by organizations at the front as being due to disinclination on the part of the centre to give speakers from the army a hearing, and has even been interpreted by certain of them as some sort of subterfuge inasmuch as the departure of Comrade Trotskii and the non-admission (by way of recall to the front) of the army deputies rendered the actual consideration of the question of military policy inapposite [that is to say, whether or not it was to be included in Congress agenda].

Trotskii replied to this 'interpretation' during the meeting, by referring to 'the extremely serious situation' that had arisen on the eastern front. A compromise was reached that involved the immediate departure of the RVSR President, but left the military delegates free to follow or to ignore his example. It appears furthermore from the minutes of this session that the Central Committee had already decided that Congress should hold a 'meeting behind closed doors' on military matters, and that Trotskii had requested – successfully – that the faithful Okulov (an RVSR member since January) might address the meeting. On the other hand, the Central Committee took the formal decision to grant V. M. Smirnov (a former 'left communist' Muscovite, currently a political-military cadre on the eastern front, and a prominent spokesman for the opposition at the impending Congress) permission to remain in Moscow, in compliance with his explicit request to do so.[12]

At Congress, discussion of military policy followed a very tortuous course. The issue was debated at public sessions, in a special session on military affairs, as well as at a plenary session behind closed doors. The proceedings of the special session and of the plenary meeting have not yet been made available. Our main sources of information therefore are the shorthand records of the public proceedings, Lenin's speech, and part of Stalin's address to the secret meeting. We also have access to incomplete and imprecise reconstructions of private and confidential discussions involving Soviet political and military historians who have presumably been able to consult the original documents. Lastly, the final resolutions of Congress are known to us, including those which were kept secret at the time.

The public debate was introduced by Sokol'nikov, who thus acted as defence counsel for the official standpoint on military affairs. His report was followed by a co-report from V. M. Smirnov, whom the opposition had selected as their representative, by means of a petition. During the public sessions, there were no other speeches specifically devoted to military policy, but only scattered references in a number of speeches – though on occasions these were lengthy and significant. The bulk of discussion took place in the so-called 'military section', which held three meetings: one on 20 March and the other two on 21 March. Lastly, on the evening of 21 March, the plenary session was held behind closed doors. The main address was made by Aralov, an RVSR member.

The Central Committee theses on military policy, drafted by Trotskii, were published at the end of February.[13] They acknowledged that 'the concrete course of development of our Red Army stands in a way in contradiction' with the principle of class-based recruiting and yet the decision taken in the spring of the previous year to switch from voluntary recruiting to compulsory conscription was fully justified (point IV). Consequently, the claim that the methods of 'partisan' warfare could represent an alternative 'military programme' was denounced as a senseless attempt to 'turn the clock back from large-scale to craft industry' (point V).[14] The theses pledged that 'sooner or later' the present army would be replaced by an industry- and class-based territorial militia. The 'regular' character of the Red Army was discreetly indicated in inverted commas, and an explicit mention was made of its provisional nature. The 'regular' army model was justified on purely empirical grounds, such as its well-proven capacity for 'defeating its enemies'. For the immediate period, the militia idea would only be applied in the formation of reserve detachments (points X, XI, XII, XIII). A start would thus be made, however, to laying the foundations of a 'class-based militia army', a vital first step towards the eventual switch-over to the pure militia, the 'universal arming of the people'.

Point XIV indicated that commissars must be communists, though the delicate wording that was actually used read: 'bearers of the spirit of our party'. Trotskii hesitated to sanction the existence within the armed forces of a party hierarchy, which might tend to operate an independent system of discipline. Commissars were placed under the control of the political departments, which took their orders directly from the Central Committee. Attention was also drawn to the importance within the detachment of the party cell. Confronted with the rapid increase in the number of party members at the front, the theses pointed to the need for greater care in recruiting, and for internal checks able to protect the party from 'privilege' hunters. It had to be made perfectly clear, as an expression dear to Trotskii put it, that 'belonging to a communist cell does not give the soldier any particular right but only places upon him the obligation to be a fighter even more full of courage and self-denial'.

While deleting the question of 'military specialists' from the list of issues that might still lead to 'disagreements of principle' among the Bolsheviks, point XV stated the need to train 'a new officers' corps' of proletarian extraction, and envisaged an increase in the number of military academies. In the subsequent section, which mentioned the disciplinary and service statutes of the Red Army (introduced in December 1918, and one of the main causes of the scandal created at Congress by the opposition), little space was devoted to arguing that their adoption had been necessary. Significantly, the 'provisional' character of the statutes was instead emphasized.

Point XVII, on the other hand, in order apparently to counter the alarmism and *sharltanstvo* of Menshevik and Social Revolutionary propaganda, insisted warmly that there was no danger of 'Bonapartism' in Soviet Russia. It is noteworthy that Trotskii attributed to this historical category a prevalently socio-political rather than military–political or institutional significance, evidently with a view to appealing to the Marxist convictions of his own party comrades.

> Bonapartism is not a product of military organization as such but of specific social relations. The political sway of the petty bourgeoisie, standing between the great reactionary bourgeoisie and lower proletarian and revolutionary strata (which remain unable to play an independent political role or exercise their own political sway) creates the necessary conditions for the birth of Bonapartism. Bonapartism seeks the support of the rich peasant and raises itself above class contradictions, which find no solution in the revolutionary programme of petty bourgeois (Jacobin) democracy.

The Red Army was only 'an instrument of the Soviet regime' and it was the existence of this regime that acted as the principal guarantee

against 'Bonapartism': 'Counter-revolution cannot under any circumstances develop from the regime of the dictatorship of the proletariat.
It can only triumph as a consequence of a direct and bloody victory
over this regime. It is necessary to develop and strengthen the Red
Army to make such a victory impossible.'

Trotskii's argument clearly went in two different directions, even if
only one of these was developed in any detail. To start with, the
Commissar for War rejected the acceptation of the term 'Bonapartism'
indicating the emergence of a prestigious leader thanks to the armed
force firmly concentrated in his hands, and on the strength of the
military victories thereby gained. Ignoring the example already provided by Napoleon I, Trotskii simply ruled out the possibility of a
Napoleon III emerging in Soviet Russia. For good measure, the last
point in the theses painted once again an ideal picture of a future
'militia of the whole people'.

Overall, the theses provided a vague outline of official military
policy and did not go very far beyond the concepts that Trotskii had
articulated a year earlier, in March 1918. The desire to provide his
adversaries with as few excuses as possible to advance further criticisms had prompted him to draft a largely defensive document,
studded with references to a victorious future where every kind of
'temporary' contradiction would finally be settled. On a number of
points, concessions were made to the criticisms that had been
advanced over the preceding months. But in their evasiveness, the
theses did not simply reflect the worries of a single leader: they
represented at the same time the lowest common denominator that
the Central Committee had felt it could put before Congress for
discussion. This view seems to be confirmed by the quasi-clandestine
form taken by another important document presented to Congress.
The new draft party programme was not in fact published prior to the
discussion and approval of the final text, and was only made public
subsequently.[15] In particular, the section dealing with military policy
confined itself to fulminating against the 'pacifism' of the Social
Democrats and of the world bourgeoisie, and to forecasting an
impending cycle of 'revolutionary wars' and civil wars throughout the
entire world.[16] In actual fact, prior to Congress, only the introduction
to this chapter had been written. What is more, the text stopped
abruptly at the point announcing the 'fundamental conclusions',
which in fact remained to be drafted. On none of the main topics of
dissension, therefore, had the Central Committee an official public
position before Congress met, or anything much more definite than a

reiteration of points 'of principle' on which of course there was a broad consensus. These were all symptoms of a desire to come to grips with the real problems in an informal way, an approach that was further encouraged by the realization that no one could hope to impose a single line on the whole range and variety of positions that had long been apparent within the party.

Sokol'nikov, in his speech, helped to bring these issues out into the open.[17] He ran through the well-known official reasons for favouring a 'regular' army and suggested that the main obstacle was the fact that many Bolsheviks still failed to appreciate the need to go beyond outdated methods of 'partisan struggle'. Even if this form of combat had played an important role immediately after the seizure of power, it now belonged to the period of voluntary enlistment.[18] Sokol'nikov summarized the points at issue under three headings: the role of 'military specialists', the election of commanders by their troops, and the 'organization of communists in the army, the rights of communist cells in the army'.[19] He stated that the employment of Tsarist officers had been justified by experience, all the more so since Soviet power was not yet in a position to replace the old commanders with a new command cadre at a comparable level of technical training. The brunt of the attack on attitudes hostile to the specialists was borne not by the Tsaritsyn group but by the 11th army, which had been engaged in operations at the extreme eastern tip of the southern front, and which had recently disintegrated during a disastrous retreat from the Northern Caucasus towards Astrakhan. G. K. Ordzhonikidze was numbered among its political and military commanders.[20]

According to Sokol'nikov, the election of commanders was ill-advised for the same reasons that the employment of ex-Tsarist officers was expedient. It was a matter not of 'principle' but of stark practical necessity. Similar steps had been taken in industry with the reinstatement of engineers and technicians employed by the former proprietors of what were now nationalized factories. As for the party cells, the speaker had no trouble acknowledging that they were not reserved any 'casting vote' in the life of the armed forces: 'On the one hand regimental communist cells were created as organs of political propaganda under the direction of the party's political departments; on the other they were conceived as combat groups of the toughest and most stoical comrades, whose job it was to drag the other soldiers along behind them.'[21]

As well as those that demanded greater powers for party cells, there was another grouping, which Sokol'nikov, adopting Trotskii's term, called the 'party syndicalists'. Just as, within the trades unions, trends had emerged that sought to take over from the state the general direction and running of the economy, local party organizations 'attempt to deliver the management of the army and the control of all the work in the army into the hands of the communists who, in their capacity as simple employees in the military institutions, are employed in the territory where the troops and the front are located'.[22] Such tasks were on the contrary matters for the party as a whole, and for the government of the Republic.

Even if Sokol'nikov upheld the principle that the command corps should not be subject to election and argued the need to centralize the party's organization within the army, he offered the opposition two areas for negotiation. First, he agreed with the theses that greater attention should be paid to the social composition of the army and that care should be taken to prevent its infiltration by *kulaki* and 'former landowners', elements that might otherwise turn the army into a fertile ground for counter-revolutionary agitation. Sokol'nikov then went further than the thesis, by stating that 'those in charge of military policy' had implemented a policy of indiscriminate recruiting in spite of 'indications and instructions' that they had received – presumably from the Central Committee.[23]

Secondly, Sokol'nikov rejected the proposal to restrict commissars to purely administrative functions (other than those of supervision), maintaining that their powers ought rather to be 'broadened'.[24] The proposal in question had been set forth by Smilga in a short paper published by the eastern front print works, before Congress opened.[25] Sokol'nikov suggested that, since a growing number of 'military specialists' were now on their way to constituting a politically reliable command cadre, commissars would be able to devote less and less of their energies on supervisory tasks and thus get on with 'political work' among the soldiers, in collaboration with the party cells. What Sokol'nikov vaguely announced (from this point onwards one of the most ambiguous and confusing points in party decisions on military affairs) was an institutional apparatus in which the communists were to spend less and less time on the technical and operational side of military life and ever more time on the purely political organization of soldiers – assuming that these two developments would not clash. What was beyond doubt, however, was that territorial party committees could not be permitted to take exclusive charge of the troops' political training especially since, when undertaken by civilian communists, this training tended to assume an ill-defined 'democratic-revolutionary' rather than a 'party' character. They might be entrusted with work of this kind in the rear but

> At the front political education shall assume two forms: either it is undertaken by the party cells, who create a party apparatus for this purpose; or, alternatively, party propaganda is implemented as the state propaganda of communism. I believe, comrades, that Congress must support the state propaganda of communism at the front, directed by the political departments of the army.[26]

Like the theses, Sokol'nikov concluded by deferring to a not-too-distant future: once 'communist society' was in a position to afford a 'communist militia', certain features of 'partisan' democratism could be 'resuscitated'. He emphasized that the theses also displayed dissatisfaction for the internal service statutes, and he labelled them 'not altogether satisfactory'. In spite of this, he expressed the hope that the harsh disciplinary regime, which had had to be established in the army, would prove a 'transitory' feature.[27]

V. M. Smirnov, the speaker for the opposition, began by avoiding anything that might indicate a desire to engage in a head-on clash. Although he observed that 'the majority' of former officers had been reluctant to join the Red Army, he denied that the question of their employment could be posed in terms of 'specialists, yes or no'.[28] Still, it had to be recognized, he argued, that the interference of commissars in administrative and strategic affairs had been provoked by the fact that Soviet power had 'inevitably' been saddled with the 'worst' of the commanders, while the best-trained and most capable had gone over to the Whites. And this was where open disagreement with the official line began. In the army and front commanders' *polozheniia*, 'the functions of the commanders have not been defined with precision'.[29] According to these regulations, commissars had been given 'supervisory' functions only. Now that commissars had acquired a greater familiarity with military matters, they should be conferred 'broader rights' of leadership in the army. As he immediately made clear, Smirnov meant by this the granting to RVS members of voting rights on 'operational questions'. Smirnov also attacked the 'internal service and discipline statutes', and the traditional pattern that these continued to impose on relations between soldiers and officers. Certainly statutes were necessary, but they should not give peasant soldiers the impression that they were still in the old Imperial Army.[30] In more general terms, Smirnov criticized the government's enforcement of compulsory mobilization, declaring that on this issue too the Red Army should distinguish itself clearly from White formations, by relying more on 'persuasion' than on 'constraint': a view that reflected the persistent preference of former 'left communists' for the volunteer system. Yet one cannot grasp why certain of the opinions voiced by the opposition, both before and during Congress, were so popular in the party and with soldiers generally, unless one considers an issue that Smirnov only hinted at: the use, since Kazan' or even earlier, of ruthless disciplinary methods to curb desertions from the Red Army. Even Vatsetis, the Supreme Commander, wrote in his memoirs ten years later that he had been deeply shocked by the extent to which Red commands employed violence and the death sentence against their troops. With hindsight, he attributed this almost exclusively to the 'style' that Trotskii had imposed.[31]

In his speech, Smirnov defined the way that political work was performed at the front as 'thoroughly bureaucratic'. The institution of the political department, providing neither for collective decision-taking nor for a wide-ranging discussion of the more important problems, could not function and, indeed, in the speaker's view, did not function. It was less a political organ, able to establish relations with the mass of soldiers, than 'an office for information and agitation'. Even more damaging, its predominant position at the front jeopardized the reproduction of the traditional characteristics of the party and of its cadres: 'it is incapable of performing any genuine party work, on the basis of which new forces might be promoted from the party grassroots. And yet this is essential to us, for our old communist reserves are becoming depleted and we shall not survive long without them.'[32]

To give the communists a solid political structure, 'bureaucratism' had therefore to be abandoned and replaced by a combination of 'appointment' and 'self-management'. Even the viewpoint of the opposition allowed for negotiation, both on the role of the commissars and on the operation and composition of the political departments, which were not rejected out of hand.

At the close of his speech, Smirnov voiced a criticism that we have already encountered in the report of 31 January that Stalin and Dzerzhinskii had made to the Central Committee regarding the fall of Perm'. Smirnov alleged that RVSR had demonstrated both its inability to effect a clear 'delimitation of functions' between the various central military organs, and its inclination to issue 'orders that contradict one another'.[33] Was the purpose of this form of 'technical' criticism to signal to the shrewdest and best-informed delegates the existence of a link between Smirnov's speech and the position of other party groups hostile to the current military leaders? The answer to this question has, I think, to be a qualified 'yes': the inclusion of this point may have represented more a quest for allies than the outcome of an already agreed platform.

Other attacks on the system of military organization were to be found here and there in speeches from delegates who criticized in more general terms the work that had been carried out by the Central Committee since the 7th Congress. Ignatov referred to the War Ministry as an extreme case of the wide currency that 'appointment from above' had gained in the Soviet state administration. Denouncing the danger of 'bureaucratism' – i.e. the risk that the party might become cut off from the masses – he predicted that

> if this disease spreads and takes root, the situation that at present obtains in a number of factories but above all in the Red Army, whereby at times the communists are not only unable to unite with the mass of the soldiers but actually become detached from them, so that they no longer manage to understand one another, might gain a hold.[34]

Sapronov drew attention to the way that local Soviet executive committees were being deprived of their authority by the government's 'extraordinary agents', above all by those of the VChK, and other central commissariats.[35] Specifically, military commissars were 'going down the same road', empowered to declare a state of war, confiscate goods and lodgings, and then to reply to indignant local administrators that 'we are accountable to the centre alone'. Sapronov laid the blame squarely on the War Ministry for having provided the first example of a state organ organized as a 'ladder', and for having discarded the principle of territorial administrative jurisdiction. The RVSs, he argued, should 'lend an ear' to the civilian powers and, if the military authorities of individual units committed abuses, the centre ought not to shrink from putting them on trial and, if they were found guilty, of having them 'shot'. The precongressional platform of the Moscow party organization had contained a similar point.

At Congress, Osinskii delivered a co-report, for the opposition, on the 'organizational question', while the defence of official positions on this more general issue was left to Zinov'ev. Osinskii insisted on the need to create two new Central Committee organs.[36] One of these would oversee strictly party work and organization, and the relations between the Central Committee and local organizations; the other body (a *voennoe biuro*) would deal specifically with party work in the armed forces. Even Ignatov gave this proposal his enthusiastic support.[37] The opposition evidently saw this measure as a guarantee that the policy of the Commissariat for War would express the will of the Central Committee and not just that of its military leaders. Following the Central Committee resolution of 25 December 1918, this insinuation could no longer be voiced explicitly, but the doubts had not apparently vanished after its approval.

The official line was also subjected to attack from positions more rigid and intransigent than its own. Iurenev led the way by proposing that the plan to combine the principle of appointment with that of the election of commanders be dropped from the party's draft programme, and that appointment be prescribed unconditionally.[38]

The available fragmentary account of the secret debates does not enable us to determine the exact order of the various interventions. We shall, therefore, attempt to sketch a rough outline of the different groupings, on the (somewhat shaky) basis of recent reconstructions carried out by Soviet historians. We have also tried to match these reconstructions with the evidence that has emerged regarding the debate of the preceding months.

The basic points over which critics of official military policy could all agree were set out in a document, drafted as an alternative to Trotskii's theses and to the platform illustrated by Sokol'nikov. All that we possess of this paper, presented to the 'military section' by V. M. Smirnov, is a number of short passages, among which there are only two points that seem to have been preserved in their complete and original form.[39] Altogether we have the names of 24 people. D. Pavlov, G. Safarov, F. Goloshchekin, A. Aleksandrov, E. Iaroslavskii, A. Okulov, A. Miasnikov, V. Miliutin, K. Iurenev, N. Tolmachev, N. Karpov, V. Mulin, S. Minin, B. Pozern, R. Zemliachka, K. Voroshilov, R. Levin, and M. Rukhimovich spoke at the first session.[40] At the second and third sessions, Safarov, Goloshchekin, Mulin, Zemliachka, and Voroshilov spoke again and A. Rozengol'ts, V. Smirnov, P. Shternberg, A. Bubnov, G. Sokol'nikov, and I. Kozlov spoke for the first time. Although only 83 names have been preserved, we know that 85 people took part in the commission.[41] Some of these, however, fall into precise groupings. First, the *tsaritsyntsy*: Voroshilov, Minin, Kamenskii, with whom Rukhimovich from Khar'kov was connected. Voroshilov and Kamenskii had been chosen as delegates to Congress by the Ukrainian party, and Minin by the town conference of the Tsaritsyn party. Voroshilov, Minin, and Kamenskii were also all members of the commission on organizational problems,[42] and thus formed a tight-nit and well-deployed group at the strategic moments of debate in Congress. Then there was a group of former 'left communists': Bubnov, Piatakov, V. Smirnov, Safarov, Sorin;[43] and, lastly, the group that at the following Party Congress (the 9th) presented themselves on the 'Democratic Centralism' platform: Osinskii, Mgeladze, Sapronov.[44]

The Tsaritsyn group, as Minin and Voroshilov stated, led the attack on the use of 'military specialists', asserting that the Red Army had in fact been built up without their help.[45] On this they were supported by Miasnikov, who, even though he wanted former Tsarist officers to be given a purely consultative role, was against Smirnov's proposal to introduce collegial operational command. Instead, he favoured one-man command, providing the commander was a party member.[46] Moreover, he proposed 'a combination of the two systems: the system of party representatives, appointed from above by the Central Committee *biuro*; and, at the same time, the use of the day-to-day experience of the party rank and file'.[47] Safarov adopted an open-minded stance, asserting that 'nobody, or at least not the overwhelming majority of our party, would dream of refusing to employ specialists', and questioned the role of the party in the Red Army.[48] Safarov felt that it was possible to discern the absence of 'any well-defined criterion for the exercise of the hegemony of the communist party over the organizational construction of the army'.

V. Smirnov, Iaroslavskii, and Safarov all spoke out against the service statutes.[49] Smirnov repeated the argument that he had previously expounded in his co-report to the public plenary session, regarding the relation between military policy and alliance with the peasantry. He obviously counted on the fact that one of the most crucial topics on the agenda of Congress was the policy to be adopted towards the 'average peasant': 'Our military policy has failed to take account of the fact that the army base consists of average peasants, whom we must win over to our side with all our energies, and whom we must not frighten with methods that remind them of the old army.'[50]

Adopting a stance rather different to that of Smirnov, Aleksandrov complained that the switch from a volunteer to a regular army had undermined its class character.[51] Goloshchekin attacked also the centralization of the various Soviet national military units under a unified Republican command, a process that had been initiated at the beginning of 1919 and which was to culminate in July of the same year.[52]

Evidently, given this chaotic overlapping of proposals and criticisms – including conflicting ones – common ground for agreement could only be found in the hostility felt towards the group of leaders that had been spearheading the reorganization of the armed forces over the previous months. The remark made by Voroshilov in 1933, that the majority of the members of the military commission 'questioned' the leadership of RVSR and that of Trotskii in particular, should be viewed either as a piece of polemical distortion or, alternatively, as self-evident.[53] Goloshchekin accused Trotskii of darting from front to front, creating chaos wherever he went with orders and counter-orders of every type: a criticism cast in a familiar mould.[54] He also accused the Central Committee of having allowed the job of organizing the army to 'slip from their hands'. Zemliachka, for her part, charged Iurenev with deploying party members responsible for political work unwisely over the front-line units.[55] To this Iurenev retorted that 'the party has no good commissars at its disposal'.[56] Okulov, Iurenev, Sokol'nikov, and Pozern, all defenders of the centre's viewpoint, were unable to stand up to the combined onslaught of their adversaries. Pozern, for his part, had his own grounds for complaint in the way he had been treated by the Commissar for War when Voroshilov and Trotskii had met at Tsaritsyn.[57] On 21 March, at the end of its third session, the military commission approved the theses presented by Smirnov by 37 votes to 20.[58] The minority walked out in protest and requested a plenary discussion. The opposition, clearly taken aback by the depth of the rift, prepared to make some alterations to the newly approved document, in readiness for a decisive confrontation. In particular, it appears that point X, advocating collegial operational command, was reformulated. On the evening of the same day, Aralov delivered his report on the country's military situation to Congress, meeting behind closed doors. All we know of this speech is that Lenin had apparently urged Aralov 'not to hide' the weak points in the construction of the Red Army.[59] Iaroslavskii reported to Congress on the proceedings of the commission. Three people were then called upon to speak on behalf of the group that had gained a majority in the commission and three for the minority: respectively, Safarov, Voroshilov, and V. Smirnov; and, Okulov, Stalin, and Sokol'nikov. Smirnov continued to insist on collegial command, and Voroshilov, in a polemic with the centre, defended the military line that had been pursued in Tsaritsyn during his stay in that town. Okulov, on the other hand, drew attention relentlessly to its weaknesses.

Stalin's speech was not made public until nine years after the

Congress had been held, and then only in an abridged form.[60] It consisted of five paragraphs with three omissions, marked by dots. Its content fully complied with the points made by Sokol'nikov. Stalin argued the need for 'iron discipline' in an army composed principally of peasants, who 'will not fight for socialism of their own accord'. He labelled Smirnov's theses 'unacceptable' and came out strongly in favour of 'a true regular workers' and peasants' army with tough discipline', apparently with the only condition that such an army should possess 'a well-organized political section'.[61] This passage confirms the trend, that had already emerged in the reports on Perm' in January, to shift the focus of criticism from Trotskii to Iurenev. But what did the passages that have never been published contain? 'It is hard to give a categorical reply', Trotskii was forced bitterly to admit in 1940.[62] Trotskii stated that at the time he had only been able to gather vague evidence that Stalin had spoken out against the Commissariat for War, but he was convinced, he said, that Stalin had in some way egged the opposition on. According to Danilevskii, Stalin seized on Okulov's criticism of the methods in vogue in the Tsaritsyn 10th army, but breathed 'not a single word' of his own attitude towards 'the party line in favour of the employment of military specialists'.[63] Yet Danilevskii believes that, even after Congress, in spite of his evasiveness in public, Stalin had stuck to his own 'mistaken' positions. Judging by what Lenin said in his intervention – probably in direct reply to Stalin's speech – Stalin had maintained that the War Ministry did not carry out Central Committee policy. This allegation the party leader once again roundly rejected.[64] It also seems that Lenin's protest against the charge that the Central Committee had followed 'a mistaken policy entailing the systematic absence of reserve troops' was occasioned by another passage in Stalin's speech. This is all the more likely, given that this point had already appeared in the well-known documents drafted by Stalin and Dzerzhinskii in January.[65] One may thus conclude that Stalin pursued the course he had embarked upon in January: to remove any elements of possible disagreement over points 'of principle' between himself and the centre; to select the technical-military field as his main focus for criticism; to distance himself resolutely from the most radical opposition tendencies; and, lastly, to set forth proposals for the improvement of the political machinery of the Red Army. Stalin used his speech to set himself up as a rallying point both for the less extreme elements within the opposition, and for any wavering supporters of the viewpoint of the centre and of Trotskii, whose mood the recent military setbacks, as well as the precarious situation that had again emerged on the eastern front on the eve of Congress, could not fail to influence.

Lenin approached many of the problems under discussion with caution, taking care to preface his remarks by saying, 'not only am I not a military specialist, I am not even a part of the military'.[66] He let it be understood that on matters such as a soldier's obligation to salute his superior officers (a point included in the Red Army service statute and attacked by Smirnov in his own counter-theses) he yielded to the judgement of men like Sokol'nikov. Yet he admitted that he had been 'appalled' to learn that this obligation had been restored in the Red Army. He spoke ironically of the circumspection of those who had drafted the rules, the shroud of secrecy under which the draft had been elaborated, and the tiny number of copies that had been circulated.[67] While not denying that there were some 'partial defects' in military policy, and stating in particular that 'no one wished to defend the [military] statutes', Lenin inveighed against the dramatic way in which such defects were denounced in Smirnov's theses. The theses apparently contained a statement to the effect that the service statute would usher in 'an autocratic and feudal order' within the Soviet armed forces. To Lenin, this was absolutely intolerable, especially since such phrases did nothing but 'bring grist to the mill of the Social Revolutionaries and Mensheviks'.[68] But Lenin touched on an important point of principle when, taking up an argument that Stalin had employed against Smirnov, he rejected the notion that to deal with the mobilized 'average peasant' a 'policy of winning over his heart and mind' could prove adequate. He then attacked point VI of the opposition theses, where he uncovered the 'marks of syndicalism', which Sokol'nikov had referred to. This was probably the section on party democracy at the front. Lenin commented abruptly: 'This can't be done in the army, where centralization is necessary.'[69]

A considerable part of his speech was given over to an assault on Goloshchekin and, in particular, on Voroshilov and his obstinate praise for the methods used in Tsaritsyn during the war against the Whites. Although it was true that the town had been 'heroically' defended, to harp on about the 'heroic traditions' of partisan warfare bespoke a failure to understand that the Soviet seizure of power had marked the start of 'a different period', in which 'a regular army with military specialists' was required. And this was true even if real cases of treason had come to light. To continue theorizing about what had occurred at Tsaritsyn was tantamount to 'violating the whole general party line' – all the more so since, as Lenin added in response to an angry interruption from Voroshilov, the human losses suffered by the 10th army might have been much less heavy, had more orthodox military methods been employed and had properly trained commanders been used.[70]

Lenin noted furthermore that all the theses of the opposition were studded with 'messages between the lines', as exemplified by the simultaneous and contradictory request for the employment of 'specialists' and for collegial operational command.[71] He drew attention to the fact that the theses had been modified following the commission's third session, without however making much difference to essentials.[72] Although it protested its adherence in principle to official military policy, the opposition, in Lenin's view, in fact raised fundamental issues at each step it took.

Finally, it should not be forgotten that Lenin explicitly defended Trotskii from the charge that he had deliberately deserted Congress. He pointed out that the decision that the Central Committee had taken on this matter had been dictated by the 'threatened situation' in which the country found itself.[73] Lenin repeated the allegation, which Voroshilov as usual had been the first to make, that Okulov had had a damaging effect on military operations on the southern front.[74] Thus, if Lenin used his authority to protect the leading group in the War Ministry and to support the general policy that it implemented, he nonetheless avoided looking too closely at individual problems, especially as regards the organization of the party in the front-line detachments. Characteristically, he believed that once the principle of rigid discipline had been accepted everything else would simply fall into place. It was not in any case his job to issue instructions on such matters. Lenin seems in fact to have considered the question of party structure in the units less a matter of principle than a problem of practical expediency. As such, its solution had to be subordinated to a clear acknowledgement of the peculiar and exceptional nature of the military situation.

Lenin's intervention brought about a distinct shift in the balance of forces at Congress. The resolution moved by those who had defended the viewpoint of the Central Committee in the commission gained the support of 174 delegates; 95 voted for the theses of the opposition, and 3 delegates abstained.[75] This success did not appear sufficiently convincing, and the desire to prevent the unity of the party from being undermined prompted the two sides to seek an agreed settlement to the affair. The following day, 22 March, a commission was elected, consisting of three representatives of the majority (Zinov'ev, Pozern, and Stalin) and two of the minority (Safarov and Iaroslavskii).[76] These men were probably selected in an effort to bring to the negotiating table those members of each faction who had displayed the greatest understanding of the viewpoint of the other faction. That very evening, Congress approved with only one abstention both the resolution on military policy drawn up by the commission and Trotskii's theses. And yet, when elections to the leading party organs were held, only 51 delegates out of a total of 301 reportedly voted for the inclusion of Trotskii in the new Central Committee.[77] Confronted with these seemingly conflicting figures, it seems legitimate to enquire who gained the upper hand at the 8th Congress. This is a question to which no firm answers have yet been supplied.[78] It is necessary therefore to examine the final documents approved by Congress.

Winners and losers

We should first take a look at the party programme. The section on 'military work', included in the draft programme, was later incorporated into the document's general introduction. A seven-point section on party policy 'in the military field' was added, which probably circulated in unofficial draft form during Congress.[79] This document featured the injunction that only 'elements from the proletariat and from the semi-proletarian strata of the peasantry, close to the proletariat' were entitled to enter the army (point I). The need to make use of political commissars and of the 'operational leadership' of 'specialists' was reaffirmed (point VI), and it was stated (for the first time in explicit terms) that they had to be 'capable and disinterested communists' (point III). Point VII asserted the principle of the 'combination' of elections and appointment in the selection of commanders, without taking into account Iurenev's declarations to the contrary. The individual sections of the programme did not go into any greater detail: they struck a sensible compromise between a factual statement of the principles on which the armed forces rested, and a blueprint for the eventual transition to a 'socialist militia of the entire people' – which was to follow the 'elimination of classes' (point I). The link between present reality and the future lay in those points that called for the immediate introduction of a form of military training in close contact with factories, trade unions, and production units in the

towns and countryside, and with as little reliance as possible on
barracks (points II and IV). One final condition regarding the training
of a future army stipulated that the command cadre should be selected
from among 'the most capable and energetic soldiers, devoted to the
cause of socialism' (point V).

With a number of significant alterations, Trotskii's theses received
the support of the commission. The point in the programme relating
to the possibility, under certain circumstances, of introducing elections to the post of commander (a point not included in the original
version of the theses) was reproduced word for word, with an
additional phrase proposing that elections for lower-ranking
command personnel be reintroduced in the near future.[80] One particular sentence, stating that attempts by party members 'to make an
issue of principle out of the question of whether or not officers of the
old army might be employed in positions of command' were 'a big
mistake', was removed from the original text.[81] At the point in the
theses where it was declared that Congress had 'adopted' the Central
Committee *instruktsiia* to party cells, the opposition succeeded in
having the important proviso 'as a whole' added.[82] The significance
of this expression may be inferred from the subsequent specific
resolutions on military policy approved by the delegates.

Under the apparently reductive title 'practical measures', a series of
sections were appended to the theses, indicating what Congress
expected their organizational consequences to be.[83] However, not all
the points listed here may be viewed as straightforward restatements
or elaborations of Trotskii's policy: indeed, they are really additions to
the theses and, in some cases, actual corrections to the line that the
War Ministry had been following up until that moment.

Whereas Trotskii's theses had merely entrusted the political departments with the task of expelling from the commissars' corps any
'careerists' that might manage to infiltrate it, the first 'practical
measure' went a step further by making it obligatory to rid the army of
all commanders who were 'not valid from the political and technical
viewpoint'.[84] Furthermore, both at the front and in the rear, special
'attestation commissions' – bodies with this name had been in existence since spring 1918 at territorial military commissariats – were to be
set up. It would be up to them to select candidates for the officer
training academies, where there should be a 'majority representation'
of party members (points III and IV). The Central Committee, in
accordance with point VI, was solemnly called upon to organize the
party forces in the Red Army, with the implication that the current

VBVK was failing in this duty. Point VII stated that 'the centre of gravity of communist work at the front' was to be shifted from the political departments of the fronts to those at army and divisional levels, in order to 'revitalize' such work and 'bring [it] closer' to the detachments. This directive, which in effect envisaged a degree of decentralization in the military political apparatus, was actually the outcome of a compromise between the majority and the opposition on a specific point of dissension that had previously emerged. During the course of a meeting held in Moscow in the second half of January, the representatives of the eastern and northern fronts had requested the immediate abolition of political departments at front level. In the end, however, their continuing existence had been accepted, on the condition that several of their functions were modified and that their power over similar lower–ranking organs was reduced.[85]

The opposition gained acceptance for its characteristic demand that 'an agreed and clear-cut set of regulations, specifying the duties of political commissars, political departments, and communist cells', be issued, as well as for their claim that it was necessary to 'redraft the *polozhenie* on commissars and the RVSs in such a way as to provide a precise definition of the rights and duties of commissars and commanders'. To appreciate the significance of this, one should bear in mind the fact that an order issued by Trotskii on the eve of Congress on the expediency of drawing up a wide-ranging document of this type still struck a very cautious and evasive note.[86] Trotskii had justified the omission of regulations relating to commissars from the Red Army service statute by arguing that 'the institution of commissars [was] not permanent' and could not therefore be codified in a text of such broad institutional scope.

Point VIII envisaged that the VBVK would be abolished and replaced by an RVSR political department which would take over its functions. This body, conceived as a vital part of RVSR, was to be headed by a Central Committee member who would at the same time become a member of RVSR. This dual role was designed to ensure regular and constant feedback between the party centre and military institutions. In all likelihood, the majority accepted this proposal partly in response to the fears that the sudden death of Sverdlov on 16 March had aroused for the future of the party leadership. As Central Committee secretary, Sverdlov had applied his organizational abilities to political work within the army. His death had placed a question mark over the continuity of leadership in this field, and at the same time had made its reinforcement essential.[87]

Point IX called for the service statutes to be rewritten and the 'archaisms' that they contained to be eliminated. As well as this further compliance with requests originating in the opposition camp – which the uncertainties and the amenability expressed by Sokol'nikov and Lenin had clearly made easier – there was also an attempt to revoke measures, introduced over the previous few months, that had granted commanders 'unnecessary privileges'.

Point X is evidence that on the question of relations between commissars and commanders the opposition scored a major success. As well as extending the rights of commissars to participate in the 'economic and administrative' life of the units, as Sokol'nikov had advocated in his speech, the commission granted them (or ratified) broad disciplinary powers, including that of arrest.[88] Despite the rejection of proposals to increase the power of commissars in operational and strategic matters, their control over armed forces service staff was increased. Congress thus reinforced both sides of the commissar's role: the political side (formerly a representative of Soviet power he now became a party man) and the administrative and service side (with the granting of greater authority in economic and disciplinary issues). In particular, the higher-ranking commissars, RVS members, were placed in charge of the *osobye otdely* (special sections), which until that time had remained the reserves of the military organs of the VChK (political police).[89] The 'practical measures' ended with the solemn order that henceforth 'statutes, regulations, and instructions of a general character' had to be submitted to the 'army's political *rabotniki*' for prior discussion.

Yet our examination of the final resolutions voted by Congress does not end here. Delegates passed a second resolution, giving the Central Committee the job of formulating and implementing other 'practical measures',[90] which began to make the points already scored by the opposition seem no more than a prelude to a still greater victory. Sections I, II, and III accepted point by point the criticisms that Stalin and Dzerzhinskii had made in their reports on the Perm' catastrophe, and appeared even to accept their proposals:

> The 8th Party Congress calls on the Central Committee to take immediate steps:
>   1 – to reorganize the *polevyi shtab* (general staff of the field units) by establishing a closer link with the fronts and a more effective leadership over them;
>   2 – to introduce regulations to improve the work of RVSR;
>   3 – to impose order on the work of the *vseroglavshtab* (all-Russian

general staff), as regards deficiencies affecting its activity (the training of detachments, the issuing of regulations, etc.) and as regards
the need to reinforce the party's representation in the said body.

A fourth point introduced the important principle that 'periodic conferences of party *rabotniki* in positions of responsibility' should be held
at the fronts; and, lastly, a fifth proposed that an 'enquiry' be set up
among the said *rabotniki* to discover what solution the various units
had found to the problem of 'the form that command corps decorations should take'.[91]

This resolution was not published with the others and only made its
first appearance in an official review of party resolutions in 1941.[92]
Though it bore witness to the success of several of the positions that
Stalin had upheld in January (and this is probably the reason why it
was published in 1941), it also featured several of the most typical
requests made by the opposition in their desire to reintroduce some
space for democratic discussion into the party, without giving way to
blackmail about the exceptional and dramatic conditions at the front.
The coexistence of these positions in one and the same document was
clear evidence of a convergence – even if unintentional – between the
policy that Stalin pursued, and that favoured by those members of the
'military opposition' who were more sensitive to questions of party
democracy. This was probably the reason why the resolution was
kept secret for so long. But it is significant that, for large groups of
party members, both inside and outside the army, this resolution was
in fact never a secret at all. Indeed, as early as the end of April 1919, it
was printed by *Voennaia mysl'*, the organ of the eastern front RVS – an
action that has all the hall marks of a benevolently tolerated breach of
the directives of the highest party assembly.[93] Even the tortuous
history of this resolution's official publication is a reflection of the
compromise nature of the military resolutions passed by the 8th
Congress.

In his *Short Course* on party history, published in 1938, Stalin made
an attempt to justify the embarrassing fact that on at least one occasion during his career he had been associated with men, some of
whom had been (and would again be) members of groups explicitly
opposed to the Central Committee. While he admitted that numerous
'left communists' had played a part in the 'military opposition', Stalin
emphasized the fact that it also included in its ranks 'some party
workers who had never participated in any opposition, but were
dissatisfied with the way Trotskii was conducting the affairs of the
army'.[94] These people apparently reproached the Commissar for War

not with his mistaken positions of principle, but with his 'veneration for the military experts' and with his 'arrogant and hostile attitude towards the old Bolshevik cadres in the army'. The *Short Course* does not, however, hesitate to disinter the story of 'numerous communists' who Trotskii had had 'shot'[95] – a story which was dramatized at the time by the 'left communist' Sorin as well as by the future Trotskyist Kamenskii.[96] According to Stalin, even if these particular grounds for complaint were valid, on the question of principle regarding 'specialists' and discipline, the opposition had adopted 'incorrect positions' which, however, were defeated at Congress by 'Lenin and Stalin'. In the Stalin years, the affair thus received the following canonical judgement: 'While rejecting a number of proposals made by the "military opposition", the congress dealt a blow at Trotskii by demanding an improvement in the work of the central military institutions and the enhancement of the role of the communists in the army.'[97]

That part of the programme and proposals produced by other ·opposition sectors and incorporated into the two Congress resolutions received, as can be seen, such vague reporting that it might easily be confused with the positions that Stalin had at that time upheld. He had sufficient decency, however, not to claim that every position of every group influenced by left-wing democratism had been rejected.

In actual fact the suspicion that a broad range of groups had joined forces to carry out a manoeuvre behind the scenes at Congress must have remained very strong during the years following 1919, for in summer 1927, at the climax of the struggle against the 'unified opposition' of Trotskii, Zinov'ev, and Kamenev, Stalin still felt obliged to clear himself before the Central Committee and Central Committee Commission of the allegation that he had belonged to the old 'military opposition'. This charge was levelled at him by Trotskii and Zinov'ev, in a desperate attempt to discredit Stalin and to explode his claims to orthodoxy, and thus to shift the balance within the leading party organs in their favour. Having declared that the transcription of Congress proceedings would demonstrate beyond doubt that 'I took a stand on that occasion, along with Lenin, against the so-called "military opposition"', Stalin had to make a small admission, no trace of which, however, remained in the *Short Course*:

> Lastly, there are people here who attended the 8th Party Congress and can confirm the fact that I spoke against the 'Military Opposition' at the 8th Congress. I did not oppose the 'Military Opposition'

as strongly as Trotskii would perhaps have liked, because I considered that in the 'Military Opposition' there were splendid workers who could not be dispensed with at the front; but that I certainly did speak against and combat the 'Military Opposition' is a *fact*, which only incorrigible individuals like Zinov'ev and Trotskii can dispute.[98]

This instant of sincerity was evidently forced upon him by the insidiousness of his adversaries' manoeuvring (at the 8th Congress, Zinov'ev had in fact sat with Stalin on the military commission entrusted with drafting the final documents!). Here again we encounter Stalin's protective attitude towards the 'magnificent cadres' who had received their training at the front-line – an attitude which we have already had occasion to remark upon in connection with the position he adopted during summer and autumn 1918. But these words also recall a number of expressions of benevolence that Lenin made on the eve of Congress, and which Stalin obviously used as a shield. An indication of the real difficulty in which the assault, launched by the opposition in summer 1927, placed Stalin is provided by the fact that immediately following the assertions quoted above, in a last-ditch attempt to demonstrate his own good faith, he did not hesitate to point to the devoted Voroshilov, then the Commissar for War, as a more appropriate butt for the allegations being put forward by Trotskii and Zinov'ev.[99]

In line with the general principle that the Red Army should possess all the characteristics of a regular army, the 8th Congress had in fact rejected the crudest and most ingenuous ideas put forward in opposition to official military policy. These had reflected, on the one hand, the more extreme positions championed by the Tsaritsyn group, and, on the other, those expounded by the more dogmatic former 'left communists'. The need for professional soldiers and rigid centralization was strongly argued. But to depict the clash that occurred at the Congress over the military question matters merely as a conflict between opposing principles would be a gross oversimplification. The resolutions drafted by the conciliation commission substantially modified the military policy that had been pursued until that moment. To some extent the changes that were made did no more than endorse or foreshadow phenomena that had either already emerged on a large scale, or that were in any case bound to arise within the Red Army, which in March 1919, after all, was still in the process of being formed. This observation, it seems to me, applies to the importance that Congress accorded to the political commissars' corps, and also to the substantial extension of their functions. But a number of other measures constituted major innovations: the explicit granting of party functions to commissars (thereby placing them beyond the reach of any sanctions from the military authorities or repressive organs); the introduction of mechanisms for the selection of commanders – over which party men would have an overriding say; the increased importance of the divisional political department; the convening of large authoritative party meetings at the front; and, lastly, the planned modification of relations within the central institutions of the army and between RVSR and the Central Committee. What this foreshadowed was an increase in the ability of party staff to exercise control over the military apparatus, and a relaxation in the centralized authority that the Commissar for War exercised over the army. That the 'secret' resolution called for the Supreme Command to be granted greater sway over the fronts and armies does not, I think, run counter to these new trends. Other directives, apparently taken for granted and obvious, in fact clashed quite openly with the policy of the Commissariat for War, for the simple reason that they appeared in a vitally important text, the resolutions of a Party Congress. This is true for example of the decision to reaffirm the leading role that the Central Committee was supposed to play in the armed forces and of the renewed emphasis placed on 'class mobilization'.

The most unwavering of Trotskii's supporters, as well as his most intransigent adversaries within the ranks of the opposition, could therefore find more than one ground for dissatisfaction in the final resolutions passed by Congress. On the other hand, those, like Stalin, whose proposals had all been accepted without their having had to trumpet democratic slogans, could exult in victory. So too could those who, in their polemics with official policy, had nonetheless displayed an awareness of the trend towards greater centralization and the introduction of strict discipline. This fourth group had in fact gained (for the time being only on paper) precise guarantees that the machinery of the regular army, dangerous as an institution and oppressive in its internal operation, could not be employed for purposes over which there was no general agreement within the party; and also that the party could at any time and at any level step in to correct any irregularities that might come to light. The influence and freedom of manoeuvre that the leading group in the War Ministry had possessed prior to Congress had been reduced; and, at the same time, necessary centralism had been tempered with a massive spread of supervisory centres under the party's control. In spite of the triumph of the majority line, advocating 'iron discipline' (there is no doubt that on this point opposition spokesmen such as V. Smirnov suffered a serious defeat), the principle that party members should play a greater role in the running of the army was endorsed. If, as seemed to be the case, party members were going to support a starkly realistic policy, there were no reasons to keep them in the background.

The viewpoint of the opposition on the accord reached in the conciliation commission was illustrated at Congress by Iaroslavskii. Given the lack of disagreements 'of principle' that had emerged in the commission, 'the practical measures put forward by comrade Sokol'-nikov and by ourselves have converged to a considerable degree'. A unanimous position had in the end been arrived at 'through corrections, and through the combination of these or those proposals'. Iaroslavskii did not of course fail to point out that 'the gravity and importance' of the situation at the front had focussed attention on the wisdom of reaching an accord, even 'independently of the fact that disagreements do or do not exist' (a remark that could in fact have been made equally well by representatives of the official line). But despite this significant rider, Iaroslavskii summed up with considerable conviction what the opposition felt it had secured from the majority:

> We believe that in future, when political work is reorganized, when political leadership is fully in the hands of the Central Committee, when local party organizations take a more systematic and active part in the management of army work, that our communist comrades at the front and in the rear will have sufficient means to exercise the influence of the party on the centres, on the committees [sic], and to alter this or that aspect of the work, with the necessary fairness.[100]

Thus, without any alteration to the Central Committee *instruktsiia* of January 5, and without any undermining of the principle of a strict and harsh military regime, Congress decisions marked a shift towards a new conception of the role of the communist military, and away from that which Trotskii had striven to impose over the preceding months. Above all since September 1918, a party structure had been outlined that pursued a rigid criterion of functionality, of adherence to hierarchy and to the service regulations that the Commissar for War was engaged in establishing. In contrast, the resolutions passed by Congress signalled a greater autonomy for party organs with respect to military bodies, entrusting the former with the task of restoring balance and of making up for the excesses that the choice of a regular army might bring about. The structurally contradictory elements that made up the Red Army were thus accentuated, far beyond the limit that Trotskii and his collaborators had originally foreseen.

The 'organizational question'

A brief examination of the course taken by discussion at Congress on the more general 'organizational question', and on the party and state machinery that were emerging under the pressure of causes beyond anyone's control and of measures that were often haphazard and inconsistent, supports the foregoing conclusion. There is a close link between the way in which Congress tackled this issue and the approach that eventually led to a settlement of the thorny military question. According to Osinskii, speaking at the end of Congress, once the commission that had been called upon to draw up resolutions on the organizational question had reached an agreement on the broader dispute over its own authority, it had not been hard to 'narrow the gap' between the positions of the majority and of the opposition on military matters.[101] Osinskii even stated that thanks to the agreement reached on the first issue, it had proved possible to incorporate the opposition theses on military affairs 'to an increasing extent, within the programme of the Central Committee speaker [Sokol'nikov]'.

The clash at the 8th Congress on the question of organization occurred between those who argued that 'the further one gets from the centre of leadership, the shoddier is party work..., the worse things go' (Zinov'ev),[102] and those, on the other hand, who, like Osinskii and Sapronov, urged the need to limit and regulate the meddling of the centre in the affairs of peripheral Soviet and party organs.[103] Moreover, whereas the speakers who defended Central Committee policy indicated that cases of arbitrary and authoritarian intervention by the central organs were inevitable in the emergency situation created by the Civil War, their adversaries expressed the fear that they might in fact be facing a full-fledged process of 'degeneration',[104] affecting the party as a whole, its mode of operation and leadership. From this second viewpoint, the causes of this 'degeneration' appeared to lie in the generalized 'concentration of powers' and in the gradual abandonment of the principle that officials and leaders, in both state and party, should be subject to election.[105] The opposition, however, demonstrated that, apart from this handful of concepts, there was not much that united them. The solutions they put forward went in quite different directions. Whereas Osinskii, for example, was convinced that it would be a good idea to include as many Central Committee members in SNK as possible, in order to ensure that the party retained effective control and leadership of state machinery,[106] Sapronov called for a greater degree of politicization of the Central Committee, demanding that its members involve themselves solely in party work.[107] Nor did Osinskii's positions constitute a fully coherent political package: while calling for the integration of the top levels of party and state, he nonetheless proposed a 'delimitation of powers' between central and local Soviet authorities, on the French pattern, thereby juxtaposing sharply contrasting models of political organization.[108] Osinskii also hoped that an 'administrative law code', of the type in force in 'bourgeois societies', would be drafted, and that corresponding 'administrative courts' might be set up to investigate the abuses of the central organs.[109] Sapronov, although he vehemently denounced the centre's bully-boy behaviour, was less 'academic'[110] than Osinskii, and bowed to the political will of the Central Committee and to its sense of fairness.[111] The range of positions championed by their adversaries gave Central Committee spokesmen plenty of room to manoeuvre. Zinov'ev mentioned Sapronov in passing as 'the most serious representative of the opposition', thus making it known that the Central Committee did not feel that it was confronted with a united front.[112]

If radically differing viewpoints might contend regarding the fate of Soviet and party democracy, both sides were agreed over another worrying phenomenon: the absorption of party cadres into the machinery of state. There was a widespread fear that groups of communists might, by pursuing the contingent and special demands of the administrative bodies to which they were attached, lose touch with the everyday life of the party organizations, and become cut off from the party as a whole. This danger seemed particularly threatening in view of the fact that Bolshevik organizations often stood in for representative and administrative Soviet organs in local government. Osinskii declared that ever since the 7th Congress 'the party [had] not had a political line': it had been too busy dealing with day-to-day necessities. Over the same period, 'even the Central Committee, as a collegial organ, [had] in effect ceased to exist'.[113]

Even though they rejected the extreme terms in which the opposition couched their polemic, those who spoke in defence of the centre's policy stated their agreement with many of the opposition's demands. They were just as afraid as Osinskii that the party might cease to 'reproduce itself'[114] as a political body capable of leadership, and that it might come merely to reflect the contrasting positions and conflicts triggered by situations in which it became ensnared. Zinov'ev gave his support to the move to provide the Central Committee with a 'technical apparatus' of sufficient size and efficiency to enable it to maintain relations with local organizations. Kaganovich, for his part, said he agreed with Osinskii that it would be a good idea for local party organizations to possess a cadre of officials devoted 'exclusively' to party work.[115] In the end, a common basis for agreement was found. Congress passed a token resolution in favour of democracy in the Soviets and against 'bureaucratism',[116] and another that supported centralization and the introduction of 'military discipline' in the party.[117] The abolition of all party organizations constructed 'on a professional basis' (in the railways, for example) was declared, in response to the broad wish to return all decision-taking processes – which, it was felt, had risked becoming isolated and one-sided – to their proper collegial and territorial bases.[118] The groups of communist deputies in elected Soviet organs were brought back under the strict control of their corresponding territorial party committees.[119]

Above all, the need to strengthen the Central Committee and to equip it with a more efficient internal organization was affirmed, as was the importance of a strong structure linking the centre with the party periphery.[120] The emergence of this practical spirit, embodied in the final resolutions, probably made it easier to reach an agreement. Many delegates and opposition members may have been induced, by Lenin's statement in his opening report, to underestimate the political aspect of the problems under discussion: 'Organizational activity was never a strong point with the Russians in general, nor with the Bolsheviks in particular; nevertheless the chief problem of the proletarian revolution is that of organization.'[121]

Yet the gulf between the two positions was real and had become conspicuous. It is symptomatic, for example, that Osinskii referred continually throughout the debate to the party regime that had existed 'before' the seizure of power. He would have liked to see the 'old rules' of the party restored, believing that they would have compelled members to participate 'personally' in the work of one of its organizations.[122] He also favoured the revival of conferences organized by the Central Committee with the attendance of active militants from the party periphery and base.[123] He even reflected longingly on the times when, thanks to the dynamic activity of the 'left communists', the internal atmosphere of the party had been 'vitalized' by lively discussion.[124] Kagonovich, on the other hand, derided proposals such as that made by Sapronov to introduce into the Central Committee 'workers tied to the masses'. Kaganovich argued that a clean break had to be made with 'before', when 'factory workers carried out party work in the evening', in their spare time.[125] Afanesov, replying to critics, elaborated a theory whereby internal democracy could no longer be the party's principal concern:

> We have ceased to be an illegal organization, we have emerged from the narrow bounds that used to hem us in. We have become the State and yet you want to shut the State in the straight-jacket of illegality, and you say that within these bounds we can go about our work as we used to. But there is no doubt that methods have changed and that we must evolve a new party apparatus to suit these new methods. This is the main position that we must argue. But to say that we must busy ourselves with self-criticism, that this is a way of improving our situation, is nonsense ... If, in the military sphere, we had tolerated as much self-criticism in the narrow circles of party assemblies as was permitted at Congress, I believe that we would not have managed to build the Red Army, which is fighting splendidly along our fronts.[126]

The agreements reached on the general issue of organization and on military affairs in fact rested on the same basis: the recognition of the need for a massive reinforcement of party machinery to enable it to perform the new functions that the older territorial and collegial organizations had found it difficult or impossible to carry out. It was also accepted that greater internal cohesion was required, backed by an increase in supervisory powers, which the party bodies should be able to exert on their own members. The centre saw these measures as a vital way of implementing its own policy, while the opposition accepted them as a safeguard against the more arbitrary aspects of state and administrative centralization. Perhaps the most significant indication of the reasoning of certain opposition groups at the 8th Congress was the development of the attitude taken by a sizable section of the 'military opposition' towards the institution of the commissar: the fact that Congress strengthened the prestige and power of the commissars, probably more than the War Ministry had previously considered expedient, demonstrated that many members of the opposition, when their other hopes had been dashed, were prepared to put their faith in this institution, despite its unmistakable and inevitably authoritarian character.[127]

Osinskii, however, wanted it to be known that the stated intention 'not to constitute, at any cost, an opposition' had facilitated the signing of the accord.[128] In his concluding speech, Lenin spoke of 'defects' in military policy, to which Congress had found remedies. Uncertainty remains as to whether his satisfaction was due more to the merits of the solutions that had been approved or to the spirit of unity that delegates of every tendency had displayed. It was on this note that Congress officially concluded its proceedings:

> We adopted a unanimous decision on the military question. Vast though the differences of opinion may have appeared at first, diverse as may have been the views of the many comrades who very frankly criticized the shortcomings of our military policy, we on the commission found no difficulty in arriving at an absolutely unanimous decision, and we shall leave this Congress convinced that our chief defender the Red Army, for the sake of which the whole country is making such incalculable sacrifices, will find in every delegate to the Congress, in every member of the party, a warm, unselfish, and devoted assistant, leader, friend, and collaborator.[129]

Trotskii's reaction

Several years later, in December 1923, during the course of a new and decisive political clash within the Central Committee, Trotskii readily acknowledged that the policy that the War Ministry had pursued in 1918–19 had included a number of unsatisfactory aspects. His retrospective assessment of the course that the 8th Congress had taken provides an outline not all that different from that supplied by Stalin in his *Short Course* – once due allowance has been made for the political slant of the latter work. Confronted with the disagreements of the final months of 1923, Trotskii clearly felt it was necessary to show magnanimity regarding those of the past:

> On problems regarding the construction of the army, we had within the party a strong and tenacious grouping. Essentially, this opposition was against the construction of a regular army, with all the consequences that that involves: a centralized military apparatus, the recruitment of specialists, etc. At certain moments the struggle became extremely acute ... Certain of the exaggerations and awkwardness of official military policy were thus attenuated, not without the influence of the military opposition, and without any damage being done, on the contrary, to the benefit of the centralized construction of a regular army. The opposition itself was then gradually reabsorbed. Not only were a very great number of its representatives called upon to work for the army, they occupied posts of responsibility.[130]

By the end of 1923 Trotskii was eager to demonstrate that there was no shortage within Bolshevik tradition of significant cases in which an internal opposition had performed a positive function by promoting its own demands and by struggling for their incorporation in the political line of the party. But at the time, in March 1919, his reception of the decisions that the 8th Congress had reached on military policy was far removed indeed from this saccharine providential vision of the salutary effects of lively internal dialectics.

Trotskii, who had asked for and been granted permission to go to the eastern front, following the disaster at Ufa and the large-scale attack that White General Kolchak had unleashed on this area, kept himself well-informed of Congress proceedings.[131] On 20 March V. Smirnov made his co-report, and on the 22nd Trotskii telegraphed to Stalin asking him to suggest to Smirnov, the official speaker for the 'military opposition', that he remain in the capital 'on party or other work' (Smirnov was a member of the eastern front 5th army RVS, the unit which, by yielding to the enemy, had triggered off the dangerous situation in the east).[132] Trotskii also demanded that Smirnov be compelled to present at the first opportunity a draft amendment to the Red Army service regulations that he had criticized at Congress, or even entirely new draft regulations.[133] The impression, however, that the Commissar for War might be inclined to take account of the dissatisfaction expressed by the opening speeches to Congress turned out to be illusory. On 25 March, on informing Lenin of the reasons for the 5th army's collapse, Trotskii voiced the categorical opinion that 'without doubt the lack of firmness, the grumbling, and the criticism encouraged from above' by those with political responsibility for the unit, had to be considered the overriding reason for the fragility that the said army had shown in combat. In particular:

> The RVS [of the 5th army] hunts for the weak points in the internal service regulations instead of apprehending those intent on disor-ganizing the army, and of setting up a solid regime ... According to my information, the army newspaper was an organ of discussion and criticism. I recommend that the critics be removed from the newspaper, and that it be turned into a military organ of firm discipline.[134]

This was an extremely effective way of pointing out to the Moscow authorities that there were really very few men who had called its policy into question at Congress, and that their actions within the army were disastrous. The following month, Vatsetis told Lenin that in his opinion the 5th army had collapsed as a result of the friction between those in charge of the party, on the one hand, and the commanders, on the other.[135] In this context, Trotskii's message to Stalin may be seen as an explicit invitation to rid the front of Smirnov and his followers. Trotskii did not express his indignation in confidential messages alone. On 24 March he wrote a searing article, which he addressed 'To the communists of the eastern front', and which appeared in the newspaper printed on his famous armoured train. Without naming any names, but evidently referring to Smirnov, he attacked the attitude of those communists who put 'their views and criticism of the military system' before their duty as soldiers. 'Orders were orders': that was all there was to it. Responsibility for military reverses was laid at their door. It was absolutely intolerable that 'the political department of an army' (the 5th?) took the liberty of 'discrediting in the military press institutions and individuals to whom Soviet power has given a task demanding responsibility'. The political departments, Trotskii suggested, should not forget that they were organs 'unconditionally subject to the RVSs' and that they had no 'autonomous' tasks other than those 'indicated and prescribed by their RVS'. His conclusions were extremely tough:

> Those who do not agree with this policy do not have the right to act in the name of the party, to abuse its name and its authority, because, in the last instance, it is of no interest to the party and to the Republic who it is that damages the internal cohesion of the army, whether it be a Left Social Revolutionary, or an insubordinate communist who abuses his position of responsibility for ends that are directly opposed to those for which he was sent to the front.[136]

The way in which the Central Committee replied to Trotskii's remonstrances indicated that something in the party centre's approach to military issues had changed and that the centre would no longer be willing to listen to the Commissar for War to the exclusion of all others, as had earlier been the case with respect to the resolution of 25 December 1918.

The Central Committee met on 25 March.[137] Zinov'ev introduced the discussion with a summary of Congress resolutions on the military question. He declared that the unpublished resolutions constituted 'the expression of the genuine wishes of Congress' and at the same time that it contained 'a concession of a kind' (svoego roda ustupki) to the opposition. This underscored the importance of the role Zinov'ev had played in the conciliation commission. In Zinov'ev's view, 'Congress had, by token of its entire line of conduct on the military question, administered a serious caution'. To whom?

The Central Committee minutes do not provide a clear answer, but Zinov'ev removes all doubts by adding: 'It is essential for Comrade Lenin to talk things over with Comrade Trotskii.' And Lenin requested that Zinov'ev's statement be put in writing and that the Central Committee append its own resolution in the form of a conclusion. The text of this resolution has not been made available. According to the most recent text-book on party history, on the following day, 26 March, it even gained the approval of the Politbiuro. Section 5 apparently read as follows: 'Inform (*ukazat'*) Comrade Trotskii of the need to pay the utmost attention to front-line communist *rabotniki*. Without their full comradely solidarity, it will be impossible to implement the military policy of the Central Committee.'[138]

Judging by these lines, the resolution was rather forthright in tone, even if not all its points were criticial of Trotskii's actions. In the elusive phrasing of the text-book, the resolution was, however, 'aimed entirely' at Trotskii.

During the session, Stalin gave his backing *en passant* to Smirnov's proposal that the Central Committee 'enquire of Comrade Trotskii as to the reasons for his having been recalled from the front'.[139]

Trotskii replied to the Central Committee between 26 and 31 March, after he had received the Congress and Central Committee resolutions.[140] Faced with the resolutions of Congress, he could not conceal a certain bewilderment (in part, as we have seen, legitimate). Although they seemed to him not to contain 'anything that contradicts the policy of the War Ministry', they were, in his view, formulated 'in supremely general (*obshchee*) and vague terms, and part of them are based on a misunderstanding'. In particular, the 'secret' resolution did not specify whether or not it recommended that RVSR be reorganized in such a way that he, Trotskii, would have from then on to 'sit at the centre' and to stop touring the fronts. Trotskii asked the Central Committee to clarify its 'understanding of this question'. As regards the resolution's second point, Trotskii explained that he and Sverdlov had never managed, however much they might have wished to do so, to find party members who were 'suitable' (i.e. who had the necessary competence) to become members of the general staff. He then went on to indicate that he would not oppose the appointment of Smilga and Lashevich, whose names had been mentioned at the time by Sverdlov himself. The proposal that regular conferences of front-line communists should be held appeared to him, for security reasons, to be 'scarcely possible'. As for the 'enquiry' into uniform and insignia, he accused the Central Committee of not knowing what they were talking about, given that insignia as such had not in fact been reintroduced.

Trotskii displayed similar bewilderment regarding Congress's published resolution: 'All these clauses amount either to merely underlining measures that either have long since been or are being taken, or to proposals for organizational changes that in no way constitute matters of principle.'[141] This comment was a way of tackling what had in fact wounded Trotskii most: the content of Zinov'ev's speech, a copy of which had been sent to him. Once again, there seemed to be something dark and ambiguous going on: 'This report lays down a special point of view on the practical proposals mentioned above and has, as it were, to fix some sort of *new line of conduct.*'[142]

Unfortunately all we know of Zinov'ev's text is its fleeting mention in the minutes of the Central Committee and Trotskii's critical reply to it. It may, however, be noted that Trotskii appeared to be worried not so much by any concrete and novel directives as by the manoeuvre that they reflected and which had actually taken place at Congress.

As far as may be gathered, Zinov'ev had sought to play down the existence of a 'military opposition', by neatly sorting its members into two categories: in Trotskii's words, 'offended gentry who count for little', and, secondly, those who, while ready to back a regular army in principle, had declared themselves 'extremely dissatisfied with my attitude'. Trotskii conceded that the first group really did exist: they were men such as Osinskii, 'largely consisting of offended Soviet officials and cases of nervous exhaustion'. But he was in no way disposed to show any understanding for the second category, in which Zinov'ev had included Voroshilov: in any case, he would have nothing to do with 'psychological case-histories'. Among the reasons for protesting against 'military specialists', Trotskii discerned a 'plebeian' and 'shabby' component, which he felt typified the men of the new regime. The issue was more than a purely military one:

> The opposition as a whole, in both its better half and in its worse half, reflects the fearful difficulties of the dictatorship of a hungry, internally-rent working class, alongside an ill-informed, discontented, and mutinous peasantry. We see these difficulties on all sides. In the military sphere they assume their most concentrated form. All the shortages, discordances and shortcomings of Soviet work, all the slovenliness of Soviet officials express themselves in their most intensified form within the organism of the army.[143]

Nor did this analysis apply only to the officials: the opposition also reflected the prejudices of a certain 'stratum of workers given to oversimplification'. It was much more important to proceed with the 're-education' of these masses than to worry about 'the Obolenskiis and Smirnovs'.[144]

It was not only a matter of reassessing the importance of competence and of specific knowhow: the army could not survive without discipline and yet the enforcement of discipline in the Red Army continued to follow 'a long and painful path'. Replying to Zinov'ev, Trotskii rejected the distinction between 'purely formal discipline' and 'comradely' discipline. Deaf to any appeal for a display of solidarity with fellow party members, the Commissar for War regarded 'comradely' discipline as that of the 'household', and as likely to lead, where implemented, to 'the complete disintegration of the army'. The difference between Trotskii's approach and the one that emerged from Congress could scarcely be illustrated in more telling terms. Indignant at Zinov'ev's flirtation with the idea of showing greater tolerance towards the more turbulent and sensitive party members in the army, Trotskii refused to consider as discipline any other relation not based on the strictest and most orthodox meaning of the word: 'I think that the party relationship of communists with one another is, in the military sphere, in fact translated into unconditional and comprehensive formal discipline.'[145]

Certainly, he admitted, the recent firing squads ordered by the 5th army tribunal were not 'comradely'. But he was encouraged by the fact that many authoritative Bolsheviks, who had left for the front as 'irreconcilable opponents of our military system', had quickly realized the need to operate in an unflinching manner. The opposition would therefore melt away as it gained concrete experience. Given the delicacy of the moment, it would be damaging to give in to those who begged for 'the screws to be eased off'. The letter ended with what sounded like a resolute condemnation of Zinov'ev and an appeal to the Central Committee to review its positions, if indeed these really were embodied in Zinov'ev's speech:

> [It] inspires the most serious apprehension that he is seeking a
> solution to the question precisely along the line of an easing-off in
> the system and adjusting it to conform with the weariness of certain
> elements in our party. Insofar as the *biuro* of the Central Committee
> has approved Comrade Zinov'ev's report, I wish to believe that it is
> not this aspect of the report that it has approved, for, if the contrary
> should be the case, I personally would not myself see any possibility

of counting on the party being successful in the severe struggle ahead of it.[146]

Very tough words, containing a clear threat of resignation. The main point in Trotskii's argument was his refusal to recognize the validity of party relationships alongside, let alone above, hierarchical relations of an administrative or state order. Likewise, he refused to subordinate the behaviour of the military organs of the Republic to narrow, one might say private ('household'), considerations. Also, one can see how this conception ties in closely with the other, i.e. with the need that the command and hierarchy be founded on a mastery of the requisite skills in accordance with which enthusiastic but ignorant militants had inevitably to be placed under the command of 'specialists'. Tinged with intellectual rigour, this assertion gave the positions that Lenin had expressed in March–April of the previous year, in his famous article 'The Immediate Tasks of Soviet Government', a markedly authoritarian and aristocratic interpretation: as was illustrated by the contemptuous and irritated allusions to the 'plebeian' character of the opposition's platform and to the 'superficiality' of the way that mass movements confronted the problems of socialist reconstruction. Trotskii demonstrated in his reply that he had understood the compromise nature of the resolutions passed by the 8th Congress, and refused to acknowledge what had formed the main ground for agreement in the conciliation commission: the guarantee that the communist military in command at various levels could enjoy an exceptional status before the commands and the central organs. Trotskii did not intend to pay the price for this compromise. Those who had drafted the resolutions of Congress would still have to do a lot of fighting to translate into practical terms some of the most important points listed therein. On the face of it, the military policy that Trotskii embodied had won the day, since many of the gains made by his adversaries remained unpublished. Over the months to come Trotskii strove to exploit this fact in order to preserve the policy of the War Ministry unchanged.

6   Rupture and reconciliation

A new emergency

Some of the measures that the 8th Congress had approved began to be implemented within a few weeks of its closure. The most important of these had to do with the central organs in charge of political work in the army. In April 1919, the VBVK was abolished and in May an RVSR political department was set up in its place, though it was given the official title PUR (the Political Administration of RVSR).[1] Smilga, Beloborodov, Serebriakov, and Rakovskii were appointed to run it.[2] With the exception of Beloborodov, who had only been voted onto the Central Committee at the recent Congress,[3] all these leaders had for a long time been members of the party's leading body.[4] In contrast, Iurenev, the head of the abolished VBVK, had never been a member of the Central Committee.[5]

General agreement had probably been reached over Smilga's appointment. As will be recalled, Kamenskii had mentioned him in his article as the man who had had the courage to stand in the way of the alleged acts of arbitrary repression ordered by Trotskii against communist commissars.[6] His name also figured among the men whom Stalin and Dzerzhinskii recommended at the time of the enquiry into the fall of Perm' as worthy to take over the command of the 3rd army.[7] At the same time, a man who on the eve of Congress had proposed the abolition of political commissars, and a transition to a system of one-man command, could in no way be suspected of harbouring excessively narrow party feelings. At the beginning of April, Trotskii himself wrote a letter to the Central Committee requesting that Smilga be appointed to RVSR.[8]

The party apparatus at the front was altered in the way the Congress resolutions had indicated. At the beginning of May, RVSR issued a general organizational model of the political departments.[9]

The 'centre of gravity' of political work was in effect shifted towards the divisional political department. Indeed, the front political department no longer had commanding power over the army and divisional political departments. The divisional political department was made directly responsible for the activity of detachment cells, and it gained the right to run its own newspaper. Regimental commissars remained, however, under the control of the army political department. A few party leaders at divisional level, probably recalling previous disputes, immediately construed the new directives as a means of suppressing front political departments: they derived satisfaction from the thought that the central organs had thus created the conditions for the extinction of phenomena involving that 'detachment from the masses and lack of vitality' that had previously characterized the work of the political departments at army and front levels.[10]

The system in force at the front was extended to the rear. At the end of March, 'administrations for political education' were set up at the *okrug* military commissariats.[11] To judge by the powers that they were granted, embracing not only the running of mass 'education' projects, but also the appointment and supervision of rear detachment commissars, these were organs similar to those operating in the field army. The territorial committees, however, were not completely deprived of their authority over the cells.

The three crucial points in the secret resolution were not, however, followed up in any concrete way. Trotskii felt confident enough to continue his policy of firmly denouncing all cases in which manifestations of left-wing dissension ran the risk of compromising the troops' ability to fight. Such was the case for example of the spate of disputes in the 3rd army, to which Safarov also belonged.[12] It was at this time that Trotskii asked the Central Committee to appoint a commission of enquiry into the 'Panteleev case', in view of the fact that it had again been raised at Congress. He argued that the full facts of the episode needed to be made known so that it might cease to act as a rallying-point for opposition to the military policy of the Commissariat for War.[13] The Central Committee granted his request. He also refocussed his attention and invective on the Soviet forces in the south, and in particular on those operating in the Ukraine. Although he commented sceptically that Voroshilov 'now seems to have become a fervent supporter of an *obshchegosudarstvennaia* military policy' (i.e. a policy no longer conducted by individual Red commanders acting in isolation, as had occurred at Tsaritsyn), Antonov-

Ovseenko, Bubnov, and Podvoiskii, all members of the Ukrainian front command, began to figure among his bugbears, and he soon requested that they be removed from military work.[14] In Trotskii's view, the southern troops and their commands stubbornly continued to take their cue from *partizanstvo* methods. At the beginning of June, he managed to convince the Politbiuro that it would be best to withhold from Voroshilov full civil and military powers in the Donets basin and to grant him narrower duties within the military sphere alone.[15] Regarding the behaviour of the Soviet commanders in the Ukraine, Lenin voiced opinions and judgements that broadly coincided with those of Trotskii.[16]

The gravity of the military situation in which the Republic now found itself, hard-pressed to the east by Kolchak and to the south with unprecedented violence by Denikin, diminished the likelihood of fresh traumatic crises within the party. At the same time, however, it placed a huge burden of responsibility on the Supreme Command, and at every step ran the risk of exacerbating just those strains that Congress had set out to soothe. The causes of these tensions had remained largely unaltered: Stalin therefore intervened to reopen the internal polemic.

Since May Stalin had been in Petrograd by order of the Sovet *oborony*, which had vested in him extraordinary powers to organize the defence of the city against the forces of White Generals Iudenich and Rodzianko.[17] As early as 25 May, he warned Lenin that neither the Supreme Command nor its general staff had a clear idea of the state of the Red units in the area, and he informed him that he had opposed Vatsetis' view that the Soviet Fleet should be drastically reduced.[18] On 4 June Lenin, for his part, informed Sklianskii that Stalin had requested the removal of Okulov, who had been transferred to the Petrograd sector of the western front.[19] Stalin claimed that Okulov was 'urging the military specialists on against our commissars'.[20] In a renewed and reinvigorated onslaught on one of his favourite targets, Stalin stated that the *vseroglavshtab* '[was] working for the Whites', a fact which documents at his disposal would make 'obvious'.[21] As confirmation of his suspicions, he cited the irregularities which he himself had brought to the attention of the Central Committee in January in the reports on the fall of Perm'. Not even the commander of the western front, a former Tsarist officer, escaped unscathed: Stalin expressed his total lack of faith in the man's ability to save the front.

All the familiar reasons for Stalin's opposition to official military policy were once again aired, including the personal resentment he felt for the upstart Okulov, who had urged that the 7th Petrograd army be brought more firmly under the command of the RVSR general staff. Okulov was the first to bear the brunt of the fresh outbreak of hostilities between the two rival groupings. He was rapidly dismissed from his post by means of a Politbiuro resolution that made 'the solid unity in Petrograd military work' the overriding priority, with a view to securing a speedy victory over the enemy.[22] As late as 3 June, Lenin – who on the following day would announce the decision that the Politbiuro had reached – called on the people of Petrograd to fall in with Okulov's orders, warning that: 'The conflict with Okulov must not be allowed to grow. Think it over well, for it is simply impossible to recall him.'[23] Unlike during the Tsaritsyn episode, Lenin and the party centre on this occasion gave in instantly to the demands made by Stalin and to those of the Petrograd party that shared his positions and agreed with his analyses.

No comment from Trotskii on this decision has survived. The impression, however, that military and political circles, with which the reader is now familiar, began at once to regain influence at the party centre, is, I think, supported by a message that Lenin sent Trotskii on 5 June. In it Lenin carefully set out the idea of sending Minin back to Tsaritsyn, which was still under siege.[24] Trotskii replied frostily that it was up to the 10th army RVS to assess the wisdom of the proposal. For his part, he was 'in general' against sending 'people acting as authorized and specially authorized delegates, with undefined functions and undefined mutual relationships' with the ordinary military and state hierarchy.[25]

On 16 June, at the end of a triumphant military operation, which he claimed he had carried off in opposition to the views of the 'specialists', Stalin wrote haughtily to Lenin that success had been secured by the intervention of 'civilians', who had not hesitated to oppose the mistaken orders of the professional military.[26] These civilians belonged, for the most part, to the Petrograd party: in the notes exchanged between Lenin and Sklianskii on the situation in the threatened city, Zinov'ev's name crops up as an adversary of those representing the War Ministry and the 'specialists'.[27] Two days later, Stalin once again began expounding to Lenin his thesis that high-ranking Soviet officers had been hatching a plot.[28] The traitors, however, were no longer deemed to be at the head of the War Ministry: it was now disclosed that they occupied positions close to the 7th army command. Thus scaled down (much to Lenin's satisfaction),[29] the plot theory appeared acceptable even to Trotskii, as may be seen from his autobiography.[30]

Half way through June, the main element in the crisis that was brewing began to reach the boil. On 15 June the Central Committee gave its backing to the plan elaborated by the eastern front RVS to follow their initial gains with a fresh counter-attack against Kolchak. Gusev, of the front RVS, had already been appointed to RVSR as the commissar of the operational general staff attached to the Supreme Commander.[31] Vatsetis was firmly opposed to this strategic approach, and proposed that the attack in the east be interrupted in order to detach from this front a number of units that could then be sent as reinforcements to the southern front, which was under pressure from Denikin.[32] Trotskii supported the Commander-in-Chief's plan and this gave the affair considerable political importance. On the 17th, in a message to the Central Committee, Lenin contested a note written by Trotskii, which had probably sought to defend the general staff's plan and to oppose the appointment of Gusev to RVSR (in fact as a supervisor of Vatsetis). Lenin declared that 'Comrade Trotskii [was] mistaken' and that the steps that the Central Committee had taken on the 15th in favour of a plan drawn up by a group of the Supreme Commander's subordinates had been occasioned by the fact that 'all is not well at Headquarters'.[33]

As for the eastern front leaders, by the time the Central Committee met to reach a decision on the strategic plan, they had grounds for deep resentment against Trotskii. At the beginning of May Trotskii had provoked their anger by removing from his position as front commander S. S. Kamenev, who had been in favour of continuing the attack that had been launched. By making a personal application to Lenin, they had, however, managed to have Kamenev's dismissal overturned.[34] The decision to appeal for arbitration to the party leader was taken by Gusev, Lashevich, and Iurenev, who demonstrated in this way that they were to be counted among Trotskii's adversaries.[35] On 20 May, having acted patiently with Sklianskii and Aralov to reach a compromise with Vatsetis, Lenin asked Trotskii to reinstate Kamenev.[36] Moreover, at the end of the month, in a letter to the eastern front RVS, Lenin warmly argued the need to conquer the Urals as soon as possible, by pushing on with the attack.[37] It is therefore likely that during this period the party centre was gradually beginning to suspect that Trotskii was 'venting his rage'[38] on the eastern front for the way in which its RVS had gone over his and

Aralov's head, by making a direct appeal to Lenin on the Kamenev case. As has been noted, this clashed with Trotskii's own attitude of 'jealous protection of the proper functioning of the military establishment'.[39] An issue which appeared to be of purely technical and strategic importance thus involved long-standing questions of principle regarding the way in which the army was to operate in the Soviet Republic.

The decision that the Central Committee reached on 15 June to back the plan drawn up by the eastern front RVS should therefore be viewed as the climax of the process whereby Trotskii and RVSR became increasingly isolated from the party centre, in the wake of developments on the western and eastern fronts in spring 1919. In particular, Trotskii was progressively alienating the commanders and political leaders (including Frunze) who, after their victorious counter-offensive in the east, were now able to insist on having a decisive say in the most vital military affairs of the Republic. To the surprised delight of those who had managed to gain approval at the 8th Congress for the 'secret' resolution, Trotskii was caught on the wrong foot at just the right moment: had not Stalin, at the very same time, uncovered yet another plot by 'specialists' in Petrograd?

Careful stock was taken of this situation at the Central Committee session held on 3–4 July, attended, among others, by Lenin, Stalin, and Trotskii.[40] First of all, this meeting decided to replace Vatsetis with S. Kamenev, as Supreme Commander of the Republic, while compensating the former with an 'honorable military position' in Moscow, on a commensurate salary.[41] Trotskii tried to have a different candidate (M. D. Bonch-Bruevich) appointed, but came up against the opposition of a majority on the Central Committee.[42] Alterations were also made to the composition of RVSR, the number of members being reduced to five, with Trotskii still in his position as president. Of the previous members, Sklianskii, Gusev, and Smilga were confirmed – although the presence of Gusev, as we have seen, cannot be regarded as a mark of political continuity.[43] The new members were Rykov and of course S. Kamenev, the former in his capacity as manager of the Republic's supplies. Danishevskii, Kobozev, Mekhonoshin, Raskol'nikov, Rozengol'ts, I. N. Smirnov, Muralov, Iurenev, Aralov, Stalin, and Satov, who had joined RVSR at different times, were all now deprived of membership.[44]

Rozengol'ts, Raskol'nikov, Muralov, Iurenev, and I. N. Smirnov had been among Trotskii's original collaborators.[45] But on their own these changes in personnel do not convey the political significance of the Central Committee's decision. The previous RVSR had been so large a body that it had been necessary to concentrate real powers in a smaller group, consisting of Trotskii, Vatsetis, and Aralov, formally legitimized by VTsIK on 30 November 1918 in the same resolution that constituted the Sovet oborony.[46] It was these men who had always taken all the main decisions. By reducing the number of RVSR members, the Central Committee evidently intended to strengthen rather than to undermine its collegial character, given that from now on only those who 'actually'[47] worked at the highest level of military affairs, as the Central Committee had formulated it, could be members. The third decision taken by the Central Committee Plenum in July, to transfer the operational general staff from Serpukhov to Moscow, was a further move to gain greater control over the activities of the top leaders in the War Ministry.[48]

The Central Committee also decided to bring into force the resolution carried by the 8th Congress calling for an *instruktsiia* to define the powers of the political commissars. The minutes of the meeting refer to a 'draft letter from the Central Committee to military commissars', submitted by Zinov'ev, which was to be sent out subject to consultation with Trotskii.[49] Later, the idea was to compile a set of instructions, which Trotskii and Smilga would be called upon to draft.

By deciding to put a stop to the 'mass dispatch of communists' to the front, the Central Committee accepted a request that had probably originated with the party organizations in Moscow and Leningrad: in future, the selection of cadres for military work would be placed on a rigorously 'personal' footing.[50] The party was obviously beginning to show signs of exhaustion in the rear. But the additional directive that from now on communists drawn from the largest organizations should be given only 'posts as commissars' or positions of comparable importance in the rear, revealed something of the exasperation of party men despatched to the front as ordinary soldiers. However much this might be justified by the increasing scarcity of available cadres, it was a further concession to a party spirit that had been extremely strong over the previous few months.

According to official contemporary Soviet sources, which do not base their assertions on specific documents, the Central Committee Plenum also came to a decision on the situation in Petrograd, and on Stalin. Recognizing the need to impose order on the relations between the civilian and military authorities in the city, the Central Committee formally appointed Stalin to the western front RVS, thereby depriving him of the extraordinary powers that he had exercised until that point.[51]

Despite this appendix, apparently designed to bring balance to the decisions that had been reached, it was clear that the Central Committee had intended not only to solve the most important strategic issue of the moment but also to grasp the opportunity to reassert the validity of the decisions taken by the 8th Congress. Trotskii construed the Central Committee's move as a polemical attack on the evasiveness he had displayed with regard to some of the said decisions, and handed in his resignation. On 5 July, the Politbiuro and the Orgbiuro held a fresh meeting to examine Trotskii's request. His resignation was categorically rejected.[52] Trotskii was given a reassurance that he would still be able to conduct in person operations on the southern front (which he considered more vitally important than the eastern front) and he was promised that the central party organs would do 'all in their power' to facilitate his work and to ensure that it 'yields the greatest benefit to the Republic'. In the document (unknown to us), setting out his reasons for resigning, Trotskii had apparently gone into matters far removed from strategic issues. This much is clear from the following passage in the resolution: 'The Orgbiuro and Politbiuro of the Central Committee afford Comrade Trotskii full opportunity of striving by every possible means after what he regards as an adjustment of the line on the military question and, if he so wishes, of endeavouring to speed up the calling of a Party Congress.'[53]

The situation had therefore come extremely close to a point of outright rupture. It is worth pointing out in passing that immediately after the Plenum Trotskii fell prey to his strange illness, the first example of that synchrony between political crises in which he was personally involved and the outbreaks of ill-health that were to occur throughout the 1920s.[54] On 9 July, Dzerzhinskii, Krestinskii, Lenin, and Sklianskii informed Trotskii that Vatsetis had actually been arrested.[55] The former Supreme Commander was released a few days later but his arrest clearly marked the culmination of an operation, developed with the backing of the Central Committee, that was designed to destroy the prestige of the military leadership that had just been replaced.

Several years later, Trotskii tried to play down the political significance of the July 1919 crisis, putting it down to disagreements of a purely technical and strategic nature. The main target of the Central Committee's measures of censure, he argued, had been Vatsetis, whereas he, Trotskii, had only been dealt an indirect blow.[56] To demonstrate that the episode had done nothing to undermine his position in the party's leading group, he cited in his autobiography the entire Politbiuro and Orgbiuro document, without adding any comment. In my view, however, the Central Committee had probably adopted a severely punitive position towards him on that particular occasion. By 1929 Trotskii had been forced to take an extreme and narrow line of defence against the Stalinist majority within the Central Committee. This consisted in claiming that his personal relations with Lenin had been based on a broad agreement between them. In this late version, the clash that had occurred in July 1918 was brushed off as no more than a sign of 'a disagreement of a purely practical nature which had of course no influence on my relations with Lenin'.[57] To provide this statement with greater credibility, Trotskii later published a document dating from shortly after the July Plenum, in which Lenin gave him a free hand to conduct operations on the southern front, and seemingly displayed the greatest possible faith in him.[58]

If Trotskii was able to assert this version many years after the events in question, this was in part due to the fact that neither the 'secret' resolution at the 8th Congress, nor Vatsetis' arrest, had as yet been made public. Indeed, Vatsetis' arrest was only mentioned for the first time in Deutscher's work after the Second World War.[59] In July 1919, the Central Committee felt it was wiser to conceal from the public the most significant aspects of the decisions it reached. *Izvestiia* reported that Vatsetis had been replaced and that a new RVSR had been established on 10 July. In an interview in the same issue, Smilga merely explained that the removal of the Supreme Commander had become necessary because, as well as other broader but unspecified 'disagreements over strategy' with S. Kamenev, he had opposed 'a decisive attack in the east'. The interview that Stalin gave *Pravda* on the 8th also touched on the Petrograd plot in extremely vague terms and did not indicate how much the Central Committee had believed they could ascertain regarding the alleged responsibilities of the two Soviet general staffs (*vseroglavshtab, polevyi shtab*).[60] Lenin helped to drop a heavy curtain of discretion around the proceedings of the Plenum and to suggest that officially the guiding principles of military policy remained, despite everything, unchanged. On 4 July he delivered a report to VTsIK in which he dealt in detail with the situation at the fronts. He announced that the Central Committee had called on Trotskii to make the report but that unfortunately he was ill and could not therefore do so.[61] From Lenin's report, which frequently named Trotskii, it is quite apparent that Trotskii's was still to be considered the most authoritative voice on military affairs.[62]

Confirmation that widespread and virulent opposition to Trotskii's policy re-emerged at the beginning of July 1919, in particular among top party leaders, is provided by the initiatives that the Central Committee took immediately following the conclusion of the session of 3–4 July. The Central Committee on that occasion followed a logic similar to that which had prompted the drafting of the two military resolutions passed by the 8th Congress. The Central Committee circulated two politically quite different documents, the first of which was more cautious and reassuring, the second more critical and forthright. In part, these two documents actually contradicted each other: one of them seemed basically to support the military policy that had so far been followed and to represent continuity between the official positions that the Plenum had voiced and previous positions; the other, in contrast, made it clear that major changes were being made to previous policy. As had occurred following the 8th Congress, the more cautious of the two documents was made public while the other was circulated secretly, even though it was as much an official Central Committee document as the first. We are referring to the 'Letter from the Central Committee of the RKP(b) to all party organizations on the mobilization of the forces for the struggle against Denikin', of 9 July,[63] (this contained the famous appeal: 'Everybody to the struggle against Denikin!'); and the 'Circular letter from the Central Committee of the RKP(b) to all party members on the strengthening of the Red Army', of five days later (14 July). This second document was not published until 1961.[64]

The letter of 9 July outlined the principal measures needing to be introduced or reinforced in order to turn the country into 'a single military camp, not in words but in deeds'.[65] It was a question of drawing the full consequences of the realization that 'the Soviet Republic is a fortress besieged by world capital'. In every sector, collegial leadership was to be limited to 'an absolutely indispensable minimum', in favour of the unconditional authority of single leaders. The style of discussions and decision-making should be as far removed as possible from 'public speeches' and should be a simple matter of 'rapid and precise information and proposals'.[66] The party was called upon to step up its propaganda among conscripts, above all those of peasant background, and among deserters. All work not directly linked to the country's military activities was to be reduced to a minimum by the party organizations in order to free as many cadres as possible for service at the front. In the front-line areas, especially in the east, where the offensive had to be carried through to complete victory, it was necessary to 'subordinate all activity, every effort, all thoughts to war and to war alone', as had recently been accomplished with success in Petrograd. 'Military discipline in military affairs as in all others' was the slogan of the moment.[67]

A special section of the letter was devoted to 'the attitude towards military specialists'. The recent, 'gigantic plot hatched by Krasnaia Gorka, the purpose of which was to bring about the surrender of Petrograd', had 'raised with particular urgency the issue of military specialists'. There was no doubt that the 'worsening of the military and food-rationing situation will for the immediate future inevitably continue to provoke an intensification of counter-revolutionary efforts'.[68] As things were, it was perfectly foreseeable that 'military specialists, as well as *kulaki*, bourgeois intellectuals, Mensheviks, and Social Revolutionaries [would] in the future account for a high percentage of traitors'. However, the document pointed out that the party programme approved by the 8th Congress 'had set forth in the clearest of terms the policy of the Communist Party' towards the 'specialists', and argued that 'to wish ... to alter the principles that underpin our military policy' would constitute 'an irreparable error and an unforgiveable mistake'.[69] Instead, it was essential to heed the views of 'the expert men who stand at the head of our War Ministry', who pointed out that wherever political work was carried out most effectively and *partizanshchina* was combated the most resolutely, 'military specialists' were automatically placed in a position where they could do no harm. Therefore, the greater the resolve to strengthen the cornerstones of the regular army and to implement official military policy (as defined, it should be remembered, by an extremely general document such as the party programme), the rarer would acts of disloyalty by officers become. An urgent call was therefore made 'to intensify political work', to 'strengthen' the role of the commissars, and to 'raise' the quality of the work they performed.[70] The events at the Petrograd front should not, that is, be allowed to undermine the foundations of the policy implemented by the War Ministry.

However, the *Letter* contained one particular passage, reminiscent of the authentic spirit of the resolutions passed by the 8th Congress, which specified that any conflicts that might arise between those in charge of political matters and 'specialists' would be resolved 'through party channels' (*partiinym putem*).[71] This meant that a settlement would be sought before such conflicts turned into full-blown clashes between different power centres over questions of authority and administration, 'as has recently happened in Petrograd'.[72] This was an explicit reference to the decision – in support of the positions of Stalin and Zinov'ev – taken by the Politbiuro (and not by the competent organ, RVSR) to recall Okulov. To the initiated, this statement would have been interpreted as a signal that the Central Committee intended to stick to the compromise line hammered out by the 8th Congress: the 'bases'[73] of military policy were not called into question, but the party would have the last word on all concrete cases. The subsequent 'Circular Letter' went a great deal further than this restatement of principle.

Unlike the first document, the 'Circular Letter' dealt exclusively with the army's internal regime. The point that distinguished it most clearly from the previous document related to the issue of 'specialists'. This time emphasis was placed on the reasons for being wary of them rather than on the reasons why it was right for the Red Army to employ them. Even the order in which the various issues were tackled was significantly inverted. In the first *Letter*, mention had been made of cases of treason only as a way of stiffening the argument in favour of the official policy, which was then expounded. Here, on the other hand, reasons for distrusting the specialists occupied the foreground. Admittedly it was restated that 'the generalized condemnation of all military specialists has nothing whatever to do with our party line', and that the Red Army 'needed' them. 'But', the 'Circular Letter' went on, 'it should not be forgotten that the majority of the so-called specialists belong to another class, hostile to us.' One could not 'shut one's eyes' to 'the events at Krasnaia Gorka, Kronshtadt, and the Petrograd front', which had shown 'just how widespread was treason in some circles of military specialists'.[74] A sure sign of the change in tone was that, in the second document, military commissars were accused of shortcomings which had until that point not often been cited in official documents, especially those signed by Trotskii. Commissars were alleged to have displayed a 'negligent and uncritical attitude to military specialists' and to have confined their activity to 'signing uncritically everything that the military specialists put before them': 'As long as a military specialist is in command, discipline requires strict submission to his orders. But this in no way implies that the military commissar, who is the representative of our party in the army, must limit his role to merely endorsing everything issuing from the military specialist.'[75]

It is also symptomatic that of the various commissars' functions indicated in the public resolution of the 8th Congress, no mention was made here of their 'administrative and economic' duties; instead, considerable stress was laid on the functions of 'control and super-vision' over commanders' activities.[76] Consistent with this approach was the fact that one of the long-term objectives formulated by the 8th Congress now reappeared as an urgent task (to be accomplished within 'a few months', as the 'Circular Letter' has it): the appointment of commanders at battalion and divisional level exclusively from among 'reliable supporters of Workers' and Peasants' Russia'.

On 8 July, Trotskii had left for the southern front. If the *Letter* of 9 July embodied his style and contained certain of his characteristic turns of phrase, the same cannot be said of that of the 14th. To which group within the party and the Central Committee might the 'Circular Letter' be attributed? The text speaks for itself: it was clearly written by people who had opposed Trotskii's positions at the Congress. But it is possible to be even more precise. It is worth comparing the above-cited passage of the 'Circular Letter' with a speech made on 5 July by Zinov'ev in Petrograd, of which the press carried a brief report: 'Although we don't go in for generalizations we have arrived at the conclusion that in Petrograd and throughout the whole of Russia it is necessary to adopt a very much more critical attitude towards those who come from a background that is foreign to us.'[77]

As may be seen, this speech anticipates several of the points that the Central Committee was to incorporate into the 'Circular Letter' of 14 July. The blow had therefore been struck from Petrograd. In his correspondence with Lenin regarding the emblematic case of Krasnaia Gorka, Stalin had been refining his arguments on this issue ever since June. Zinov'ev took advantage of Trotskii's extreme political weak-ness following the Central Committee Plenum to draw from the events at Petrograd lessons that might be deemed applicable to all the fronts.

In substance, what I am suggesting here is backed up by the relevant information furnished by the editors of the fifth edition of Lenin's *Works*. The draft appeal 'To the struggle against Denikin', i.e. the first *Letter*, was written by Lenin and given to Central Committee members so that they could comment upon it. Zinov'ev and, in particular, Stalin criticized the original text, arguing that it ought to state explicitly the need to review the party's attitude towards 'mili-tary specialists', together with its whole military policy. Apparently – in contrast with Lenin's oft-repeated stand on this matter – Stalin even went so far as to deny that the issue of employing former Tsarist officers was basically the same as that of employing 'bourgeois specialists' in civilian and economic fields, on the expedience of which he was obviously in agreement.[78] Disagreements on strategy had thus cleared the way for political dissensions and for a fuller expression of personal rivalries. On drafting the 'Circular Letter', the Central Committee had taken into account the opinions, both old and new, of those men whose prestige had been strengthened by the successes scored at Petrograd.[79]

But there were still further differences between the two documents. Although it began by stressing that party 'collectives' should not set themselves up 'in competition' with the commissars, and that membership of a collective did not entail any right to 'the slightest privilege',[80] the 'Circular Letter' carried out a hard-hitting criticism of the regime that had been established among the communists at the front. The view was expressed that 'our political departments have here and there become infected with bureaucratism'.[81] Their functionaries, buried under heaps of red tape, had begun to lose touch 'with the soldiering masses'. Pointing out that it was their job to act as 'the political leaders of the soldiers in each unit', the political departments were urged to become 'as popular as possible in the regiments'. The importance of the divisional newspapers was also emphasized, and soldiers were called upon to become involved in their production, even by writing letters 'illustrating the army's defects'.[82]

The difference between the political standpoints adopted by the two documents became strikingly apparent at the end of the 'Circular Letter'. The demand that official military policy be recognized as valid and pursued without any modification was flatly rejected: 'Life has necessitated a number of corrections to our military work. These corrections must be made rapidly and in a planned and organized way'.[83]

Despite the impression created by the two resolutions passed by the Central Committee, the crisis of July 1919 was not confined to the points of difference that had emerged at the 8th Congress. It was the disagreements over strategy, which had come to light between May and July, that set the stage for the subsequent debate on the 'single military doctrine' (see chapter 8 below). The men who had been in positions of command on the eastern front in spring and summer 1919 (Frunze, S. Kamenev, Gusev, Tukhachevskii) in the subsequent debate supported a systematic 'theory of the offensive'. Moreover, the dramatic circumstances in which Vatsetis and other top Soviet officers had been arrested carried a variety of extremely grim and disconcerting political and strategic implications. The *Cheka* had accused Vatsetis of not responding promptly enough to an attempt by his subordinates on the general staff to create a counter-revolutionary organization in coordination with Kolchak and Denikin, with the aim of overthrowing Soviet power. As a short-term aim, this group had apparently set out to reorganize the RVSR High Command. Then, at the beginning of October, Vatsetis was judged guilty only of 'extremely unstable . . . behaviour' and of having been 'superficial in his relations, despite his position of authority'. The following month, the *Cheka* called for the others involved in the affair to be liberated too.[84] If nothing else, this indicated just how bitter the struggle in July 1919 had been. But the main conclusion to be drawn from the foregoing account is that the most influential opponents of Trotskii's military policy proved that they were able to carry the majority of the Central Committee with them on several of the most hotly-debated issues. Trotskii took stock of this setback, and his actions soon began to reveal a greater awareness of the actual balance of forces within the leading Bolshevik group over military policy.

Trotskii changes his stand

On 9 July, from Voronezh, behind the southern front-line, Trotskii issued the following order:

> Articles are appearing in the press about the treacherous plot hatched by part of the command corps of the Petrograd front, which are being interpreted as signs of a change in Soviet policy on military affairs, above all as regards the question of military specialists. According to the reports filed by the *politrabotniki*, such rumours are widespread among officers, and are arousing a sense of alarm and uncertainty. I therefore consider it necessary to clarify matters: Soviet military policy remains unchanged, for the simple reason that it is not the product of the excogitations of a handful of individuals or groups, but rather the result of the experience of many hundreds of thousands of workers and peasants.
>
> Soviet power will continue to trust and support Red Army commanders who are honest – and the vast majority of them are so –, acknowledging their precious collaboration in positions of the highest responsibility.[85]

This was perfectly consistent with the first Central Committee *Letter*, issued the same day. Trotskii defended the policy that he himself embodied, with a declaration of confidence in the former

Tsarist officers. At the same time, Trotskii made yet another veiled reference to the Central Committee resolution of 25 December 1918, which now appears to have been the only occasion on which the party's top leading organ espoused his positions in their near-entirety.

The order of 9 July articulated a number of concepts that Trotskii had already voiced the day before in a brief note written at Kozlov. He argued that to put the military defeats that had been suffered on the southern front down to 'the methods of constructing the Red Army' that had so far been practised, was to indulge in 'small-minded gossip'. At the same time, he made the point, reiterated in the Central Committee *Letter*, that there was no need to review the official attitude towards 'specialists'.[86]

Initially, therefore, Trotskii clung to his own positions, reacting to Plenum decisions by drawing attention to elements of continuity. Indeed, the Central Committee *Letter* of 9 July seems, wholly or in part, to have been inspired by him. On 12 July, in his capacity as president of RVSR, he addressed a long letter to the Republic's army and front RVSs. Here he strove to present the military setbacks in the south as the straightforward consequence of the shortfall in supplies. All the other rumours that had been put about, and 'the excess of "criticism" that had been directed against the foundations of our military construction', were the work of party members who were by now well-known for their rebellious opinions: some turned up now and then on one of the fronts and proceeded 'to peddle their superficial views as if they were the latest discoveries of military science'; others were characters who had had to be removed from their positions of command because of their 'blatant unsuitableness' for military work. This state of disinformation and deliberate 'distortion' of reality had been exploited in an attempt to raise once again the question of 'military specialists', even though this no longer constituted 'a problem'.[87]

This document then assumed the form of a fully-fledged *instruktsiia* to the combatant units, with the result that it has sometimes been identified as the regulation on relations between military and political authorities within the army, which the Plenum of 3–4 July 1919 had requested of Trotskii.[88] If this was the case, one cannot help observing that once again Trotskii was putting the decisions of the Central Committee into effect after his own particular fashion, demonstrating that he had not grasped the real political significance of the request. In actual fact, neither at this juncture nor during the months that followed were any formal regulations issued, and this in itself was a clear response to the Central Committee's instructions. But there are other aspects that need to be examined.

In the message of 12 July to the RVSs, Trotskii continued to reject the proposal that periodic conferences be organized for party leaders at the front. This idea had originated in the 'secret' resolution of the 8th Congress, and more recently the Central Committee Plenum had called for its implementation.[89] Indeed, Trotskii actually justified the sending of his own letter-regulation by saying that such meetings were 'extremely hard to organize' and that – as he himself was doing – one should think more in terms of a different kind of relationship, 'an exchange of opinions, resolutions, and so forth, dealing with the most pressing and important issues of military construction'. As soon as he began to take a close look at a number of the problems, there emerged a third reason for rejecting the policy that Congress had recommended. While the tendency to make the divisional political department the linchpin of the army's political machinery was 'wholly correct', Trotskii warned against the 'almost total liquidation' of army political departments. Wherever this occurred, it would destroy any 'possibility of exerting continuous control on the work of communists' in the units. Trotskii stated that the essential task of the army political department remained that of providing commissars above company level with leadership.[90] He then went on to refute a line of argument that the Central Committee was to accept, two days later, in its 'Circular Letter' of 14 July. Trotskii wrote: 'In some party circles, the complaint has been made that commissars sometimes restrict their role to keeping a formal check on the work of military specialists in order to head off any counter-revolutionary actions, while failing to take a closer look at things.'[91]

This is a clear reference to the criticism that Zinov'ev had made in his speech in Petrograd on 5 July. Trotskii's solution is markedly different from that proposed two days later by the Central Committee. In his opinion, it was not a matter of tightening up their 'supervision' of officers, quite the reverse: commissars should seek, as far as possible, to 'complement' their commanders, and should display greater initiative in the 'economic field', by seeing that the material needs of the regiment were properly satisfied. Sokol'nikov had taken exactly the same view at the 8th Congress. Commissars should of course be more dynamic and vigilant, but they should work 'hand in hand' with the commanders and in no case attempt to take their place. They were urged to 'win for themselves a leading position within the regiment' but not at the expense of the officer's authority.

Issued on 14 July, the Central Committee's 'Circular Letter' did not have an immediate influence on Trotskii's positions. In an article published in a Ukrainian newspaper on the 17th, he inveighed with characteristic fury against the press and the military political administration of Khar'kov, which had, respectively, printed and tolerated articles that blamed the difficulties faced on the southern front on acts of treason committed by 'specialists'.[92] The group that had formed in the Ukraine around Voroshilov was keen to take advantage of the Republic's military plight to restoke smouldering issues, and to exploit the unwillingness of Ukrainian communists to take orders from Moscow. Trotskii retorted that *partizanshchina* methods had caused the Republic much more trouble than cases of treason among the officers. In particular, Denikin's gains had been made possible by the collapse of the 11th Northern Caucasus army, which had enabled the White forces to create a direct link between their front-line in the Ukraine and in central Russia, and their rear in Kuban.[93] Referring to the Central Committee's *Letter* of 9 July, Trotskii warned that the party had spoken out against any change in military policy. He cited the example of two armies on the southern front, the 8th and the 13th, whose communists had declared their support for the line that had been followed up to that point, and their opposition to its revision.[94]

The decision to fight the manoeuvre, which his traditional adversaries were evidently preparing during his absence at the centre, emerged clearly in Trotskii's reply on 19 July to two articles signed Tarasov-Rodionov (printed in the 3 and 10 July issues of *Izvestiia*). In his view, beneath the moderate veneer, a public attack on official military policy was being mounted.[95] As early as 14 July, Trotskii had complained to the Central Committee about the article-writer's 'disruptive agitation' in the press, and had requested that he be posted forthwith to take on practical work on the southern front.[96]

But the tone of Trotskii's writings altered noticeably after 19 July. In an order that he issued on that day to the 13th army, he stressed that, although it was not the commissars' job to give commands, they should 'take steps to replace' commanders whenever they proved to be 'incompetent' or politically 'untrustworthy'.[97] An order to the 14th army, issued on 9 August, reflects a radical reassessment of the importance of the divisional political department, to which Trotskii was at last willing to entrust control of regimental commissars.[98] But above all, towards the end of July, Trotskii engaged in a debate against the theoreticians of military professionalism, with whom, up until that point, he had not considered it necessary to enter into open polemic. He published two articles, on 24 July and 5 August, in *Voennoe delo*, a paper that brought together many of the former general staff officers who had opted to cooperate with the Bolsheviks. The first of the two articles relaunched the polemic against *partizanstvo*, in the form in which Tarasov-Rodionov had presented it. Significantly, however, Trotskii distinguished between two possible conceptions of partisan warfare. While it was vital to combat the claim that ill-assorted bands of men could conduct a war more effectively than a regular army, Trotskii conceded that guerrilla warfare (*malaia voina*) could, 'in certain conditions, [be] an effective weapon in the hands of both sides in civil and class war'.[99] Providing it was resorted to 'under the strict control of the operational general staff', guerrilla warfare could constitute an appropriate method of combat for specific purposes: not the outright destruction of the enemy, which only a regular army could aim to accomplish, using the tactic of the large-scale 'trench warfare', but its 'attrition'.[100] Guerrilla actions might be considered the form of warfare most advantageous to the weaker side. It would in any case be an absurd error to regard partisan struggle as in any way intrinsically 'proletarian', or the regular army, on the other hand, as a typically 'bourgeois' organizational model.[101] The form of warfare that was most appropriate in any given conditions should not be made an ideological issue or a question of principle: it was a matter of suiting means to a given purpose and to what was actually possible.[102]

While, on the one hand, this line of argument undermined the opinions of many of those who had swelled the ranks of the 'military opposition' at the 8th Congress, it also introduced a number of points that were distinctly unorthodox in the theoretical quarters inhabited by the editors of *Voennoe delo*. Trotskii rounded off his piece by suddenly striking a much more idealistic note:

> Without in any way minimizing the importance of technique in the organization of the operational leadership (on both sides, as we have seen, a certain levelling out is occurring), it is safe to say that in the last analysis the decisive factor will turn out to be which organs of propaganda will prove to be the most powerful, i.e. which idea will demonstrate its ability to convince the broadest mass of people and to keep them spiritually united, for without this no army can exist.[103]

To counter the arguments of professional military science, Trotskii thus invoked higher political ideals. Quite apart from the theoretical significance of his remarks, it is worth recalling that he made them for the first time in the political conjuncture of summer 1919.[104] One cannot help concluding that the Commissar for War wished to draw attention to the fact that he now accepted a number of positions which he had hitherto always relentlessly rejected *en bloc*. The reasons Trotskii gave for this about-turn were original and personal, and also probably reflected his complex and sometimes contradictory personality.

In the second article, his new stance is even more clear-cut. Here Trotskii takes on A. A. Svechin, former *vseroglavshtab* member and professor at the Military Academy,[105] who, writing in *Voennoe delo*, had praised the superiority of barracks-training as compared to militia-style training. In Svechin's opinion, even if party spirit had at the outset (spring–summer 1918) 'replaced' the discipline provided by the barracks as an agent capable of welding together and galvanizing the Red troops, it was nonetheless essential at a certain point to switch to methods of training characteristic of the regular army.[106] Trotskii, on the other hand, denied that the party had ever played such a role. It was true only in an extremely limited sense:

> Barracks are coercive; the party is a union that from every point of view is voluntary. Barracks are hierarchical; the party is an ideal democracy ... Party discipline, despite all the strains, has never wavered and is truly unshakeable. The constraints of party spirit are of a purely voluntary, non-coercive nature. The party is the direct opposite of the barracks.
>
> Professor Svechin pretends he has forgotten that the underground revolutionary party, with its voluntary discipline, came into conflict with the miraculous autocratic barracks, conquered it, and seized power from the grasp of those classes which had relied on the brutalizing (and 'miraculous') constraints of the barracks.[107]

As a result, the militia, imbued with the feeling of close solidarity that the party afforded its combatants, urged that citizens be provided with basic training in the use of weaponry, without the ideology of hierarchy and submission to orders. *Esprit de corps* was not the product of typical barracks-training methods: the harmonious combination of the 'spiritual development of the broad masses', 'a good schooling', and 'physical work', that the militia system was expected to ensure, could secure even better results.

Trotskii's polemic with those 'military specialists' who agreed with the most orthodox positions of the *Voennoe delo* editors was also related to the schemes that RVSR was drawing up for the next phase of military construction at the end of July. On 27 July, RVSR put the *vseroglavshtab* in charge of the preparation of a demobilization plan that would take account of the fact that the army, at the end of the war, would have to be reorganized along the lines of a territorial militia army.[108] Significantly, it was at this very moment, at the end of July, that RVSR issued an order setting out precise criteria for the recruitment of Red Army conscripts. A new kind of questionnaire was introduced, designed to 'pinpoint more clearly the class background of the conscripts', and one of the questions explicitly enquired whether or not the respondent lived 'from the work of other persons'.[109] One of the traditional demands made by Trotskii's adversaries thus received an official sanction from the very bodies that had once been the butt of their accusations.

In an interview that appeared in *Izvestiia* on 26 August, Trotskii made a series of statements that certainly sounded more convincing than those he had couched in a similar language on the eve of the 8th Congress:

> The disagreements between us at the time of the 8th Congress have now completely vanished. Many misunderstandings have been cleared up during the course of events, and numerous prejudices have faded away. We now work hand in hand with those comrades who, it once appeared, were separated by an unbridgeable gulf from 'official' military policy, and no one even dreams of bringing up past dissensions.[110]

These sentiments were echoed by part at least of the opposition, as Miasnikov, one of the opposition's keenest representatives at the time of the Congress, clearly demonstrated. At the end of July, addressing an audience of soldiers stationed in Moscow, Miasnikov spoke out in defence of the former Tsarist officers; and at the beginning of August, in *Izvestiia*, he sang Trotskii's praises for having scored a resounding victory over *partizanshchina* methods in the construction of the army.[111] Through the breach that the July Plenum had opened in the War Ministry citadel, the spirit of the 8th Congress began to make itself felt in the Red Army. In August 1919, Stalin made up his mind to comply with one of the last outstanding commitments that RVSR had so far failed to fulfil, and personally wrote an *instruktsiia* to the commissars and to the cells. Although this was not formally ratified by the centre, it was distributed on the southern and western fronts. Soviet military historians have drawn attention to what is probably this document's most interesting feature: the commissar was defined not only as a party representative but as the 'father and soul' of the regiment.[112] Thus, yet another point championed by the 'military opposition', reflecting a very distinctive and unbureaucratic way of conceiving service relationships, gained full respectability among the Soviet armed forces. Lastly, it should be remembered that in the second half of 1919 a review was carried out of rates of payment for the various categories of serving soldiers. The scale drawn up in November narrowed the gap considerably between the pay of officers up to divisional level and those of ordinary soldiers and NCOs.[113] After the crisis of summer 1919, criticisms of the War Ministry assumed a less formal and more episodic character, even if they by no means disappeared, remaining widespread among the ranks. Apparently, however, serious divisions among the main military leaders and Central Committee members no longer emerged.

One significant piece of evidence testifying to the degree of unity achieved in approximately this period is the famous *ABC of Communism*, which Bukharin and Preobrazhenskii began writing in summer 1919, and which they completed in October of the same year.[114] A chapter illustrating the way the Soviet armed forces were organized was included in the 'practical part' of the book, edited by Preobrazhenskii.

While declaring that the ideal would be a 'class army', Preobrazhenskii argued that the necessary recruitment of 'middle peasants' did not undermine the Red Army's social character. The Red Army was 'an army of all the working population'.[115] The principle of 'coercive discipline' was accepted, though this would be soon replaced by 'the workers' voluntary acceptance of the discipline of the Civil War'. In the Soviet Army, military orders were 'backed . . . by the whole Workers' and Peasants' Republic', though with the important rider that orders had to be 'reasonable'.[116] As for the role of communist cells, Preobrazhenskii claimed that they were entitled to 'watch how their own commissar and other commissars perform their communist duties'.[117] Thus, 'without any infringement of general military discipline', the communist party could 'secure complete control over all its members and prevent any misuse of power on their side'. This easy-going attempt to reconcile institutionally conflicting approaches came to grief as soon as mention was made of the political departments, towards which an unquenchable aversion again made itself felt. It was alleged that they had become too bureaucratic, and that they were 'a refuge for idlers and incapables who belong to the party war-office officialdom'. Lastly, a plea was made in favour of the militia system, which, it was argued, would 'approximate the structure of the Red Army to that of the productive units of the workers.'[118] In the long term, it was hinted, even the election of officers might be reintroduced.[119] Despite the various reservations that it contained, this text, written as a semi-official comment on the party programme adopted at the 8th Congress, was extremely well-received by the political and military authorities – to judge at least by the fact that, as late as the end of 1921, it was still being prescribed by the party centre as a text-book to be used in the political education of the masses.[120]

Disagreements on strategic issues also assumed a more technical and confidential character after July 1919. Moreover, the scant evidence that scholars have so far been able to examine shows that, following this date, the alignments we have so far encountered were in part overturned. It is true that, following the July Plenum, Trotskii and others (Sokol'nikov, for instance), who remained convinced that the old plan of operations in the south drawn up under Vatsetis was still valid, strove to influence S. Kamenev's plan, which had won the approval of the Central Committee, accordingly.[121] But immediately after this, Trotskii and Stalin found themselves on the same side when a decision had to be reached on the possible evacuation of Petrograd, in autumn 1919. Opposing Zinov'ev, they both favoured a defence of the threatened city, to the bitter end.[122] Again, in summer 1920, albeit for different reasons, they both displayed scepticism regarding the wisdom of transforming the Polish campaign from a defensive war into an offensive one, aimed to conquer Warsaw.[123] Not only were some military experts (including former members of the old eastern front RVS, like Kamenev and Tukhachevskii) keen on this policy, so were Lenin and a majority of Central Committee members.

The last months of the Civil War

In the first half of December 1919, three important meetings took place: the 8th Party Conference (2–4 December), the 7th Congress of Soviets (5–9 December) and the 1st All-Russian Congress of military *politrabotniki* (11–15 December). I shall attempt, within the constraints of the evidence available, to provide a review of the military question at this date.

The 7th Congress of Soviets, and the 8th Party Conference, which prepared the ground for it, noted with satisfaction, and considerable surprise (Lenin spoke of a 'miracle'),[124] that victory in all the main theatres of the Civil War was now within sight. Even the semi-legal parties, represented in the Soviets, shared in the general enthusiasm, in the hope that they would soon witness the introduction of greater political pluralism. On the first day of Congress, Dan' expressed his solidarity with the Bolsheviks, while simultaneously calling for a reinforcement of the 'single revolutionary front' of Russian workers' parties.[125] Lenin cheerfully observed that the 'popular' nature of the Soviet army was now recognized even by those who had originally opposed its constitution and had voiced scepticism about its ability to secure victory.[126] In the 6th of December issue of *Pravda*, Safarov too remarked that the Bolsheviks' political opponents in the Soviets had ceased to consider the Red Army a 'Praetorian Guard'. Trotskii, for his part, noted that the 'Soviet opposition' (i.e. the other parties) were now full of praise for the success of the army that the Bolsheviks had built.[127] The 7th Congress of Soviets conferred on the Supreme Commander, S. Kamenev, the highest honours of the Republic.[128]

In this triumphal atmosphere, Trotskii spoke enthusiastically of the vital contribution that had been made by two fundamental components of the armed forces: the 'specialists' and the commissars. The latter, Trotskii said, represented 'a new communist order of Samurai'.[129] He remarked that a generation of 'proletarian commanders' had now come of age, and predicted that their appearance on the scene would spell the final resolution of the strains that had previously dogged the army: the men he referred to by name were Frunze, Sokol'nikov, Tukhachevskii, and Budennyi.[130] The undisciplined Ukrainian formations, traditionally inclined towards the methods of the *partizanstvo*, heard their most intransigent adversary reproach them with uncustomary affability.[131] Nor did Trotskii shrink from heaping warm praise on cadres sent to the Red Army by the other parties, whom, as he put it, the War Ministry had welcomed as brothers.[132] He finished by declaring that, in view of the approach of final victory, it would be reasonable to give concrete consideration to the replacement of the regular standing army by a territorial militia.[133]

The sense of triumph in the air did not prevent new criticisms from being directed at the armed forces. At the 8th Party Conference, Mgeladze (of 'Democratic Centralism') denounced the political departments and military organs in general for 'not taking account of the opinions of local organizations', and complained also of the leaden insensitivity of the Central Committee towards requests for a precise disciplining of their relations both in the rear and at the front.[134] Zelikman cited the example of the executive committee of the

Tula Soviet, which, according to him, the army had completely divested of its authority, when the city had been directly threatened by
Denikin.[135] Sapronov, who followed Vladimirskii with a co-report
that focussed on the problems posed in the organization of the state,
approached the same issue within the context of the broader one
regarding the degree of power that, in his view, ought to be granted to
local Soviet authorities in normal circumstances. Sapronov argued
that these authorities should enjoy greater independence and be
defended from the interference of the central *glavki*, including the
army.[136] He also alleged that the military commissars and RVSs had
proclaimed the state of siege without asking the local Soviet for its
consent. At the previous Party Congress, this accusation had
appeared on the banners of a section of the opposition.[137] Sapronov
accepted that centralization was necessary, providing it was achieved
via 'unitary' party and state structures, and as long as it did not lead to
a proliferation of arbitrary power centres.

In actual fact, in October the Central Committee had already turned
its attention to the problem of relations between military organs and
civilian authorities, and had passed a resolution on 'the relations of
the RVSs and general staffs with the party organization'.[138] But, as
Mgeladze rightly observed at the Conference, this document revealed
a clear bias in favour of the military. Indeed, the Central Committee
had even urged civilians to consider the paramount importance of
'defence interests', and had warned darkly that if local authorities put
up any opposition, 'the Central Committee [would find] means of
backing the interests of the army'.[139] Now that the war seemed to be
drawing to an end, the right moment had come to revive the issue,
and to review the previous rigid position. The 8th Conference was
thus faced with a proposal that a nine-member commission be elected
(three military experts, three territorial committee and *guberniia* representatives, and one spokesman each from RVSR, PUR, and Central
Committee), with the job of drawing up a new regulation.[140] The
delegates felt that this composition was too heavily weighted in
favour of the military, and when it came to voting for the proposal
(moved by Zinov'ev), they decided to add two more representatives
from territorial party organizations.[141] Accordingly, the commission
now consisted of Dzerzhinskii, Smilga, Gorbunov, Volin, Sapronov,
Kaganovich, Mgeladze, Teodorovich, Poluian, Potemkin, Vetoshkin,
and Maksimovskii.[142] The commission met to examine the two items
on the agenda: '1) Relations between local civilian and military
powers; 2) Relations between political departments and party organi-

zations.'[143] A resolution was passed, which was temporarily to remain secret.[144] This reaffirmed that territorial authorities were to comply with any requests that the military authorities made to them. However, to ensure that the positions of the civilian authorities were respected, it was also determined that military *party* organs would keep in close touch with civilian *party* organs. In this way, while safeguarding the principle that the military should take precedence in administrative questions, it was also decided that any conflicts that might arise should be settled through party channels. The *nachalnik* of the political department would be appointed to the corresponding territorial party committee with full voting rights. Party members in the military units stationed in the area would be 'registered' at the appropriate territorial organization, which would be able to propose to the political department that they be employed 'in various types of temporary work'. Lastly, if there existed a 'party commission' – we shall take a closer look at this new body below – attached to the political department, it should if possible include representatives from the territorial committee.

These decisions, taken at the 8th Party Conference, show that attention was beginning to focus on the issue of the 'non-territorial' status of party organizations in the armed forces and on their compatibility with the ordinary structure of the civilian party. The issue of compatibility was a similar and, one might even say, parallel problem to that regarding the relations between the vertical and 'non-territorial' structure of the command existing in the units of the regular army and the local state and representative organs. This was not a new problem, but now that the party appeared to have grown less anxious about relations within the military structure, it came to occupy the centre of public debate. Even though the party seemed reconciled to the existence of an apparatus with the peculiar features of PUR, it still hesitated formally to acknowledge its existence in the most solemn document of the Soviet institutional system: the party rules. The new version of the party rules, approved at the 8th Conference, made no mention whatever of the norms relating to Bolshevik military leaders. A chapter devoted to 'the party organizations in the Red Army' was only to appear in the subsequent version of the rules, approved by the 14th Congress in December 1925, more than seven years after the Central Committee resolution that had abolished the ordinary party structure within the army. Only then would PUR be formally defined as the 'military section' of the Central Committee.[145]

The first session of the Congress of the *politrabotniki*, on 11

December, dealt with relations between central and peripheral PUR organs, as well as with those between the said peripheral organs and territorial party organizations.[146] But the most important topic on the agenda was that tackled in two speeches from Smilga and Trotskii, devoted to the problem of whether or not collegial command should be maintained within the Red Army. This issue would come to have an increasing weight in military affairs, even if it was a much less dramatic problem than at the outset of the Civil War. Smilga gave a brief summary of the army's construction, dwelling in particular on the institution of the commissar.[147] He seemed close to Trotskii's characteristic position when he justified the failure to issue a precise service regulation on the grounds both of the 'temporary character' of the commissars and of the numerous changes in their functions, since their introduction. A precise definition was also hard to supply because, depending on the concrete conditions that might obtain and depending on the personality of the commanders, 'the commissar is at times nothing, and at times everything'.[148] Smilga poured scorn on the plan, presented to Congress by delegates from the southern front, and written 'in part by Stalin, who wished very much indeed to draw up such a regulation'.[149] In Smilga's view, they were witnessing a process whereby the commissar's role as a political watchdog 'was slowly dying out', as a consequence both of the appearance of a growing number of 'Red commanders', and of the political loyalty displayed by the majority of former Tsarist officers, who had remained at their posts in the Red Army. It was therefore becoming possible to raise more forcefully than in the past the question of a transition to one-man command:

> We must now consider how to abolish the institution of the com-
> missar. In particular, the army RVSs have now outlived their useful-
> ness. The principle of collegiality in this instance leads to compro-
> mises, and compromises are not called for in military affairs. Instead
> of the RVSs, we could have army commissars, who could take direct
> charge of the political department, the *osobyi otdel* and the revolution-
> ary tribunal. We could then get rid of the apparatus of commissars
> attached to the *otdely* and in those institutions headed by communists.
> The institution of the commissar is dying out and I think this needs to
> be discussed openly. This won't undermine the role of communists in
> the army, quite the reverse: they will be turned from an organ of
> control and supervision into organs that directly run army life.[150]

Commissars were thus to be absorbed gradually into the army's ordinary service structure, and assimilated in every way into the command staff. This line of argument was reminiscent of that used by Sokol'nikov at the 8th Congress, even though on that occasion Sokol'nikov had attacked the view, expressed at that time by Smilga himself, that commissars should be abolished immediately.[151] Smilga now specified that the one-man command system should be introduced by accentuating those of the commissars' functions that complemented the work of commanders, and by giving commissars a free hand in all political work and policing.

The speech gave rise to 'lively discussions', as the reporter put it. Trotskii, who arrived late at the meeting, and had not heard it, replied to objections raised by those who intervened after Smilga. While 'defending the principle that every section be headed by a commander', without any 'duplication' of authority over operations, he cautiously expressed his view of Smilga's proposal.[152] Addressing those who had objected to the scheme, Trotskii stated that commissars were not a fail-safe device against officers' treason, cases of which had continued to occur even over the previous few months. Commissars, Trotskii maintained, had had a different role: to act as 'intermediaries' between soldiers and their commanders, and to provide a 'political guarantee' of a much more general kind. On the other hand, the suggestion that one-man command be introduced immediately, by means of a straightforward order from the War Ministry, troubled him. How many commanders would be able to wield adequate 'moral and political authority' over the men? And even if the more limited principle were accepted that only communist commanders could do without a commissar, what of politically 'neutral' commanders, or ones who had only been in the party a short time?[153] Trotskii proposed that initially one-man command be introduced in units in charge of supplies and in other institutions in the rear that were 'less crucial' than the combat detachments. No sweeping changes should, he thought, be made to hierarchical relations at the front, for the time being. What was needed was a prudent 'step-by-step approach'.[154] The Commissar for War also opposed Smilga's proposal that the job of the commissar, an RVS member, be merged with that of the *nachalnik* of the corresponding political department, since there existed a 'practical antagonism' between the two posts: whereas commissars mainly had to carry out operational tasks, *nachalniki* were mainly charged with 'political education'.[155] Overall, Trotskii assumed on this occasion a standpoint that was far removed from that of the implacable enemy of the commissars, attributed him by his adversaries.

The meeting of the *politrabotniki* resolved simply to 'accept the report [from Smilga] as a basis for discussions to be held within the party and army'.[156] But in the subsequent sessions also, discussion continued to concentrate on the role of the commissars. Pavlunovskii, in obvious agreement with Smilga, argued the need to create 'the closest possible coordination' between the political departments and the *osobye otdely*, as well as between the *osobye otdely* and the commissars, and gave two reasons why this was so vital: first, in order to prevent the *osobye otdely* from turning into 'professional bodies of investigation', with the danger that they might end up by 'generating criminals and bandits among the investigating agents themselves';[157] and, secondly, in order to enable the commissars to take more effective action against 'counter-revolution'.[158] In his intervention, Trotskii had stated his opposition to this approach, which would tend, in his view, to turn the commissar into a straightforward 'Cheka functionary'.[159]

Once again Smilga's plan had been judged untimely, though on this occasion it was given more serious consideration than at the 8th Congress.[160] The arguments that Trotskii marshalled amounted to a cautious reassertion of a number of points that the War Ministry had already made. Indeed, at the end of May 1919, a formal order had been issued introducing one-man command into military institutions in the rear.[161] If the 'technician in charge' was a communist, instead of being forced to work alongside a political commissar, he would now have an 'aide for the political field' (*pomoshchnik po politicheskoi chasti*). The difference between these two posts lay in their service positions: the aide was, in terms of military hierarchy, subordinate to the commander, whereas the commissar was answerable to the political department alone.[162] A few weeks later, another decree contributing to the establishment of one-man command was passed. This, rather than assigning political responsibilities to military staff, attacked the problem from the other end: henceforth, military commanders attached to (territorial) commissariats in the rear were formally restricted to playing a role as 'aides in the technical field' to the commissar in charge.[163] The discussion that the Congress of *politrabotniki* had called for in December 1919 was, however, launched, and in fact it continued publicly up until the 9th Party Congress (March–April 1920). War with Poland, in May 1920, made this debate even more topical. At the end of 1919, Miasnikov had spoken out in support of one-man command, though without completely ruling out collegial decision-taking ('even Napoleon, the greatest of *edinonachalniki* commanders, had recourse to *kollegii*').[164] At the beginning of 1920, a newspaper article made the same point with greater force and doctrinal authority. 'That command has to be concentrated in the hands of one man', the article began, 'is one of the few eternal military laws.' In view of the fact that the revolution had uncovered considerable military qualities in numerous squads of workers and peasants, there should be no hesitation in putting into practice the rallying-cry: 'The way is open to talent' – especially now that obstacles of a social nature no longer hindered the promotion of officers from the ranks. But above all, the article exhorted readers to bear constantly in mind the lesson provided by the 'countless' military defeats suffered by 'the revolutionary French Army between 1792 and 1795'. According to the author, these had been caused by 'the presence of commissars of the Convention who meddled in the leadership of the sections'.[165] Iurenev disagreed: a 'political campaign' of debate might moreover have damaging practical consequences on the state of mind of commissars and commanders alike, demoralizing the former and strengthening the hand of the latter to such an extent as to put an unbearable strain on the delicate internal equilibrium, established by experience.[166]

Lastly, the Congress of *politrabotniki* debated an *instruktsiia* to the military party cells that specified in greater detail, and in part modified, the relations already stipulated in that of 5 January 1919, which the 8th Congress had approved 'as a whole'.[167] First and foremost, the new *instruktsiia* brought several things up-to-date. A point was introduced concerning the inclusion, with full voting rights, of the *nachalnik* of the political department in the territorial party committee, in the area where troops were quartered. The new post of *politruk*, 'aide to the [regimental] commissar', was also created, and its role was defined by RVSR in an order promulgated on 14 October 1919.[168] More importantly, the party structure was altered by the new regulations. Henceforth, the *nachalnik* of the political department, rather than the commissar, was the 'party representative' in military units. Commissars now enjoyed this status only in relations with party cells, and their authority now was derived explicitly from an act of investiture performed by the political department. In this way, the importance that the political machinery had acquired only one year after it had been officially set up was sanctioned, and the reluctance of the War Ministry to define the enigmatic post of commissar in an unambiguous and conclusive way was reconfirmed. The new *instruktsiia* envisaged the creation of cells at company level, with an elected leadership. These cells were intended to decentralize party organization, which had until then been founded on regimental cells. Elected by these regimental cells, the *biuro* received new rights of political leadership and control, which it was to exercise jointly with the regimental commissar. Lastly and most significantly, legitimacy was granted to the newly created 'party commissions', attached to political departments, which in some cases had already been in existence for several months.[169] To these 'commissions' was entrusted the task – previously the exclusive province of the political departments – of 'confirming' enrolments and expulsions, and of furnishing an opinion as to the expediency of disbanding undisciplined cells, a function that had formerly been the prerogative of the commissars. At army and front levels, the commissions were composed of two members appointed by the respective political departments, and a third, representing the territorial party committee; at divisional level, the three members were all named by the *nachalnik* of the corresponding political department.

Overall, the new regulation embodied an attempt to give ordinary party members a chance to play a more active role in the party, while providing the party's primary organizations with stronger guarantees of their political prerogatives. The existence of 'party commissions' would henceforth ensure that communists within the army had a specific forum to which they could resort in any particularly serious disputes with commissars and political departments; and also that the ordinary territorial party structure would have its say on problems regarding the internal life of military organizations. Perhaps for the sake of caution, the *instruktsiia* was not issued at once. At the end of December, Iurenev was still busily stressing the issue of relations between the party's military and territorial organs. On the face of it, his article did no more than recommend the elimination of aspects of 'competition' that might flow from a party organization within the army, 'parallel' to the ordinary committees. Yet he did not miss the chance to declare that the allocation of greater influence to the territorial organization was the only sure way of preventing the emergence of a 'caste' of leaders, unaccountable to the party as a whole.[170]

Judging by the nature of political debate in December 1919, the terms of the 'military question' had shifted considerably in a matter of months. The internal organization of the Red Army no longer aroused the widespread interest that had prompted the left of the party to lead the battle for its overhaul in the winter of 1918–19. The compromise reached at the 8th Congress proved a success. Despite its persistent and increasing disciplinary rigidity, official military policy had proven sensitive to the criticisms that continued to be directed at it. In particular, the issue of democracy in military party organizations had ceased to be a question of principle, even though it was not to vanish from the scene altogether.

The opposition's new approach emerged clearly at the 9th Party Congress. The main topics discussed were the policy of the militarization of labour, and the steps devised to centralize further the administration of the state and the economy – a subject which we shall consider briefly in the next chapter. Those who, at the previous Congress, had spoken out against the militarization of the party in the army were now too busy combating the proposals to extend military patterns of organization to economic and everyday life to reopen the old question. They may also have felt that nothing more could be done to modify that policy. By this time a distinct rift had presumably developed between, on the one hand, the old slogans of Bolshevik discontent, and, on the other, the low level of political and cultural sophistication of the young and increasingly numerous new members, whom it was often hard to tell apart from the growing mass of conscripts. And for the latter, war and discipline had become part and parcel of a single reality, which might be eluded by deserting, but which could not be radically questioned. Moreover, many former members of the 'military opposition' may have felt that their proposals had won a satisfactory degree of recognition since the previous Congress: a view that, as we have seen, was not unfounded.

Both Sapronov and Osinskii, for example, refrained from criticizing the way the party was organized in the army, seeking instead to oppose the introduction of the political departments system into the main branches of industry. This step, they argued, was bound to undermine the authority of territorial party committees, factory cells, and elected Soviet organs.[171] Syrtsov, a delegate from a coal-mining region (the Donbass), where a special coal-industry political department (the so-called Podonbass) had been in operation since the beginning of 1920, asserted that it was necessary to 'confine the system of political departments exclusively to the military field', the only place where political departments were genuinely required.[172] And V. Smirnov, opposing 'the application of military methods' to the party as a whole, implicitly acknowledged that the existence of forms of party organization specific to the army was now taken for granted.[173] Iurenev raised the issue of the relations between party organs in the army and in civilian life, in areas where units were stationed. He put forward draft regulations whereby, in the rear at least, political work among communists in the army would be directed by special 'military sections', under the control of the territorial party committees.[174] At the front, the political departments would retain their leading role 'until [regular] party committees could be set up' in the areas liberated from the Whites. Iurenev conceded that at least at the outset the political departments should not be accountable to the ordinary committees. The Saratov party organization, on the other hand, prior to Congress, had passed a more extreme resolution calling for the 'political departments to be placed under the control of the territorial committees.'[175] Despite everything, there remained a determination to maintain and if need be to restore the principle of territoriality in the overall party structure, when the emergency that the war had imposed came to an end.

7   Peace or war

Extension of military methods to the economy

Towards the end of 1919, the Soviet authorities began to focus their efforts on the development of means of mobilizing urban and rural manpower, based on the obligation to work ('universal compulsory labour'), and on the introduction of military-style discipline in the major branches of industry and the economy.[1] The first moves in this direction were made right at the beginning of 'War Communism', and the War Ministry was one of their main promoters. In July 1918, VVS had stated its support for the decision 'to place under its [own] command, and to militarize, the staff of the railways, and in general that of means of communication, such as roads, troop transport vehicles, military supplies, and evacuations'.[2] In November 1918, Trotskii had asked government, party, and Transport Commissariat officials to have the railway system 'militarized', since 'the introduction of military discipline on the railways is a matter of vital necessity'.[3] Pursuing an already familiar line of argument, Vatsetis, in February 1919, explicitly urged Lenin that the various different Commissariats should cease 'to lead separate lives', and that it be acknowledged in political and organizational terms that 'the Commissariat for War is the motive force of the current period'.[4]

The militarization of labour was the government's overriding commitment during the months leading up to the outbreak of hostilities with Poland. Lenin himself, at both the 8th Party Conference and at the 7th Congress of Soviets, had placed this objective squarely on the agenda. Now that victory on the battlefields was within sight, it was essential to 'direct all the experience gained in war towards the solution of the main problems of peaceful construction'.[5] Lenin emphasized that this applied, in particular, to the way 'specialists' had been employed in the war effort. But as well as restoring the

authority of industrial leaders and technicians, it would soon be
necessary to direct the deployment of available skilled and unskilled
labour, to suspend workers' freedom to move from job to job and
from place to place, and, with the collaboration of trade-union organizations, to impose strict discipline. By way of recompense, militarized
workers would receive the same food rations as Red Army soldiers.

On 20 December 1919, the Central Committee sent a letter to all
party organizations, calling upon them to mobilize the population by
age-groups, with the goal of combating the 'fuel crisis' that was
threatening to paralyse transportation, and with it the whole
economic life of the country.[6] On 29 January, SNK extended mobilization to cover all citizens fit for work, and the broadest range of
special jobs.[7] While, on the one hand, labour was coming increasingly
to resemble military service, on the other, a number of Red Army
units no longer engaged in combat were beginning to turn their hand
to large-scale public works. An example was set by the eastern front
3rd army, whose leaders resolved to proceed, at the beginning of
January, with a radical conversion of their unit's tasks. Trotskii
greeted the proposal with enthusiasm, and promised to give it his full
backing at the party centre.[8] On the whole, Lenin too welcomed the
move, if somewhat coolly.[9] The first 'labour army' had been born, to
be swiftly imitated by other formations stationed in numerous regions
of the country.

The formations retained 'their own organization, their own internal
framework, and their own spirit' of genuine military units.[10] The only
limitation on their freedom of manoeuvre, as far as their new tasks
were concerned, was that they were advised to seek an 'understanding' with the local Soviet organs and to establish 'comradely and
cooperative relations' with the civilian workers mobilized through
labour conscription, and in particular with the trade unions.[11] The
political apparatus of the armed forces and the political commissars
were enjoined to reach an agreement with the civilian organs as to the
most effective ways of utilizing the troops in economic work.[12] Subsequently, the labour army RVSs were turned into fully-fledged territorial organs, and placed in charge of the management of the
economy. Representatives of the principal commissariats and government ministries were appointed to the said bodies, which were given
sweeping powers over the local authorities.[13]

The most striking example of the trend towards the militarization of
labour is provided by the alterations made to the administration of the
Commissariat for Transport and to the organizations of the commun-

ist rail-workers. In this sector, the process had begun back in November 1918, during the initial phase of large-scale militarization throughout the country, with the introduction of 'extraordinary military commissars' on all lines.[14] Appointed by RVSR, these commissars came under the control of the highest military organs, via the Commissariat for Transport, who became a member of RVSR. Immediately afterwards, with the creation of the supreme 'Council of Defence' (Sovet oborony) the military, supplies, transport, and war industry administrations were united under the command of none other than Lenin, in his capacity as president of SNK.[15] With a similar degree of resolve, the 'military regime' was introduced into each of the said key-sectors. This of course was translated in precise alterations to the way the corresponding party structures were organized.

Following the example of the Red Army, a Commissariat for Transport political department was created immediately the 8th Congress came to a close.[16] It was during this period that political departments were set up along the railway lines.[17] By the beginning of 1920, a PUR-type body was operating in the railways: its job was to direct political education, to deploy railway politrabotniki, and to 'institute political control over all the work of the railways'.[18] The existence of this body was sanctioned by a directive issued in January 1920 and which referred to it as the Glavpolitput' (Chief Political Railway Administration).[19] The Central Committee entrusted the Glavpolitput' with the task of taking control of 'all communist forces working in transport'. A vertical hierarchy of political departments, appointed by the Glavpolitput', marshalled and directed the party cells and the individual members at the three territorial levels of raion, uchastok, and railway liniia. The territorial party organizations attached to railway installations were under orders to furnish the political departments with 'all the cooperation and help possible', and to ensure that their opposite numbers in the Soviet organs did likewise. The setting-up of communist rail-workers' organizations, attached to the territorial party committees, was categorically prohibited, with a reference back to the 8th Congress's ruling on the issue.[20]

A subsequent decision, taken in May 1920, provides a more detailed picture of the extent to which the railways had already been militarized by the time the power of this system reached its peak.[21] In contrast with what happened in the Red Army, party cells of communist rail-workers continued to belong to the territorial organizations. Those in charge of the political departments became members of the ordinary committees, but with a consultative vote only. And yet 'the right to deploy all the *politrabotniki* in the railways, and to redirect communist rail-workers to political work, and the ability to appoint the commissars of every line office, [was] granted exclusively to the Glavpolitput' and to its local organs'. Despite pretences to a residual 'Democratic Centralism', the organization that was being created was modelled essentially on that of the combatant army. The fact that in the railways, unlike in the army, political commissars were often also in charge of 'technical' matters within their own administrative section,[22] does not detract from the overall identity between the forms of direction and organization within the party.

By the time the 9th Congress was convened in March 1920, the Glavpolitput' was only the most obvious case of a very widespread system of militarized management. As V. Smirnov commented a few months later, the political department had come to be seen as a 'magic means' of boosting a whole series of administrative and industrial sectors.[23] As a particularly significant example, Osinskii pointed to the Podonbass that Stalin was running in the Ukraine,[24] thus importing into the all-Russian forum the echoes of a battle that had erupted at local level. At the 4th Congress of the Ukrainian party (March 1920), the 'Democratic Centralism' group had rejected Stalin's report on the militarization of the Ukrainian economy, and had put forward its own programme. This accepted the principle of militarization as long as it was not taken to mean 'the mechanical transfer' into the economic sphere of 'all the organizational forms and administrative methods' typical of the army. The industrial manager's right to exercise one-man command was also accepted, providing he were flanked by a 'commissar', chosen by the trade unions, to whom would be granted the exclusive right to dictate disciplinary sanctions.[25] At the Congress, Osinskii denounced what 'Democratic Centralism' feared was the intention of Trotskii, who at the beginning of March had been placed at the head of the Commissariat for Transport:[26] 'to replace party organizations with political departments not only in the railways but also in all the main branches of industry'.[27] Sapronov accused the Central Committee of considering ordinary party committees 'a bourgeois prejudice' tinged with organizational 'conservativism'; whereas 'the new line involved the replacement of party committees with political departments, the leaders of which take the place of elected committees'.[28] Opposition censure on this issue was interwoven with attacks on the introduction of strict one-man command in civilian administrations and on the generalized spread of the system of 'appointment from above (*naznachenie*)'.[29] Once again there were those who, like V. Smirnov, although they protested their willingness to take into consideration the arguments in favour of stricter discipline across the board, continued to oppose 'the application of military methods in the form of party political departments', i.e. the militarization of the party itself.[30]

At the Congress Trotskii illustrated the Central Committee's theses on the introduction of labour conscription, and defended the creation of the Glavpolitput' as an emergency organ confined to the railways and to rail-workers, 'the most backward section of the working class'.[31] At the same time, he tried to dispel delegates' fears by stating that it was a temporary body and would cease to exist as soon as it had performed its specific tasks in the field of transportation, i.e. within a matter of months. L. Kamenev, who spoke on the 'question of organization', presented a draft resolution, which Congress later approved, whereby territorial party committees were given a say in the selection of *nachalniki* to sit on the railway political departments.[32]

These assertions and adjustments had little real effect on the new methods of political, trade union, and administrative management. Before the organs of the Glavpolitput' were abolished and the transportation emergency declared to be at an end (which happened in December 1920 during the debate on the role of trade unions in the Soviet state),[33] the Central Committee came very close to making equally sweeping innovations in the workings of party organizations in the 'factories, workshops, businesses, institutions, and other of the Republic's economic organs': in other words, in the very heart of the party. In July 1920 the decision was taken to abolish or drastically to curtail the powers of the industrial cells' elected organs of leadership. In their place, or alongside them, *organizators* were introduced, responsible for the activity of each cell, and backed up by an 'elder' whom they themselves appointed. In his turn, the 'elder' was responsible for the communist 'groups', engaged in compulsory labour.[34] Territorial committees in the factory area were to employ representatives of their own to direct the work of the cells. But the most significant point in this *instruktsiia* was the one that altered the functions of factory-based party organizations, restricting them to propaganda and to the fight against violations of work discipline. Meanwhile, they were prohibited from 'interfering' in companies' affairs, and their only right of appeal was to the 'labour commissar' of the factory. The analogy with the status of military cells couldn't have been clearer.

The battle at the 9th Congress over militarization had several other important implications. Once again a general political issue, of an almost constitutional nature, caused alarm among a broad section of the party; the fear was abroad that the War Ministry was about to take control of economic and civilian affairs. This allegation was formulated in very clear terms by Osinskii, on whose sensitivity to institutional matters we have already remarked.[35] Trotskii dismissed such suspicions, noting that the new militarized type of organ in charge of economic management was run not only by military leaders but also by staff from other ministries. He also attempted to demonstrate that the tendency to grant broad authority to technicians and to leading cadres did not constitute an arbitrary and improper extension of military methods, since the move to make greater use of 'specialists' had in actual fact originated in industry as early as spring 1918 – earlier than in the army.[36] Trotskii labelled the opponents of one-man command and militarization carriers of the *partizanstvo* and *kustarnichestvo* spirit,[37] failing to make any distinction between those who were critics at the 9th Party Congress, and those who, at the 8th, had attacked official military policy. But the fact that the Commissar for War delivered a second report on the introduction of a territorial militia system, far from reassuring those who harboured fears about his ambitions, added to their misgivings. Given Trotskii's overall positions, even this reform, originally an expression of anti-militarism, could seem threatening:

> The Red Army has fulfilled a considerable part of its tasks, and will also fulfil those that it still has before it. The Red Army is undergoing transformation, the army of defence is moving closer to labour: labour is being militarized, the army is being industrialized. Labour and the army shall be united and crowned with an armed forces militia system ... These conditions of union between labour and defence, defence and labour, are the basis that shall make the Soviet Republic the most powerful country on earth.[38]

At the moment when the Red Army reached its peak of prestige and influence, it was not the fascination of military power alone that dominated Trotskii's thinking. He continued to view the army, first and foremost, as the prototype of efficient state bureaucracy. A few days after the conclusion of the 9th Party Congress, at the 3rd All-Russian Trade Union Congress, the Commissar for War defended labour militarization from attack from the Menshevik grouping, and did not hesitate to declare that it was necessary 'to learn something from militarism, especially from German militarism'. To the workers, both from a political and from a classical socialist standpoint, the army might constitute either 'an apparatus of oppression and repression' or 'an instrument of liberation and defence', depending on whether it was led by the workers themselves or by the bourgeoisie.

> But – Trotskii went on – the unquestioning subordination of the parts to the whole is a characteristic common to every army. A severe internal regime is inseparable from military organization. In war every piece of slackness, every lack of thoroughness, and even a simple mistake, not infrequently bring in their train the most heavy sacrifices. Hence the striving of the military organization to bring clearness, definiteness, exactness of relations and responsibilities, to the highest degree of development. 'Military' qualities in this connection are valued in every sphere. It was in this sense that I said that every class prefers to have in its service those of its members who, other things being equal, have passed through the military school.[39]

Owing precisely to the universally formative value of military experience, political commissars, for example, could be used to equal advantage as union cadres on the labour front.

In a subsequent interview, given to an American journalist, Trotskii stated that 'in all areas of life and creative work certain common methods are applied . . . in the area of administration a good administrator of a factory or plant will also be a good military administrator'.[40] By way of proof of this 'basically nineteenth-century philosophy of administration',[41] the Commissar for War, with disconcerting candour, confessed that neither he nor the valorous Frunze, for example, had ever received any military training as such, and that in order to organize and run an army all that was required were 'a few administrative and political qualities'. In all likelihood, most of the other Bolshevik leaders, suddenly finding themselves involved in the governing of an immense country, entertained a similar conviction. But not so many of them can have been willing to conclude from this that the Commissar for War should assume the greatest managerial and organizational responsibilities in the economic and civilian sphere.

Militia or standing army?

The resolutions passed by the 9th Party Congress on the transition to a militia army aroused the enthusiasm of the group headed by Podvoiskii. A disciplined military cadre with vast experience of 'partisan' warfare in the Ukraine, Podvoiskii was above all a convinced advocate of the Red Army's reorganization as a militia, at least once the war came to an end. The Petrograd Vsevobuch saw 'a colossal difference' between the theses passed by the 8th Congress and those proposed by the 9th. The dual basis (militia and regular army), on which the Red Army had until that moment been constructed, was about to be eliminated.[42] But this optimism was the result of a misunderstanding, and was destined to be disappointed.

A document in which Trotskii expounded his own theses on the militia had appeared in December 1919.[43] The connection that he traced between the next stage of military construction and the militarization of the economy was succinctly expressed in the title to the theses: 'The Transition to Universal Labour Conscription in Relation to the Militia System'. It is probably in this close correlation that lies the key to the apparent paradox whereby the man who had always stood out as the most consistent supporter of the regular army now appeared to embrace the opposite viewpoint.[44] It is not a matter of grasping how one abstract model of military organization was all of a sudden replaced by another: indeed, it should not be forgotten that the Commissar for War had always portrayed the militia, even in the theses he presented to the 8th Congress, as the ultimate ideal goal, which would be achieved once communist society had at last been founded.[45] It would perhaps be more accurate to say that once the conviction began to gain ground – not only in restricted army circles or in Trotskii's own mind – that the armed forces were emerging as the soundest and most viable arm of the state, it appeared expedient to adapt them to meet the needs of peacetime. And now that the mobilization of labour was to provide the workforce with military discipline and training, it was plain to see that the conscript workers' units constituted a territorially based levy.[46] In other words, the seeming triumph of the militia idea towards the end of the Civil War was to a considerable degree only one aspect of the ambiguous nature of 'War Communism', under which responses to concrete needs could be mistaken for harbingers of a future ideal society. The expediency of using the army in economic reconstruction and of imposing a military-type discipline on the working population might prompt the thought that the moment had been reached when the distinction between armed forces and labour forces, between army and country – a distinction characteristic of the regular standing army – was coming to an end. If nothing else, the conviction that it really was this that was occurring could be turned to some use in rendering the prospect of militarization palatable to the more sceptical workers and party members.

However, the introduction of labour service was accompanied by a resurgence of activity and of interest among the military (including professional soldiers) in the launching of a militia system that might be combined with the gradual demobilization of the gigantic combatant army (numbering almost 5 million men at the end of 1920). The militia idea was not just an idealistic banner covering a harsher and more prosaic reality. From November 1919 onwards, special commissions created by the supreme organs of the War Ministry intensified their examination of the forms that the transition should take in the fields of mobilization, training, and unit formation.[47] It was at this juncture that Podvoiskii triumphantly asserted that, in the course of personal talks between himself and Lenin and Trotskii, 'it has been determined that from now on the Vsevobuch will no longer be an auxiliary organ of the Red Army but will assume control of all the forms and means for the transition to a militia army'.[48] In the course of this relatively lengthy discussion (for obvious security reasons, highly confidential), one section of Soviet military leadership doubtless displayed considerable affection for the militia model and fought hard to have it adopted. Nonetheless, orthodox circles as well as the most prominent party leaders in the War Ministry successfully opposed these efforts. When, finally, the dispute was settled with the adoption of a 'mixed' system,[49] entailing a reduction in standing armed forces to a minimum considered indispensable, and the setting up of a certain number of units at a territorial and industrial level (with extensive non-barracks training), the outcome was as much a result of economic pressures as of principle. With its commitment to reconstruction, Soviet Russia in the early 1920s simply could not afford to maintain on a permanent basis all the armed forces that were felt to be required for its defence.[50] With the gradual abandonment of 'War Communism', from December 1920 onwards, the most exciting of the theories regarding the impending merger of administrative, economic, and military apparatuses also faded away. By far the most significant episode at this time was the defeat that Trotskii, in his advocacy of 'state control' over trade unions, suffered at the 10th Party Congress in March 1921.

Following the conclusion of the 9th Congress, war with Poland made the militia question seem less important and pressing. When the debate resumed, in the autumn of 1920, it seemed at first that those who backed a full-blown militia system might gain the upper hand. A Central Committee resolution, passed in September, marked a first decisive step in this direction.[51] Referring back to the decisions

taken by the 9th Congress, the resolution reaffirmed the determination to move towards 'the institution of a new army on militia
principles'. Provision was therefore made for the combination of the
existing system of military training for industrial workers (Vsevobuch)
with 'special task detachments'. Created in April 1919, these detachments were considered to be more politically reliable: during the Civil
War, they had been employed both in battles against regular White
forces and in repressive actions in the rear, e.g. in cases of mass
insurrection and 'banditry' against Soviet power.[52] Composed prevalently of party members, these formations had initially taken the form
of direct offshoots of territorial Bolshevik organizations. From this
point on, while the Red Army was struggling with the difficulties
posed by demobilization, these detachments were consolidated and
utilized to repress the revolts that occurred above all in certain rural
areas of the country, during the first years following the end of the
struggle against the White armies. The resolution of September 1920
removed the job of 'training and directing' the 'special task detachments' from the party committees, and gave it to the Vsevobuch.
Steps were also taken to merge these sections with the units trained
by the Vsevobuch. Buoyed up by the increased authority of the
organization that he directed, Podvoiskii sought in vain to persuade
the Central Committee to free the Vsevobuch from its humiliating
dependency on the 'regular' military organ in charge of the training of
the Red Army, the *vseroglavshtab*, and to grant the former an autonomous position within RVSR. At the same time, he proposed that
territorial commissariats be abolished, asserting that, if his recommendations were accepted, they would become superfluous.[53] If
Podvoiskii's scheme had been accepted, the Vsevobuch, he argued,
could have immediately established a thoroughgoing and unadulter-
ated militia system.

The course of the RVSR commission proceedings displayed a trend
very different from that pursued by Podvoiskii. In December, during
an important conference of military leaders, a majority of delegates
proved to be much more sensitive to arguments in favour of the
preservation of a sizable standing force and of the existing system of
organizing the supreme commands.[54] The Commander-in-Chief, S.
Kamenev, was among those who expressed this viewpoint with the
most energy and authority.

Prior to the 10th Congress, there was very little public debate. At
the 8th Congress of Soviets, in December 1920, the Menshevik Dan'
made an unsuccessful attempt to spark a discussion by alleging that

the new 'professional Soviet soldiers' were opposed to the militia for egoistic reasons of self-preservation.[55] At the 10th Congress, debate was limited to a series of commission sessions closed to the public.[56] This happened despite the request, formulated by one of the delegates at the start of proceedings, that no special 'military section' be formed to discuss the 'question of the organization of the army and the fleet'.[57] According to this anonymous speaker, 'this issue [concerned] not only the military *rabotniki* but all communists in general'. The Congress voted down the proposal to form a special section, and the compromise put forward by a second speaker was probably accepted: any delegate who wished to attend the soldiers' meeting would be free to do so.[58] But on 10 March, Trotskii appealed to the Congress Presidium to order that each debate be held in a special secret session, from which all non-delegates should be strictly barred, with the threat that party sanctions would be inflicted on any participants who later disclosed any of the materials of the said sessions.[59] These measures were necessary because, Trotskii argued, the matter in hand as usual contained no issues 'of principle' and did not therefore come within the authority of the Congress in its plenary and public forms.

The press had reported some of the conflicting positions that had come to light, though it had concentrated mainly on the two vaguest and most schematic ones. In early January 1921, *Izvestiia* published Podvoiskii's platform: 'The Soviet System and the Militia. For the Reorganization of the Armed Forces'.[60] A quite different treatment was reserved for Tukhachevskii, champion of the regular army, whose theses 'On the socialist Army' were published by *Pravda* right in the middle of Congress,[61] after another article of his, refuting the claimed superiority of the militia, had appeared at the end of February.[62] Each strove to demonstrate that his own system was preferable not only from the point of view of the state budget, but also from that of military efficiency. Finally, the issue was discussed at a series of locally-held pre-Congressional assemblies. Reports in the most authoritative press gave the impression that the idea of an immediate transition to a militia army, on the lines that Podvoiskii had expounded, was relatively unpopular. Then, at the Moscow *guberniia* Party Conference, a resolution prudently stressing the 'gradualness' of such a transition won majority support.[63] At the same time, it was noted that Tukhachevskii had been given an enthusiastic reception at the Conference of western front communists.[64] It is not hard to imagine that in this instance animosity towards their Polish neighbour may have played a part.

Finally, the 10th Congress indicated the solution that was pro-
visionally adopted:

> As for the militia system, the party has no reason whatever to review
> its own programme. The form, the methods, and the speed of the
> transition to a militia army wholly depend on the situation abroad
> and at home, on the continuation of the period of peace, and on
> relations between town and countryside, etc.
>
> At the present time, agitation by certain comrades for the *de facto*
> liquidation of the existing Red Army, and for the immediate tran-
> sition to the militia, is mistaken and dangerous on practical grounds.
>
> For the time being, the foundation of our armed forces must
> remain the present Red Army, freed as far as possible from the most
> elderly age classes and strengthened in its proletarian and commun-
> ist component.[65]

The party did not renounce its long-term position, but regarded the
introduction of the militia as dependent on two fundamental conditions. First, that for the near future there should be no conflicts
between the Soviet Republic and other states: the uncertainty that
Congress expressed in this regard made it appear wise to maintain a
respectable fighting force that could be rapidly mobilized and
deployed. Secondly, that an attitude favourable to Soviet power
should be seen to have developed among the peasantry. This condition was a clear expression of the fear, by no means devoid of
foundation in spring 1921, that a universal and territorially based
training system might promote the spread of discontent in rural
areas,[66] and that this discontent would be armed. The demobilization
of the Red Army should therefore go ahead, while paying attention to
the quality and political reliability of the remaining cadres in the
standing units. Even Podvoiskii came round to agreeing with this
point, as can be seen from the platform that he put to Congress.[67]

One important consequence of the decision to maintain a regular
standing army was Congress's acknowledgement that military professionalism was now a respectable skill in the Soviet Republic. This
was an idea that had traditionally been abhorrent to the more dogmatic backers of the militia system. Though in reluctant and wavering
terms, this step was marked by the inclusion of point 9 in the resolution 'On the military question': 'Since, now that the war at the fronts
has ceased, officers are no longer called upon to serve on a temporary
basis but to practise a long-term profession (*dlitel'naia*), steps need to
be taken to improve their material circumstances, and above all those
of NCOs.'[68]

The defeat of Podvoiskii and of the other Vsevobuch leaders was of course also a consequence of the lack of clarity of the scheme that they supported. It is not hard to imagine the misgivings created in the High Commands by frequent assertions in the pro-militia press that, for example, recommended the models of military organization of Cromwell's army, of the armies of the French revolution, of American armies during the War of Independence, of anti-Napoleonic formations mustered in Germany and Spain, and of those used by Garibaldi, all of which were bundled together under the militia label.[69] Bolshevik political and military leaders had cause to be dismayed when they read in the pro-militia press not only the mottos of Jaurès, regarding the desirability of the militia system, but also those of Bebel and Kautskii.[70] Even greater political concern was aroused by certain slogans that the supporters of the militia were spreading among the soldiers, calling, for example, for the abolition of commissars in the future militia army.[71] Disquieting too were the ingenuous theses that Podvoiskii himself continued to expound, even before the highest military organs, regarding the replacement of professional commanders with non-military cadres drawn from party organizations and from the trade unions.[72]

Podvoiskii's plans may be fairly viewed as the last echoes within the RKP(b) of the anti-militarist idealism that was widespread in the parties of the 2nd International prior to the war. What distinguished them from this tradition, however, was their unmistakable inclination towards forms of military organization involving the population as a whole, and for a much vaguer strand of pacifism. In this period, however inconsistently, Trotskii used the term militia to cover a variety of other meanings. To judge by certain of his speeches, he viewed with interest the kind of army, based more on quality than on sheer numbers, that General H. Von Seeckt advocated for Germany: a small professional and regular group which, at the right moment, would be able to broaden its ranks to accommodate conscripts who had already undergone a rapid course of training.[73] In these circumstances, militia-type training might have a complementary role to play. This notion did not, however, hinder him from presenting on occasions the 'mixed' system as a prudent application of 'Jaurès' ideas': a Swiss-type militia army, corresponding closely to the Vsevobuch conception. When it came to the crunch, however, Trotskii proved to be a lukewarm supporter of the militia system. In December 1920–January 1921, he opposed Podvoiskii's proposal that two separate High Commands be established, one to take charge of the militia and the other of the standing forces, deeming it preferable that the former remain subordinate to the latter. He recommended that the experiment of periodic training on a territorial and factory basis be started with the minimum possible number of units. With characteristic vagueness, he even spoke at this time of the future militia as 'a regular army, constructed on certain territorial principles and closely tied to labour'.[74] He showed greater enthusiasm for militia formations only when, in 1922–3, they began to be organized on a broader scale, in compliance with the decisions taken at the beginning of 1921.[75] But it is disconcerting to find that, in some of his writings of 1936, he expressed a negative judgement on the period when the development of the militia system within the Soviet armed forces, promoted by Frunze in 1925, reached its height: it was, in his opinion, a further sign that the Soviet regime was finally shelving the prospect of world revolution.[76] This demonstrates that Trotskii basically accepted the view that had gained ground among Bolshevik military leaders at the end of the war, that a 'pure' militia army was a wholly inadequate instrument for waging war.

Demobilization and the fate of PUR

While the military organs debated the future form that the armed forces should assume, several aspects of their internal organization began once again to attract the attention of broader party circles. The 9th Party Conference was held in September 1920, following the dismal conclusion of the war with Poland and only a few weeks prior to the opening of peace talks. The Conference marked a retreat from the positions that had won the day at the 9th Congress, which had favoured a thorough militarization of party structure. As can be gathered from Zinov'ev's address to Conference and the resolution passed on 'The tasks of party construction',[77] it was the Central Committee itself that raised the issue of a change in policy.

It was against this background that Khataevich, a PUR delegate, unleashed a forceful attack on the 'bureaucrats' communism' that was rearing its head within the Red Army.[78] He did not, however, raise the old issue of the party's methods of organization within the army: 'as regards the political departments in themselves, there is nothing to be said'. It was the people not the institutions that were the problem. Those in charge of the majority of political departments, in Khataevich's view, were doubtless good administrators, but they were not 'experienced party leaders'. This created 'an unhealthy atmosphere' in PUR and resulted in the lack of any 'lively organizational leadership'. The complex hierarchical apparatus of PUR was beset with difficulties of internal coordination, in particular between the divisional and higher levels. Khataevich complained also of the 'separateness' (*obosoblennost'*) of PUR from the rest of the party. The solution that the 9th Party Congress had recommended, regarding relations between Bolshevik military and civilian organs, had not led to any marked improvement. The moment had therefore come for the Central Committee to take a more direct hand in PUR affairs. Khataevich received the backing of Preobrazhenskii, who confirmed that the political departments were staffed with a new 'type of highly disciplined communist bureaucrat, who scrupulously carries out all the orders he receives, but whose work bears no trace of party spirit'.[79] In Preobrazhenskii's opinion too, the weakest point was the low calibre of divisional political leaders.

Conference resolutions urged party organizations to play a more active role in party member assemblies, and to ensure that their leading functionaries took part in them.[80] The trend towards 'appointments from above', which had prevailed at the 9th Congress, was offset by providing greater scope for elections. Altogether, the resolution was written in the spirit of a 'greater equality', in the party and in the country at large, between the 'commanding heights' and the 'base', between 'specialists' and workers, between leaders and those they led – and also between one ministry and another. It was bound to be interpreted as a polemical volley aimed at the extraordinary powers that the Commissariat for War had amassed.[81]

A special section was devoted to the Red Army. Significantly, the watchword of 'iron discipline' that had thus far enjoyed wide currency was now dropped in favour of 'revolutionary discipline', more attuned to calls for a struggle 'against the routine of the old military system and against manifestations of any form of bureaucratism'.[82] Political commissars and party members in the RVSs were enjoined to live 'as far as possible ... among the mass of soldiers and workers'. An amendment, proposed by Khataevich, was even included, whereby the Central Committee undertook to step up its involvement in the internal life of the armed forces:

> Conference draws the Central Committee's attention to the need for it to assume more direct control of the organizational work of the Red Army's and Fleet's party organizations, as well as to the fact that any further isolation of the life and work of our organizations from the general life of the party is not to be tolerated.[83]

At the end of October, in a *Letter to the RVSs*, Trotskii himself repeated these ideas and recommendations, recognizing the need to foster 'a comradely relationship' between ordinary soldiers and command personnel.[84] On 5 October, PUR had issued an order to commissars and political departments to 'draw closer' to the party cells. The hope was expressed that 'more frequent and regular' meetings for communists would be arranged, and those in positions of political responsibility were urged to hold discussions with the men about the issues that lay closest to their hearts.[85] As soon as the Conference ended, the south-western front political department issued a directive carrying even more precise instructions: at party meetings, following leaders' speeches, 'debates are desirable'; all collegial party meetings ought to be open to party members; disciplinary sanctions were to be inflicted with particular severity on 'responsible party functionaries' found guilty of abuses of power.[86] Lastly, at the beginning of December, PUR promulgated an order that called for the strict limitation of privileges, a struggle to prevent the re-emergence in the detachments of 'the discipline of the stick', and the realization of genuine 'communist equality' in the Red Army: in this way it would be easier to counter occasional 'demagogic moves' among the troops.[87] As in December 1919, in the autumn and winter of 1920–1 the approaching cessation of large-scale military operations triggered a slackening of the party regime throughout the military organizations, and a relaxation of discipline in the units. Once the immediate danger seemed to be passed, there was a risk that the soldiers, regardless of whether or not they were communists, might cease to see the need for the most oppressive aspects of discipline, for the authority of the command corps, and for disparities in treatment according to rank. Efforts were made to prevent the eruption of virulent forms of discontent. Yet the special meeting of military delegates to the 9th Conference made no major alterations to the organizational structure of PUR. Party cells retained their status as 'working organs' without any power to take decisions. Also, the right to perform political work in the rear remained the prerogative of the political departments and was denied to ordinary party committees.[88]

A more concrete result, on the other hand, was achieved by recommendations that the Central Committee's control over the armed forces be increased: this was one of the most traditional and time-honoured of demands made by the communist military and by opposition groupings. In September 1920, the Orgbiuro of the Central Committee granted itself the authority to 'confirm' front, army, and divisional RVS members, and insisted that it be kept informed of any transfers that might occur.[89] The same body also resolved that those responsible for army political departments would be nominated by the corresponding RVSs, but subject to the 'confirmation' of the Central Committee.[90] During this period RVSR issued an order that boosted the ability of the political departments to influence the selection of commanders by presenting the candidacy of commissars subordinate to them.[91]

The meetings held at RVSR in December 1920 also studied the schemes that the most intransigent advocates of the militia system had proposed for reorganizing PUR.[92] All we know of this matter is what can be inferred from one single passage in the programme that Podvoiskii put before the 10th Congress, probably drafted to prepare the ground for a radical reorganization of the army's political machine. The passage in question spelled out the need for 'political work in the army to be closely linked, wherever the military situation allowed, with the general work of the party as a whole and with that of its local organs'.[93] A majority of the military leaders, however, voted in favour of preserving PUR in its existing form, rejecting the idea of a 'merger' of political work and military training, which Podvoiskii's group presumably favoured.[94]

The need to review relations between military political organs and civilian party organs, and the whole question of relations between different army bodies, were formulated by the 2nd Conference of *politrabotniki*, in the second half of November 1920. Smilga, in his address to Conference, not only mounted a determined assault on risky 'experiments', such as the introduction of the militia, but also questioned the role that the party should play in the army during the transition to peacetime.[95] Smilga argued that it was important to 'distinguish clearly between purely party work and the general work of political departments', and he championed the introduction of 'those forms of work that exist for the civilian population'.[96] Smilga thereby appeared to attack the close ties linking administrative and political military organs, and to denounce the curtailment of Democratic Centralism that this entailed within the armed forces. His definition of a communist-at-arms as the 'party pariah', the 'semi-legal communist', seemed to point the way to a proposal for the reorganization of PUR, which, however, he did not make. Yet he spoke in explicit terms of the need for 'democratization'.[97] But a few days later, Smilga hinted at just how reluctant he had been to give a degree of verbal satisfaction to the 'critical mania' that had taken PUR by storm since demobilization had got under way.[98]

The delegates to the Conference of *politrabotniki* hurled at PUR an avalanche of criticisms, very similar to those voiced at the Party Conference in September. Trotskii declared that he was not willing to go into such matters. He spoke of the 'inevitability' of a closer tie with territorial organizations, in which, however, army representatives would have an increasingly important role to play. Unlike Smilga, Trotskii approved of 'the prudent attempt to move towards a militia system' decided upon by the military authorities. He also called on delegates to resign themselves to the inevitable decline of the army's influence in the life of the country, caused by the advent of peace and demobilization. If the army were to try to preserve 'the independence of its own organizations with respect to the party as such', the said organizations would find it impossible to ensure even their own internal cohesion – or indeed their very survival. All the more so, added Trotskii, given that 'critical mania in the army is growing'. A marked openness towards the territorial organizations had therefore to be accompanied by a greater recourse to 'democratic methods', and an increased willingness to take criticism itself seriously, provided this in no way compromised the specific make-up of military machinery. Trotskii stressed, however, that he saw no contradiction between democratic and 'military methods'.[99] This emerged as one of the crucial points in Trotskii's arguments during the debate on trade unions, and indicated just how little importance Trotskii in fact attributed to democracy in PUR.

The Conference expressed a low opinion of PUR's recent work. 'Anarchy' had apparently reigned, and PUR had not even been able to guarantee efficient links with the political sections.[100] Smilga could only make a feeble attempt to clear himself of personal blame by citing the numerous commitments with which the party Central Committee had saddled him over the previous months. These had made it impossible for him to concentrate his attention on the body that had been placed in his trust.[101]

Reorganization

In January, apparently at his own request, Smilga was removed from office.[102] Following a brief transitional period, during which Solov'ev was head of PUR, Gusev took over the job at the end of March.[103] This was a significant appointment: between the end of

1919 and the beginning of 1921, Gusev had acted as the spokesman of a group of communist military leaders which had now managed to place its own candidate at the head of the armed forces. The long march that these men had embarked upon, towards the final dislodgement of Trotskii from the post of Commissar for War, culminated in January 1925, when he was replaced by Frunze. As demobilization commenced, Gusev seemed to embody an answer to the problem of how the armed forces should be organized and what role they should play – an answer able to take account of the party's principal concerns. A supporter of the realistic formula of a 'mixed' structure for the Red Army, Gusev was also the most fervent promoter of the view that PUR should in all essentials be preserved 'in the shape in which it has developed over three years of war'.[104] At the beginning of 1921, he reminded those who favoured a radical reform of the political apparatus that PUR was the most effective bulwark against any 'Bonapartist moves' that might find encouragement in the country's internal breakdown and international isolation.[105] Gusev's tenure of a leading post in the army must have helped to reassure those Bolsheviks who, during the debate on trade unions that shook the party from November 1920 to March 1921, were hounded by a menacing image of Trotskii, ever intent on grabbing for himself vast new powers throughout the country.

Nor could Gusev be accused of taking an excessively novel line on any of the main problems regarding the structure of the armed forces. As far as the implementation of one-man command was concerned, his position did not differ from the prevailing approach, supported also by Trotskii, which stressed the necessary 'gradualness' of the process.[106] In line with the approach that Bukharin was later to take at the 10th Congress on the issue of party democracy, Gusev did not rule out the possibility of an 'internal democratization' of the military political apparatus in the short term. Providing the 'autonomy' and 'centralization' of PUR were not placed in jeopardy, Gusev was also in favour of 'a close tie' with territorial organizations.[107] There were no traces in Gusev's own political past of 'anti-specialist' positions. Indeed, prior to the 8th Congress, he had spoken out firmly against the sensational declarations that Sorin and Kamenskii had made.[108] Gusev had played a prominent part in the clash that occurred in summer 1919 between the eastern front RVS and Trotskii. The row had focussed above all on strategic questions, but other people had then taken advantage of the situation to reopen broader political issues. Relations between Gusev and military circles close to Stalin seemed, on the other hand, to have worsened, after the momentary convergence of the two groups at the July Plenum. After July, Gusev had fallen out with Stalin over the deployment of forces and the conduct of operations on the eastern and southern fronts. Then, at the end of August 1920, following the army's defeat in Poland, he had been appointed to the south-western front command, taking the place of Stalin, who had just been removed from his post.[109]

Once again the choice of the top political leader of the Red Army had been finely balanced. Evidence of Gusev's professional and political maturity is provided by a number of statements he made at the end of 1921 on the institutional problem of party–army relations. In his view, not only did the Central Committee and the Party Congress not have the right to meddle in 'strategic-operational' questions,[110] the party should manage its own military organizations exclusively through the political departments – organs that were protected from the interference of bodies 'external' to the army itself.[111] Making himself heir to an important part of the tradition whose development Trotskii had decisively influenced, Gusev insisted that the party's military organizations should preserve their 'closed character'. Nonetheless, his continual references to the dangers of 'Bonapartism' (dangers to which he also drew attention in the theses he submitted to the secret military meetings at the 10th Congress),[112] signified that Gusev and his group continued to share the widespread mistrust of unrestrained professionalism. Under his leadership, PUR, over the months that followed, pursued an extremely flexible organizational line which, while safeguarding certain vital features of the apparatus, came to terms with mounting pressure for the decentralization of political work among the armed forces.

Straight after the December *politrabotniki* Conference, which had called for the standing army to be maintained, a second and similar meeting, held at the beginning of January 1921, endorsed the principle that PUR should also be retained in the future.[113] This Conference indicated the possibility of to some extent decentralizing political work at regiment and company level. In mid-January, a session of the Central Committee outlined in very general terms its agenda for the future. By cautiously espousing something of the 'militia spirit', it sought to reconcile the preservation of a barracks-based army with the preference, typical of supporters of the militia system, for greater identification between the army and the country:

> The barracks cannot and must not lead a separate life, shut in upon itself. Between the barracks and the factory, the barracks and the

Soviet, the party cell in the detachment, and the overall organization of the party, an indissoluble link must exist. But the convergence of the Red soldiers and the workers and peasants must in no case come about at the cost of even the slightest weakening of revolutionary order in the detachments.[114]

In February, these recommendations were restated with greater precision in instructions that the Central Committee itself released. A special resolution emphasized that close contact had to be fostered between military and civilian organs, and that the military authorities needed to pay greater attention to the soldiers, to their needs and to their protests.[115] From this point on, commissars, for instance, were to be chosen 'in greater contact' with *guberniia* party committees; the company *politruk* now came to have a rank closer to that of an ordinary soldier than to that of a member of the command staff; military and civilian authorities were enjoined to strive to satisfy the soldiers' material needs, to ensure that the men received everything to which they were entitled, and to draw attention to cases of 'illegal conduct' by Soviet authorities. In particular, in an implicit reference to the worries fuelled by the presence in the Red Army of an overwhelming mass of peasants no longer engaged in military operations, it was decided that the denunciation and punishment of abuses committed by local authorities, in relation to food requisitions, should be given greater priority. The political departments had to supervise the enforcement of 'the principle of equality between soldiers, commissars and commanders'. Service relations were also significantly reinterpreted:

> Make it obligatory for all commanders and *politrabotniki* to check that military discipline and the internal life of the soldiers [*sic*] corresponds to the rules laid down in the military statutes of the Red Army. To this end, it is necessary to request only that which does not exceed the limits of the statutes and of a reasonable notion of discipline.[116]

Clearly the purpose of these injunctions was to ease the pressure that was otherwise likely to build up in the army, which, even though it was undergoing demobilization, could not but be affected by the political and social tensions of those months, as well as by the conditions of dire want and poverty then afflicting the country.

We shall shortly be turning our attention to the limited democratization of party organizations within the army; as can be seen, this process was already hinted at in the resolution quoted. As regards the decision to encourage greater contacts between the army and the area where it was stationed, a second resolution, passed in June 1921 and devoted to 'relations between the political departments of the Red Army and the organizations of the RKP(b)', should first be mentioned.[117] This resolution declared that the political departments were fully entitled to monopolize political leadership in the detachments, but it also ruled that their *nachalniki* had to 'carry out their work in coordination with the corresponding party committees in the area where the military units [were] deployed'. Furthermore, the *nachalniki* were to make 'periodic reports' to the *guberniia* committees on the work they carried out in the units, thereby introducing the notion that the political departments were accountable to the territorial organizations. The military cells were to register at these local organizations, which might entrust them with the performance of general political tasks – on the sole condition that this met with the agreement of the corresponding military commissars. With the same proviso, the military cells could take part in political campaigns launched 'on the initiative' of the local committees. Communist soldiers too could take part on equal terms with civilian party members in all assemblies and elections held at the territorial organizations. In comparison with the previous arrangement, the biggest change was that whereas local organizations could now exert considerable influence on the internal life of the army, there was no guarantee that this relation was reciprocal: the political department *nachalniki*, though still included in the corresponding territorial committee, lost their full voting rights, now enjoying only a consultative vote. It appears that this particular measure encountered the determined but in the end unsuccessful protest of Ukrainian political and military leaders.[118]

Given the nature of the period during which these decisions were taken, it is perhaps easier to understand why even those PUR leaders who felt least sympathy for the hegemonic claims of the territorial organizations were induced to grant them a very considerable role in the political life of the Red Army. As demobilization got under way, countless party cadres left their political posts in the units. In part, the central and peripheral civilian organizations dispatched them to the peacetime 'fronts' of economic reconstruction.[119] This did not, however, take place in a planned and gradual way: indeed, it soon took the form of a headlong flight. The decision to maintain a sizable standing army thus ran the risk of miscarrying for purely practical reasons, and the Central Committee had to step in repeatedly and energetically. As early as the second half of 1921, a drastic effort was made to halt the demobilization of the *politrabotniki*.[120] The end of enemy pressure on the fronts also led to a sharp change in the way resources were allocated. As the army no longer received priority treatment, there was an immediate worsening in soldiers' living standards. The resolution passed in April 1922 by the military delegates to the 11th Party Congress, with its single-minded insistence on the need forcefully to combat desertion, draft evasion, and insubordination, and with its recommendations that military courts resort to tougher repressive measures, was an eloquent indication of the chaos that deteriorating conditions caused within the armed forces.[121] Territorial Soviet and party organizations were therefore urged both to provide material and financial backing, and to continue their political and supervisory activities.[122] It is therefore noteworthy that the organizational machinery referred to in the resolutions of winter and spring 1921 in fact concealed a situation much more complex than the straightforward decision to maintain a regular army nucleus might lead one to suppose. PUR adapted itself to the demands of the new period, creating closer links with the armed forces and the country at large, above all through the appropriate party organs. Although the militia idea failed to take root, the existing political apparatus proved flexible enough to reconcile the principle of territorially based organization with the upkeep of a vertically organized regular military structure.

One example of the difficulties and risks that this line could pose for the centralized army structure and its internal regime is supplied by events in the Baltic fleet, as demobilization got under way. Party committees had survived longer on the ships at Kronshtadt than in the infantry, and the powers that the party collectives had arrogated were traditionally much wider. RVSR and the Baltic fleet political department (PUbalt) had had to work hard to implement the organizational methods and the pattern of authority in force in the Red Army.[123] At the end of 1921, the radical trends characteristic of the sailors, broadly reflected in their party organizations, were demagogically exploited by Zinov'ev to support his and Lenin's platform, and to undermine the position that Trotskii had taken in the debate over trade unions. Zinov'ev had not hesitated to extend the Petrograd party committee's right to interfere in the political activity of the fleet, to the detriment of the autonomy and authority of the PUbalt.[124] The Petrograd Bolshevik leaders had long cherished the ambition of placing the armed forces of the region under their control.[125] Thus, at an important meeting in January 1921, after a speech from Trotskii and then one from Zinov'ev, Raskol'nikov (the fleet's supreme political commissar) rose to accuse those present of attempting to conceal behind their support for the Lenin–Zinov'ev position on trade unions their dogged resolve to see *komitetchina* reintroduced on the ships. Zinov'ev rejected this allegation with a great display of indignation, but his protestations remained somewhat unconvincing.[126] What the Petrograd example clearly demonstrated was that a hardening of the principle of territorial organization could go hand in hand with – or even give rise to – impulses towards more profound and dangerous alterations to the life of the armed forces. The Kronshtadt rebellion (28 February–18 March 1921) appeared to vindicate Raskol'nikov.

At the 10th Congress and in the months that followed, the need to redefine the internal life of the Red Army was tackled with greater caution than had been shown in the creation of a new framework of relations between military and civilian organs. Partly of course this was a reflection of anxieties within the party caused by the Kronshtadt affair. In his speech, Bukharin stated that the 'Workers' Opposition' group would be agitating for the reintroduction into the army of the 'elective principle'.[127] This was denied by Maksimovskii (of 'Democratic Centralism'), who said that to his knowledge the group referred to had not reached any such decision.[128] Smilga then made things worse by informing the delegates that in some areas soldiers had already held elections not only of political leaders but even of commanders.[129] This, however, is not the only evidence to suggest that something resembling a movement for the democratization of PUR and of the armed forces was afoot at the start of 1921. Among the restless Red units of the Ukrainian Republic, the demand that Bolshevik political organs be made elective and independent of the military organs was once again heard.[130] Prior to the 10th Congress, the PUR leader of the military *okrug* of Kiev, Degtiarev, had cited a number of specific cases. The communists of an entire division (the 58th) had proposed that the PUR organs be split into: party organs, functioning in accordance with the principle of 'Democratic Centralism'; and administrative 'political education' organs, which would be placed under the control of the territorial centres of Glavpolitprosvet (Central Administration for Political Education).[131] One might also add the demands made by the Kronshtadt rebels for the abolition of the political departments and political commissars. These demands, expressing a widespread feeling, formed part of a broader attack on the one-party system.[132]

At the 10th Congress, Smilga referred explicitly to the Kronshtadt uprising. From his position of authority as co-reporter together with

Bukharin, who had been given the task of presenting the positions of the Central Committee, he attacked the Central Committee theses on the transition to a regime of 'workers' democracy' in the party. This, he said, was empty and dangerous 'demagogy'.[133] As a consequence of his intervention, Smilga came under fire from many of the subsequent opposition speakers. Smilga had even called into question the resolutions passed by the 9th Conference, which he alleged had yielded 'opportunistically' to desires at the end of the war in both the party and the country as a whole for a greater measure of détente.[134] 'Democratization' could provide no solution to the crisis that racked the party. Its causes were to be sought in the rift that had opened between ordinary people and party members, between the mass of the workers and the factory cells.[135] The 'privileges' that the resolution moved by Bukharin sought to grant Bolshevik cells had therefore to be eliminated, including the faculty to 'interfere' by administrative means in provisions taken by company managements.[136] Smilga thus reaffirmed the need to maintain and extend the party regime characteristic of the Red Army. To bolster party popularity, its members needed to be placed on an equal administrative footing with ordinary citizens, without, however, undermining in any way the principle of strict hierarchical subordination. Once again the principle of a greater separation between party organs and state organs featured prominently both in the arguments of the most authoritarian trends within the party and in those of certain opposition circles.

At the opposite political extreme from Smilga, the fact that it was Maksimovskii who led the attack on those who allegedly wanted to grant the party's military cells 'the right to influence the composition of the political departments and RVSs'[137] should be viewed as evidence that these extreme positions, however widespread they may have been among communist soldiers, by this time had only a very slight following among prominent party cadres. Controversy over this issue had begun to die down perceptibly as early as autumn 1919. The revolt that simmered in large areas of the country, and the isolation of the party in spring 1921, must have seemed to embody powerful new arguments in favour of preserving consensus in the sensitive military sector too.

The document that 'Democratic Centralism' presented to the 10th Congress gives a very precise idea of the margins within which dissensions between the various currents on the military question might vary at this point in time. Several passages deserve to be quoted in full, given that this text was, as far as we know, the last original plan to reform the structure of PUR that was considered by an RKP(b) Congress:

> The existence of particular conditions in the combat army imposes the need to limit the principles of Democratic Centralism in party work. Despite this, there is no doubt that a certain broadening of the democratic forms of party and political work in the army is necessary.
>
> In view of this, the Congress resolves that:
>
> 1 – Party commissions in the brigades, divisions, armies, at the fronts, and in the *okrugy* shall be elected by the corresponding conferences.
>
> 2 – Party commissions shall be attributed the following functions: a) the acceptance and expulsion of members; b) the examination of conflicts and appeals; c) the review of party work undertaken by the political departments.
>
> 3 – The political department *nachalniki*, inasmuch as they are the official representatives of the party, are accountable to the respective conferences.
>
> 4 – Should the Conference pass, with respect to the *nachalnik*, a resolution expressing a formal lack of confidence in him, the said resolution must be presented to the superior organs of the party in order that disciplinary measures be taken against him.
>
> 5 – As for the performance of party obligations by commissars and RVS members, the Congress confirms that the resolution of the September All-Russian Party Conference must be strictly adhered to.[138]

Point (1) apparently met with the approval of the military delegates to the Congress, a majority of whom, in their secret session on 17 March, voted in favour of the 'complete electivity' of party commissions.[139] With a greater measure of caution, Congress resolved in its plenary session that: 'Considering it desirable to establish – with the necessary guarantees – the electivity of party commissions in the army, the Congress calls upon the Central Committee to check the existing material on this subject with a view to drawing up a regulation as soon as possible.'[140]

The Central Committee responded to this call the following June.[141] Of the scheme that 'Democratic Centralism' presented, the principle that the commissions be elected by the conferences, and that they take charge of enrolments and expulsions, was accepted. The commissions' authority to settle conflicts was, however, strictly confined to the realm of relations between individual party members and the cells to which they belonged, and could only be exercised providing the causes of the proceedings 'involved the breach of general party obli-

gations' (which implicitly excluded the entire sphere of service relations). The commissions would not have their own apparatus for this,
but would make use of that of the political department. Every type of
decision taken required the *nachalnik*'s endorsement. To compensate
for this, it was stated that this regulation did not have to be enforced
in 'large centres', as long as the *guberniia* party committee gave its
go-ahead.

This resolution bore all the marks of its political parentage. It
broadly incorporated the position expressed by the Ukrainian military
leaders prior to the Congress in a detailed programme, written by
Gusev and Frunze. The programme raised all the main points that
were repeated in the document that Gusev and Frunze attempted to
force the secret sessions of the 10th Congress to discuss. Unlike this
later version, the original programme also contained a special chapter
on the reorganization of the party in the Red Army, which was not
put before Congress.[142] The proposals in question had clearly been
affected by the criticisms and ideas elaborated by 'Democratic Centralism'. The Ukrainian military leaders had in fact clashed with this
group before the start of the All-Russian Congress. The 'Democratic
Centralist' Mgeladze (Vardin),[143] who had taken part in the Polish
campaign as the *nachalnik* of the 1st cavalry army political department
(RVS: Voroshilov, Budennyi, Minin), was carrying out agitation in the
Ukraine.[144] On the problem of one-man command also, the original
Gusev–Frunze platform seems to have been the cue for other PUR
measures introduced at this time. Gusev and Frunze had emphasized
the need to use 'a certain prudence' in implementing the programme,
and had called for a restructuring of those posts that gave greatest
power to political staff in the units and detachments. In their view, the
functions of the divisional commissar and of the *nachalnik* of the
corresponding political department should be exercised by one and
the same person. Similarly, where one-man command was in force,
the commander's *pompolitchasti* should also be the political department *nachalnik*. A new commissars' *polozhenie*, issued by PUR in
January 1921, took the same approach.[145]

According to a distinguished Soviet military historian, the resolution on party commissions signified 'the elimination of a certain
militarization – caused by the war – affecting the activity of party
organizations in the army'.[146] This probably overstates the case, and it
would definitely be wrong to assert that it was only the communist
soldiers' organizations that suffered such restrictions during the war
years. Nonetheless, if one also considers the regulation governing the

operation of army cells, issued the following October, the change in outlook, compared with previous years, is unmistakable. The characteristic rule forbidding party cells to meddle in administrative and operational military affairs remained in force, while the commissar and political department lost none of their power over party life, especially in standing formations. But the cells were made doubly accountable: to the territorial committees as well as to the superior military organs of the party. Meanwhile, the general assembly of party cell members was granted exceptional importance, and its right to discuss matters was considerably extended, especially in the rear. The structures of the Red Army and of PUR were not in this sense demilitarized, but the party was given greater scope to perform independently certain elementary functions normally discharged by civilian organizations. As well as a certain degree of decentralization, a cautious distinction was introduced between the administrative functions of PUR and the 'political' functions of the party. The moderate requests made by 'Democratic Centralism' to render the political departments more accountable to the party members were doubtless rejected both because it was inevitable and desirable that the said functions overlap at this level, and because a relation of accountability might in practice have led to a restoration of electivity.

Glavpolitprosvet

At the end of the Civil War, the organizational integrity of PUR came under threat not only from supporters of the militia system, from latter-day 'military syndicalists', and from territorial party committees seeking to concentrate control of military units in their own hands. The Commissariat for Education, whose requests for cadres and resources had until then been sacrificed to the superior demands of national defence, had long since set its sights on the armed forces' powerful propaganda and indoctrination machine: this it regarded as an instrument perfectly tailored for the performance of its own tasks among the population.

The appetites of those in charge of the education system were far from unjustified. The Bolshevik political and military *rabotniki* had realized early on that 'no serious political work [was] conceivable without the assimilation of elementary general knowledge'.[147] PUR's educational work (*prosvetitel'naia rabota*) presupposed the establishment of schools in which the soldiers were taught 'Russian, Literature, Mathematics, History, and Geography',[148] for without a basic grounding in these subjects political propaganda could not take root. Although teaching was undertaken 'in the spirit of Marxism', it remained a separate activity, paving the way for the 'party political' education that was also one of the duties of the army's political organs. A dense network of schools, with teaching staff attached to the units themselves, operated throughout the army both at the front and in the rear. In 1920 the Baltic fleet alone possessed 1500 elementary-level schools, with over 1000 teachers and nearly 28,000 students. The schools, moreover, were supplemented by other cultural bodies, such as libraries, study and discussion 'clubs', and so on. The number of detachment libraries rose from 3000 to approximately 10,000 between the beginning of 1919 and the beginning of 1920, and almost half of these were at the front. Altogether, 3 million books were available for loan.[149] Every front army published its own newspaper, produced by its political department. The newspaper of the 1st mounted army, which was particularly famous, distributed almost two and a half million copies in April and May 1920 alone.[150] One of its regular writers was Isaac Babel, then a young *krasnoarmeets* fascinated by the personality of Budennyi and by his wild and picturesque unit.[151] By summer 1920 there were 400 'dramatic societies', and 500 'choral and musical societies' at the front. If one includes the rear, the army had roughly 1000 theatres and musical associations. It was not therefore surprising if PUR leaders affectedly declared that 'the complex political apparatus of our army is without precedent in military history'.[152]

The manoeuvre of the Commissariat for Education took a long time to evolve. In February 1920, SNK issued a decree setting up Glavpolitprosvet in order to bring together in one centre work formerly carried out by different bodies up and down the country: the Commissariat for Education first and foremost, but also PUR, VTsIK, the Glavpolitput', the Central Trade Union Council, and the Komsomol Central Committee: all of which organs were involved in mass 'political education'.[153] In particular, close coordination with PUR was envisaged, with the inclusion of its representatives in the corresponding territorial organs of Glavpolitprosvet. The two apparatuses (which the decree, in line with the tendentious approach taken by the Commissariat for Education, defined as 'parallel') were supposed gradually to merge. As for the military political departments in the rear, 'the general management and supervision' of their educational work was to be transferred forthwith to Glavpolitprosvet.

The 9th Party Congress did not discuss education at its plenary session. Instead the issue was addressed at the closed meeting of army delegates, which passed the first of a series of resolutions that over the months that followed kept repeating the same concept:

> Considering that the tasks of the Red Army not only are not termi-
> nated but that, with the transition to the principle of labour conscrip-
> tion and to the militia system, are becoming even more complex, the
> apparatus of PUR needs to be maintained without in any way
> subdividing it according to the various commissariats and institu-
> tions of the RSFSR.[154]

It seems therefore that the February 1920 SNK decree was not put into effect at once; indeed, the leaders of the Commissariat for Edu-cation had repeatedly to demand that it be implemented.[155] In October 1920, VTsIK endorsed the setting-up of Glavpolitprosvet, stating that it should incorporate the apparatus of PUR, with the sole exclusion of front political departments.[156] Given that the initiative continued to remain no more than a scheme, in November a new decree, drafted by Bukharin and Preobrazhenskii, once again ordered that it be established.[157] This time it appeared that negotiations with PUR might benefit from an improved understanding between the two commissariats: indeed the Commissariat for Education was now headed by Natalia Trotskaia.[158] While Glavpolitprosvet began to assume responsibility for teaching in the rear, a military section was set up within its own organization,[159] in spite of the fact that the army delegates to the 9th Congress had previously rejected a proposal to this effect.[160] This did not fail to arouse the indignation of the military. At the 2nd Conference of political workers in December, Smilga explained his intransigent opposition to the transfer of functions from PUR to the new body by stating his certainty that the military political apparatus would fall to pieces once it was placed under the control of local civilian organs.[161] In the final resolutions, the Conference accepted in principle the VTsIK decree, but introduced a series of conditions designed to safeguard their own organization. Only 'cul-tural and educational' (kul'turno-prosvetitel'nyi) functions might be transferred to Glavpolitprosvet; the structure of the political depart-ments was to remain unchanged; and the PUR nachalnik was to become the Glavpolitprosvet second-in-command. Lastly, PUR alone would be able to issue orders to the military section of the new body, and at local level the nachalniki of the political departments were to become members of the leading organs of Glavpolitprosvet, with full voting rights.[162]

In January 1921 PUR began to issue a number of decrees to this effect.[163] In compliance with certain of the decisions taken by the Conference of political workers in December, PUR ordered that the party functions discharged by the rear political departments at *guberniia* level be transferred to the corresponding party committee in order to facilitate collaboration between the said political departments and Glavpolitprosvet.[164] But this did not go far enough to satisfy those in charge of education whose ambitions became clearly apparent at the 10th Party Congress, when Preobrazhenskii presented, on behalf of the Commissariat for Education, an impressive scheme aimed at bringing under centralized state control all those activities relating to education and political propaganda carried out by the different state and party organizations. The idea was to implement 'state communist propaganda' on a vast scale, by 'mechanizing' its methods and approach.[165] Within this exciting and original framework, Preobrazhenskii justified his demands for hegemony over PUR by denouncing the way in which PUR had gradually assumed 'functions that bear no relation whatsoever to its original job, i.e. to the maintenance of 'political cohesion' in the army.[166] A degree of 'parallelism' had emerged in the work of PUR and Glavpolitprosvet, even a kind of 'competition', which was liable to lead to the insufficient use or indeed to the waste of enormous financial and material resources (one of the considerations closest to the hearts of the leaders of the Commissariat for Education). According to Preobrazhenskii, not only should the merger of the two apparatuses in the rear be deemed irreversible – even if another war broke out, the apparatus of PUR in the standing units should also sooner or later follow suit and be transferred to Glavpolitprosvet. PUR would finally become a kind of RVSR 'Inspection' with the job of merely overseeing the way in which Glavpolitprosvet discharged its educational functions in the army.[167]

Preobrazhenskii's extreme proposal betrayed an ancient and deep-seated distrust for the powers of the War Ministry. But it failed to take account of a series of problems which had a decisive influence on toned-down decisions that were actually taken. It was not easy to distinguish between the political, educational, and administrative functions that PUR discharged, and the military organs clearly intended to keep any activity relating to the political indoctrination of soldiers firmly under their own control. Furthermore, in the armed forces PUR coincided with the party structure and the interference of a civilian body risked introducing a perilous organizational dualism. It was no accident that Preobrazhenskii, at the end of the merger with Glavpolitprosvet, pointed out that PUR as a specifically military political organ would virtually disappear.

The arguments marshalled by the Commissariat for Education at the Congress were firmly rejected by Gusev. The fate of PUR could not be decided in such simplistic terms, since it was still far from clear whether or not a militia system would be adopted in the future.[168] Moreover, the very principle whereby the army, according to circumstances, should adopt radically different forms of organization, was mistaken:

> There cannot be two ways of organizing the army; in peacetime and in wartime there cannot be two different types of discipline, because the army is prepared for war and therefore its organizational structure must be properly designed for waging war. The experience of all the armies in the world shows that the organization of the army in times of peace has to be just the same as in times of war.[169]

Gusev thus expressed at the same time his own preference for a regular standing army. In Gusev's view Glavpolitprosvet's request that the political departments of the military *okrugi* be liquidated,[170] in order to make room for its own territorial organs at the same level, actually masked the territorial party organizations' old ambition to gain control over the military units.[171] Gusev went on to mention cases in which *guberniia* party committees had not only sought to run political work in the armed forces on their own, but had even appointed commissars. The organizational model represented by Glavpolitprosvet therefore seemed to Gusev to be either a nebulous and abstract drawing-board project, or, even worse, a Trojan horse for the advocates of the militia system. All that PUR was willing to do was to establish 'a relation, a contact, but not a full merger'. Solov'ev went even further, rejecting out of hand 'all the demands made by Glavpolitprosvet to disband the political departments'. This distorted way of characterizing the positions of the two sides clearly had a polemical purpose.[172] In its final resolutions, the 10th Congress made no mention of any 'merger' of the two bodies, merely repeating that 'on the whole' the management of political education in the army was a matter for Glavpolitprosvet, and referring the problem of concrete organizational relations to a special conference.[173]

Both the meeting of the political department *nachalniki* in May 1921, and the All-Russian Conference of military *rabotniki* in December of the same year, issued a whole range of detailed orders and complicated regulations.[174] The Glavpolitprosvety at *guberniia* level were provided with military sections entrusted with educational work in the armed forces. But these bodies too were made accountable to the corresponding political department. The regulations of the 'education commissions' in the detachments at company, regiment, and battalion levels specified that they were 'organs auxiliary to the party cells' in the detachments, operating under their orders, and not under those of organs outside the army. The new system probably did not even have time to establish a regular mode of operation. By April 1922 the military delegates to the 11th Party Congress were already complaining of Glavpolitprosvet's inefficiency and inability to fulfil its duties in the armed forces.[175] This was the beginning of a counterattack from PUR, which towards the end of 1922 managed to secure the incorporation within its own organization of the apparatus that Glavpolitprosvet had created for its work in the army. Collaboration between the two bodies thus finished in a way that was diametrically opposed to that hopefully foreseen by Preobrazhenskii at the 10th Congress. PUR was to preserve its own institutional physiognomy intact, and its political independence from any authority other than RVSR and the party Central Committee.

8   Continuing political tensions

The 'single military doctrine'

It became clear at the 10th Congress that the most important military decisions would in future be overwhelmingly pragmatic, having little to do with matters of 'principle'. The military question, which during the first two years of Soviet rule had played a prominent role in party debate, was no longer one of the 'great political issues'. In spite of this, at the end of the 1921 the Republic's top military leaders became engaged in a lively controversy, centring on the tenets of the 'single military doctrine'.[1] On one side were ranged some of the most illustrious Bolshevik commanders of the Civil War period; and, on the other, Trotskii, at times isolated and at times given the embarrassing support of non-Bolshevik orthodox military theorists. Trotskii doubtless went too far when he suggested that his adversaries represented a resurgence of the 'military opposition' of 1919.[2] Yet it could not be denied that men such as Minin and Voroshilov led the support for Gusev, Frunze, and Tukhachevskii.[3]

The topics of debate had changed since the 8th Party Congress. At that time, issues had been raised that reached far beyond the military sphere. Attention had been focussed on the principal planks of party policy, and the foundations on which the Soviet state and the RKP(b), as the party of government, were being constructed, had been submitted to scrutiny. Arguably, at the 8th Congress, any specifically military 'culture'[4] or military grouping was still at the embryonic stage among Bolsheviks. And it was perhaps precisely because military affairs were so loosely distinguished from others that this topic aroused such broad and varied interest among party members. This is reflected by the crucial place that it was accorded during the proceedings of that Congress.

The implications of the 1921–2 controversy were more limited. The way Trotskii interpreted the positions of his adversaries, by high-lighting some of their general consequences, helps one to appreciate the genuinely political aspects of the problem.[5] This also means that under pressure Trotskii was obliged to 'politicize' the discussion, thereby exaggerating at times the significance of issues that his rest-less collaborators had sought to frame in narrowly technical and strategic terms.

Trotskii's writings following the 9th Congress display a growing concern with problems of economic and civil construction, and a declining interest in those relating directly to the army. In 1918–19, the construction of a combat force was still the main task on the agenda. Now, however, peace was raising fresh problems: it was to these that the versatile Commissar for War turned his attention. In his writings of 1920–2, there are very few references to the events examined above in chapter 7. From the end of 1919 onwards, his efforts were concen-trated instead on the application to the economic field of the organi-zational lessons of his experience of managing the masses in the Red Army. Discussion on the role of trade unions in the Soviet state, the only issue tackled by Trotskii in his speech to the 10th Congress, had clearly shown his growing interest in the economy.[6]

The controversy over the 'single military doctrine' therefore appeared to be irrelevant and gratuitous.[7] There are numerous viewpoints from which this debate may be examined. It may seem of greater interest in relation to the main theoretical positions assumed by Trotskii and his adversaries than as regards a reconstruction of their political activity in the early 1920s. The theoretical implications of Trotskii's distinction between war as 'art' and as 'science' are, however, beyond the scope of the present work;[8] nor can I attempt to give any judgement here as to the military importance of the theories of tactics and strategy that Trotskii and his adversaries expounded. The present and the following sections will focus instead on those aspects of the controversy that tie in more directly with the topics handled in the foregoing chapters.

The policy documents drafted by Frunze and Gusev prior to the 10th Congress maintained that it was necessary to elaborate a sys-tematic theory of the lessons of the Civil War, covering tactics, strategy, and training.[9] The Soviet army needed to clarify and assert a set of unanimously held views in this regard, and, just like the French and German armies before the First World War, it had to build and strengthen its character by adopting clear-cut and uniform points of view on the way that war should be conducted. Frunze and his comrades in the old eastern front RVS thus joined in the theoretical controversy that even prior to the First World War had divided the high-ranking officers of the Imperial Army in their quest for a specifically Russian military doctrine. As early as 1918, the distinguished 'specialists' who had agreed to collaborate with Soviet power raised this topic anew in the pages of *Voennoe delo*. The controversy had started as an attempt to study the lessons 'inflicted' on the Imperial Army by the war with Germany, and had continued for some time without reaching any broadly accepted conclusions. Frunze's intervention was designed to bestow academic dignity on the new group of Soviet military leaders and to steal the initiative from the old members of the general staff, by succeeding where it seemed that they had failed.

In the mature form in which the new 'military doctrine' was debated at the meeting of military delegates to the 11th Party Congress (22 March–2 April 1922), it appeared to hinge on two basic assumptions. First, an eruption of 'revolutionary wars' (i.e., wars between states, accompanied by civil wars) was thought to be imminent world-wide. During the course of these wars, as had happened during the Russian Civil War, political and spiritual factors would play as important a role as technical and military ones. The second assumption was that the best way for the Red Army to prepare for such an eventuality was systematically to prepare its men for 'offensive' operations, and to teach its cadres a strategy of 'manoeuvre' rather than 'position' fighting. It was argued that the wisdom of such a policy was demonstrated by examination of the tactics that had made it possible to win the Civil War in Russia. These had been based on the employment of large cavalry units and the continual movement of troops. It was on these grounds that Tukhachevskii had combated the positions of Podvoiskii regarding the immediate transition to the militia system. By its very nature, a militia army could only conduct 'defensive' operations. In particular, a militia army would be quite unable to come to the active 'assistance' of any revolutions that might occur in the Western countries.[10] Added to these points was the conviction that Marxism could contribute to the elaboration of a body of theory capable of constituting a military 'science', genuinely proletarian and Soviet, in opposition to an allegedly 'bourgeois' one. Ukrainian Bolshevik military circles also complained that the 'central Soviet organs' (and first and foremost Trotskii) had neglected the needs of the army at the end of the Civil War, thus adding the accusation of inaction in the field of theory to that of negligence in financial and material matters.[11]

This line of thought first emerged in 1919. This suggests that it formed a focus for many of the concerns and dissensions (disguised or deliberately toned down) regarding official military policy, which had been manifested in their full virulence at the 8th Party Congress and at the July 1919 Plenum. As the Civil War spread, and became more complicated, involving a rising number of forces on both sides, Bolshevik military leaders sought to blend the experience of war with the ideological stock of the revolution. They thus attempted to give the Bolshevik viewpoint on questions of tactics, strategy, and military training a certain theoretical dignity. The first serious step in this direction was taken by Tarasov-Rodionov, who, as we have already seen, was involved in a polemic with Trotskii during the weeks immediately following the July 1919 Plenum. A month earlier, Tarasov-Rodionov had published, in the journal of the general staff 'specialists', his theses on 'military construction'. These began by accepting, albeit with various reservations, the severe disciplinary regime in force in the Red Army. The author then went on to outline various principles which in his view should govern the conduct of military operations. The author declared that he was in favour of a 'war of manoeuvre' founded on initiative and attack. He accused the former Tsarist officers of the supreme military organs of being incapable, owing to their training, of waging this type of war. Politics and military technique could not, in his opinion, be regarded as separate and distinct. The 'war of manoeuvre' was an expression of the 'revolutionary activity of communist soldiers', and as many Red Army commanders should be recruited from this group as possible.[12] Similar ideas had been surfacing for some time on the eastern front and, as we have seen, had played a role in the anti-Trotskii campaign before and after the July Plenum. In February 1919, a certain 'S. K.' (S. Kamenev?), writing in *Voennaia Mysl'*, had expressed the opinion that, in a civil war, the tactics of a revolutionary army should be those of 'attack alone'. Greater power had to be vested in RVS military and political leaders during a civil war than during a national one, and technical and strategic leadership had to be subordinated to their instructions.[13]

This current of thought was anything but uniform. 'S. K.', for example, said that he was extremely sceptical about the possibility of applying the techniques of partisan warfare successfully, whereas Tarasov-Rodionov was utterly convinced of it.

During the main debate on the 'single military doctrine' at the meeting of military delegates at the 11th Party Congress, Tukhachevskii came down firmly on Trotskii's side. He denied that there was any such thing as a 'proletarian' conception of war. This provoked an embarrassed reaction from Frunze, who also took a stand against the views of Tarasov-Rodionov.[14] But these were not the only men to adopt ambiguous positions on this issue. Podvoiskii, for example, had been a supporter of Trotskii's military policy, and for three years had subordinated his own convictions regarding an ideal militia system to the achievement of victory by means of a standing army. At the beginning of 1919 he was a member of the command of the Red forces in the Ukraine. At that time, he held that a proletarian army needed to be superior in numbers, courage, and 'fanaticism' in order to wage a civil war against an adversary superior in organization, knowhow, and equipment ('technique'). The continual use of 'assault' tactics could keep the enemy under constant pressure. This in itself would create a 'legend' capable of 'terrorizing' and breaking up the enemy forces even before any armed clash occurred. In this sense the principal weapon of the revolution was 'the word'. Podvoiskii was in favour of an army that relied wholly on its audaciousness, unheedful of its losses because able to fall back on 'boundless reserves' among the insurgent masses. But these views, probably reflecting certain features of peasant warfare in the Ukraine, were mingled with a variety of outlandish notions, certainly very far removed from the sobriety and realism of Trotskii, Frunze, or Tukhachevskii. In a way, however, they anticipated Tukhachevskii's well-known propensity for the creation of a world-wide general staff of revolutionary armed forces:

> Our Red Army must be the nucleus of a world proletarian army, the nucleus to which the insurgent masses of other countries and the disintegrating armies of the bourgeoisie shall flock.
>
> But to achieve such a revolutionary build-up of forces we must act rapidly and with resolve, with armies of millions of men; we must lead against the oppressors masses such as the world has not seen since the great migrations, since the time of Attila and of Alaric, when the Roman legions were demoralized and destroyed by millions of 'barbarians'.[15]

After the disastrous conclusion of the war with Poland, the main points in the 'single military doctrine', discussed in 1921–2, began to emerge more clearly. Defeat at Warsaw had profoundly disconcerted the Soviet High Command and the communist party, and had immediately sparked off recriminations.[16] The row exploded at the 9th Party Conference in September 1920 and took a significant course.

It was straight-away clear from their speeches that both Lenin and Trotskii were anxious to avoid any detailed public discussion of the causes of defeat. Hopes that a clash might be avoided were, however, frustrated by Iurenev and Minin, who demanded that an enquiry be held into the actions of RVSR. Minin, in particular, did not miss his chance to launch yet another attack on the 'military specialists' and to restate his distrust of them, using words that seemed long since banished from Bolshevik usage. But it was Bukharin's speech that marked a turning-point in the debate, by disclosing a new issue of principle. In his opinion, the decision to march on Warsaw, reached with the agreement of a majority on the Central Committee, had solved the dilemma as to whether or not it was 'legitimate' for the 'proletariat' to employ 'offensive tactics' in revolutionary politics. Stalin, on the other hand, denied that a clear line could be drawn between 'offensive' and 'defensive' tactics, at least in military matters. He defended the decision to attack Warsaw and added that defeat could not be blamed on the political leadership that had taken the decision but rather on the failure of the military organs to carry out Central Committee instructions properly. He also joined Minin in his call for an investigation. In his reply, Trotskii hit back at Iurenev and Stalin. He attributed the main responsibility for the decision to Stalin, who, he alleged, had misled the Central Committee with baselessly optimistic information on the state of disintegration of the Polish army. He stated that he personally had been much more 'sceptical', thereby disassociating himself from the responsibility of his Central Committee colleagues. Lenin, clinging to the concept that Bukharin had articulated, stoutly defended the decision to attack: communists had the right 'to attack actively'. He mentioned nonetheless the negative effects on military operations of the grudges that Stalin and the south-western front RVS (Stalin, Egorov, and Budennyi) had harboured against the command of the western front (Smilga, Tukhachevskii). Stalin, in his turn, denied that he had given any backing to the most audacious positions, and laid the blame squarely at the door of the Commander-in-Chief.[17]

In the months that followed, Lenin abandoned the line he had pursued at the Conference and explicitly labelled the Soviet decision to advance on the Polish capital an 'error', caused by an over-estimation of their chances of success. In this, he was imitated by Trotskii who espoused and expressed with particular force Lenin's argument that the defeat was due to the inefficient organization and inadequacy of supplies for the Soviet armies.[18]

The contrasting assessments of the Polish campaign drove a broad wedge between the Tukhachevskii–Gusev–Frunze and Stalin–Voroshilov–Budennyi groups, with the result that the supporters of the 'single military doctrine' could not, even in 1921–2, be regarded as a totally cohesive block. Let us take another example.

By this time Minin had evolved the theory that the Western armies' large-scale introduction of 'technique' would weigh them down to an increasing extent and as a result would reduce their capacity for 'manoeuvre'. Consequently, '[for] us, inhabitants of Eastern Europe, the way ... of waging war is that of a revolution occurring in a backward country' and it was therefore best to place all one's trust in mobility and troop morale.[19] This characteristic underestimation of the importance of 'technique' was itself a telling indication of the distance separating Frunze and Tukhachevskii from novices, former *tsaritsyntsy*, etc., who advocated the doctrine of the offensive. In the course of the debate, however, even Tukhachevskii proved somewhat unwilling to back Frunze in the boldest of his speculations regarding the relation between the spontaneous 'attacking' spirit of the revolutionary proletariat and the Red Army. The Commander-in-Chief, Kamenev, took care not to embrace the strategy of the offensive without reservation. His remarks on the objective circumstances that formed a background to the theoretical trends expressed by certain of his distinguished colleagues amounted to a plea for a more cautious approach. In Kamenev's view, one of the prominent features of Soviet strategy during the Civil War had been the frequent recourse to the *udarnyi kulak* (literally the 'assault fist'). This involved the concentration of forces in a small area of the front, deemed on each occasion to be the most important, even at the risk of causing temporary setbacks in other areas and on other fronts which had thereby been weakened. 'Decisiveness and risk-taking' were the psychological factors that had given the Red commanders their propensity for large-scale 'manoeuvre' operations. And besides, this blend of attitudes was counselled by the need to maintain and stiffen discipline among the troops, by keeping them permanently engaged – a vital consideration, given the Red Army's extremely high desertion rate. A passage in which Kamenev defined the typical outlook that the Red command had acquired during the Civil War years was particularly significant: 'The inevitability of these occasional setbacks and losses, with the prospect of correspondingly greater gains when this front [the enfeebled front] again received priority treatment, has created in the Red Army a psychological state whereby setbacks are viewed as temporary phenomena followed as a rule by even greater successes.'[20]

To demolish the arguments of his adversaries, Trotskii launched a two-pronged attack. He set out to ridicule the claimed strategic scope of the new principles and simultaneously to demonstrate that they were incompatible with the more general principles that presided over the internal and international policy of the Soviet state, at a time when it was adopting the 'New Economic Policy'. Trotskii doubtless encountered some difficulty in differentiating his opinion from that of such 'military specialists' as Svechin, who displayed scepticism for any form of doctrinal system-building, merely judging 'the era of revolution . . . an era of empiricism'.[21]

Pouring scorn on his adversaries, Trotskii argued that the theory of the 'offensive' could not be deemed an exclusive feature of the Soviet army, but was indeed familiar to the military leaders of a variety of countries. It therefore possessed no essential class character, and, furthermore, it was not always victorious.[22] Frunze continually harped back to the disagreements over strategy that had emerged in May–June 1919 between the eastern front command and Vatsetis, as to an emblematic episode in the clash between a theory of the 'offensive' and a theory of the 'defensive'. Unavoidably sensitive to the personal element that this introduced into the debate, Trotskii's reaction was caustic.[23] Replying indirectly, he did not fail to point out that the wars that the Republic had so far waged in fact taught the opposite: that 'if our commanders suffered from an illness at the end of the Civil War, it consisted in an excess of manoeuvre warfare'.[24] This comment went hand-in-glove with Trotskii's observation that 'with the march on Warsaw we attempted to make a revolutionary sortie into Europe, but it did not meet with success'.[25]

Moreover, how could an 'offensive' spirit be inculcated in the army, at a time when Soviet Russia clearly needed to avoid any further wars, and when Soviet power was wholly committed to making 'concessions' to foreign capital and to implementing a drastic 'retreat' from War Communism?[26] Faced with the danger that some military circles (which, by virtue of their particular formation, constituted at the same time a political body) might eventually develop a position in conflict with the government's foreign policy, Trotskii recalled that 'the Red Army is *merely* a weapon to guarantee the possibility of realizing the communist programme'.[27] The army, in other words, did not have any independent political purpose. For the first time, Trotskii had voiced a suspicion regarding his adversaries, which for years influential party circles had harboured regarding his own intentions.

The resolutions of the 11th Congress bore no trace of the debate on military doctrine. At the previous Congress Trotskii had refused to discuss the issue even in closed session, and had impelled Gusev and Frunze to withdraw their theses.[28] A point appeared, however, which for the initiated constituted eloquent, albeit isolated, evidence of the debate in which the Commissar for War had been personally involved at the meeting of military delegates:

> 2. The Red Army observes and understands all the efforts that the Soviet government is making to maintain and strengthen peaceful economic relations with the bourgeois states. The ability further to reduce the size of the Red Army and to lighten the burden of military service on the toiling masses will wholly depend on the successes of the Soviet government in this work of strengthening its peaceful relations.[29]

After the defeat which he had suffered at the 10th Congress on the trade-union issue, Trotskii probably saw the controversy with the supporters of the 'single military doctrine' as a useful opportunity to spell out his positions not only in his capacity as Commissar for War but also as a front-ranking political leader. The risks involved were minimal. Trotskii was clearly one of the party's greatest orators, and his intellectual superiority was beyond doubt. The debate enabled him to intervene in foreign policy from a certain distance. It was certainly no accident that one of Trotskii's articles, demolishing the premises of Frunze's doctrine, was printed in the paper of the Communist International.[30] He asserted that the theory of the 'offensive' was an attempt to import into the military sphere the 'leftism'[31] displayed by some of the delegates who had intervened at the 3rd Congress of the Communist International. As one of Trotskii's supporters explained, it was understandable that Tukhachevskii had urged the International to form a world general staff, during the days of enthusiasm triggered by the advance on Warsaw. But what sense could this exasperated 'offensive' spirit have now that the 3rd Congress had changed its tactics and proclaimed the 'united front'?[32] With regard to internal policy, the debate gave Trotskii a chance to express a conception of NEP that placed particular stress on its character as a 'retreat', in line with his cautious assessment of the international situation. There was also an evident relation with the isolationist position in economic policy that he was defending at this time.[33]

Old antagonisms, new situation

One of the issues raised by the advocates of the 'single military doctrine' was the proper purpose and content of the political education and leadership of PUR among the armed forces.[34] It was above all Gusev who assumed the task of confronting Trotskii on this ground. He fired the first shot by publishing an article in *Pravda* in December 1921, and then a few days later held a meeting with representatives of the military press. During the same period, a similar article appeared in the PUR journal.[35] Gusev's central assertion was that PUR's aim should be 'to turn every peasant into a communist'. Accordingly, PUR's programme of activities had to be given a clear ideological character, designed to promote 'the spirit of internationalism' among peasant soldiers, to overcome their 'rural narrowness and petty-bourgeois limitations', and to combat any 'trends in favour of political and social restoration'. In terms of the country's internal situation, this was a way of eliminating the 'counter-revolutionary' tensions that had already erupted in the violent Kronshtadt and Tambov rebellions. In terms of the country's defence, strict indoctrination alone could induce peasants to support a 'war of attack'. It would certainly be much more difficult to persuade peasants to die in a 'revolutionary war' than – as had been the case in the Civil War – in the direct defence of their land from returning landowners. The peasants had to be convinced that, 'unless revolution triumphed in the West too, they would lose the land and the freedoms they had acquired'. It was necessary to 'de-peasantize' (*razkrest'ianat'*), or, more exactly, to 'workerize' (*orabochit*)[36] young recruits from the countryside. To stiffen the loyalty of the armed forces, Gusev proposed that the membership of military party organizations be considerably boosted, even doubled.[37] Like Trotskii, a man with very broad political interests,[38] Gusev regarded the barracks as a 'communist youth school', which could be used 'literally to regenerate the countryside': 'To train the Red Army in revolutionary warfare and to gain political and ideological influence over the peasant: these are the two great and important tasks before the Red barracks and the political work that is carried out inside them.'[39]

In Gusev's view, the Civil War had demonstrated that 'with a high percentage of communists in the detachments, no enemy [could] stand up to us, not even a better-armed one'. This was an extreme version of the thesis, included in the platform that Frunze and Gusev had presented to the 10th Congress, which stated that 'only by raising the

political consciousness and military training of individual combatants
can one compensate for the insufficient quantity and quality of Red
Army command cadres'.[40]

Minin held views similar to those of Gusev. In mid-1921, Bubnov
and he became the *pompolitchasti* of Frunze, the commander of the
Ukrainian military *okrug*; then in spring 1922 Gusev was appointed
head of PUR in the Ukraine.[41] Minin was obsessed by the numeric
predominance of the peasantry in both the Ukrainian and the Soviet
armies, something which he considered 'a tragedy'. Only by giving
party work in the units a massive boost could the danger represented
by this lumbering mass of peasants be averted. He felt, however, that
the prevailing line within PUR was likely to reduce the party's role in
the army to that of 'an organization of radical democratic intellectuals', involved exclusively in such elementary tasks as the running
of literacy campaigns among the soldiers. Minin also declared his
resolute opposition to one-man command, which he considered a
request typical of the 'bourgeois' strata of the population, which,
owing to NEP, were managing to rear their heads in every field of
activity right throughout the country.[42]

On each point, Trotskii's views were the diametrical opposite of
Gusev's, in terms both of political analysis and of concrete proposals.
Trotskii was convinced, however, that the army, in a country like
Russia, could and ought to exert a direct influence on youth and in
particular on peasant youth.[43] But in contrast to exalted plans to
'de-peasantize' the army in preparation for a 'revolutionary war of
manoeuvre', he proposed an ostentatiously base and lowly task: to
teach soldiers first and foremost how to look after their weapons and
kit, how to 'grease their boots'.[44] Ever since the days when the
outcome of the Polish campaign had hung in the balance, Trotskii had
focussed the attention of the military on the Red Army's negligent
attitude to the supply and storage of essential goods, vital to
operational efficiency and to the soldiers' morale. Stalin attempted to
ridicule the War Commissar's convictions regarding the importance of
'shirts' and 'boots' to winning the war.[45] With an insistence that must
have struck his critics as clear provocation, Trotskii repeated indefati-
gably that 'negligence', 'ignorance', 'incapacity to carry out orders',
and 'personal sloppiness' were the main defects bedevilling not only
the army but Russia as a whole – given that 'all the aspects of a people,
the positive as well as the negative ones, come together in the army'.[46]
The example set by Peter I who, in his sacred longing for 'cleanliness
and order', had commanded that following the German manner all

beards should be shaven off, expressed in unambiguous terms the underlying concept dear to Trotskii.[47] Nor did Trotskii refrain from striking a note that to the Bolshevik commanders must have sounded particularly polemical and perhaps even threatening: 'If a future historian turns his attention to the defeat of our army at Warsaw he will find many causes that brought it about; but I have no doubt that one of the causes he will note will be the fact that the soldiers' boots were not properly greased.'[48]

As for the reasons for the Red Army's victory in the Civil War, Trotskii warned against falling prey to excessive illusions. Russia had been able to triumph thanks to its 'enormous expanse', because it was 'not a State, but a continent'.[49] The Bolsheviks had managed to build and lead the armed forces directly from Moscow, with lines of communication in territory under their own control. The political and propaganda apparatus of the Soviet state and army paled into utter insignificance in comparison to the organizational capacities and wealth of means that the economically and culturally more developed European countries had been able to command in the field of propaganda. This fact had been amply demonstrated by the French during the First World War: 'Were we Bolsheviks the inventors of propaganda? Not at all! Every religion has been propaganda. Even Tsarism knew how to make propaganda: orthodoxy, autocracy, and patriotism! Take a look at what the French have achieved in the realm of propaganda and we shall seem like wretched pigmies alongside them.'[50] And yet this scorching accusation of provincialism, directed at Gusev, was probably exaggerated. Gusev, in December 1921, had in fact noted:

> It is highly probable that the grandiose approach to political work in the Red Army is a peculiarly Russian feature and that in a Western European red army there will be no need for such pressure. But inasmuch as the backward strata of the proletariat and a part of the peasantry will also be conscripted into this Western European red army, it will be necessary to organize political work.[51]

Trotskii's contemporary speeches and writings on the 'military doctrine' and related topics were inspired by a down-to-earth vision of the dramatic circumstances in which Russia found itself at the end of the Civil War. This vision was also embodied in the instructions that the Commissar for War passed on to the party's military organs. It should be noted that these instructions were very similar in tone to those that Lenin was issuing on broader non-military matters during the same period. At the 2nd Congress of *politprosvety*, in October 1921,

Lenin had highlighted the 'semi-barbarous' state in which the population was living, and had singled out illiteracy as one of the main enemies of Soviet power. The programme of cultural tasks that was proposed as a remedy might appear extremely traditional and unrevolutionary, but there is no doubt that Lenin considered this elementary sphere of activity to be of fundamental importance. Talk of 'political education' in Russian post-war conditions provoked in Lenin reactions of ill-disguised irritation for the pretentiousness that this term revealed. The noun by itself indicated the genuine and pressing job: education *tout court*, an attempt to 'civilize' the population:

> The task of raising the cultural[52] level is one of the most urgent confronting us. And that is the job that the Political Education Departments must do, if they are capable of serving the cause of 'political education', which is the title they have adopted for themselves. It is easy to adopt a title; but how about acting up to it?[53]

It was on the same occasion that Trotskii, scorning the use of the ideological terminology on which Lenin had commented ironically, invited PUR 'to unite the work of military instruction with that of general education (*obshche-prosvetitel'nyi*)'.[54]

At the 11th Congress, Trotskii openly attacked Gusev's theses:

> In the barracks one has to take as one's point of departure the fact that the peasant has become a soldier. Why? For what purpose? This is the main point; this is a new period in his life, and it is this fact that has to constitute one's point of departure, not the attempt to turn a 19 or 20 year old peasant into an ideal communist, in accordance with an abstract and ideal programme. Instead, one has to explain to the young periah [*sic*] of Saratov and Penza, whom the workers' state has torn from the countryside and placed in a regiment, and who above all wants to understand what is going on, why this has happened; the explanation must be straightforward, concrete, political, but not 'didactic'.[55]

On one side of the dispute were those who considered that the Soviet state, and therefore PUR also, should be responsible, among other things, for civilizing the Russian population, thereby bringing it into line with Western European cultural standards. Ranged against them were those who viewed ideological indoctrination and the existence of the party as a substitute, almost an alternative, to educational work which, in the terms envisaged by Trotskii, struck them as excessively prosaic and conventional. These were differences of emphasis, and not necessarily head-on political clashes, but that makes them no less relevant to the present analysis. The positions that Gusev expressed immediately recall the integralist and intransigent spirit that had inspired the attacks of at least one wing of the original 'military opposition'. Now, however, new accents had been added in the form of the stimulating theories of the 'offensive' elaborated by turbulent Bolshevik commanders in search of a blend of military professionalism and political militancy. Seemingly defeated in the preceding years, this spirit now reasserted itself, cropping up even in the positions of some of those who had fought for the constitution of a regular army. But was not this a result of the ambiguous character of the compromise reached at the 8th Congress?

The concept of discipline that Frunze considered appropriate to his own military programme in 1921–2 was, for example, of great significance. Unlike in the Tsarist Army, discipline was merely 'each man's voluntary and conscious performance of his own duty' and had to be founded on certain essential assumptions:

> First of all, the awareness of the part played by the mass of soldiers, by their communist cells, by the *politruki* and by all the officers, by their temperament, by their devotion to the revolution, by their spirit of self-denial. Secondly, the ability of the commanders to form bonds with, to reach out to, and to blend in with the broad mass of soldiers. Thirdly, the correctness of the technical and political leadership, the strengthening of the faith of the mass of soldiers in their commanders' complete fitness for their position . . . Of course, it is impossible to do without some measure of coercion, but its use must be very limited. Only he who commands complete submission to his own will without taking any coercive measures whatsoever may be acknowledged a true Red commander.

And again:

> The psychology of the new class in power is reflected in the internal life of the Red Army. The concept of discipline has changed. Mechanical submission, founded on fear and violence, has been replaced by the newly created discipline of the soldier citizen, who senses intimately the need for submission. The barriers raised by differences in rank drop away. The Red Army is the most democratic army in the world.[56]

In contrast with what one might term 'party patriotism',[57] typical of Gusev's conceptions, Trotskii championed a sense of civic duty, in equally traditional terms. It was necessary, in his view, to educate the peasant soldier 'in the spirit of Soviet citizenship', 'to bring out in him the Soviet citizen',[58] 'to teach him to love Soviet Russia'.[59] One ought 'to treat him, in other words, as a citizen who is serving the colours',[60] and 'to stimulate in him a soldier's ambition'.[61] PUR's activity and propaganda needed therefore to illustrate the national and popular character (in the broadest possible sense) of the Soviet state. It should play a primary role in material and civic mass education.

These instructions seem fully consistent with those Trotskii issued on the policy to be adopted towards the Red Army command corps. In December 1921, at a meeting of Bolshevik military cadres, he spoke repeatedly of the traditional distrust felt for officers who were not in the party. At the time of the 10th Congress, this feeling had seemed to be dying away. Trotskii was faced with attempts to restrict the influx of non-Bolshevik candidates into the military academies. There is nothing in Gusev's writings to suggest that he supported these positions. To Trotskii, however, to refute the arguments of those who favoured a continuing distrust of non-Bolshevik officers seemed a logical continuation of his struggle against those who advocated that the army be 'de-peasantized'. He argued that it would be unwise 'to entrench oneself, as they say, in the communist positions in the institutes for higher education'. Instead, he suggested that a more flexible and 'practical' line be taken.[62] It was more a matter of regulating the access of 'non-party' commanders (who at that time accounted for a full 95% of all officers in the Red Army)[63] to the academies. To anyone who might have thought of citing Kronshtadt in support of the more 'distrustful' position, Trotskii replied that the revolt had in fact been caused by 'elements foreign to us', which a wrong-headed policy had encouraged to join the party: 'This should be a lesson to us. If the party sought a communist monopoly of education, it would thereby prompt a lot of people to change their colours and to worm their way into its ranks; while, at the same time, it would put off honest non-party people, and become isolated politically.'[64]

This opened the way to those of Trotskii's critics who had the longest memories. They now accused him of according greater importance to officers' *kompetentnost* (professional qualification) than to their *nadezhnost'* (political reliability).[65] It is uncertain whether or not it was possible, in the political climate of 1921–2, to distinguish – as Trotskii sought to do – between non-party supporters of the Soviet regime and fully-fledged communists. This distinction tied in closely with another one: that between the 'Soviet' and 'non-party' climate that Trotskii would have liked PUR to establish in the armed forces, and the heavily politicized atmosphere preferred by Gusev. Nor can this difference of opinion be simply seen as a clash between opposed principles; account needs to be taken of the political and social strains existing in Russia at that time. Trotskii clearly realized, for example, that it would be wise not to give too wide a rein to exhibitionist and sectarian tendencies within the party. For otherwise certain strata of the population might become even more exasperated with the authority of the only legal party. However, Trotskii felt that, independently of these pessimistic assessments, there was evidence that the cultural policy he was pursuing was correct. The actual nature of this evidence, however, was sure to scandalize his opponents. The publication (abroad) of the famous book *Smena vekh* demonstrated, Trotskii maintained, that there was by this time a widespread conviction within the country that 'other than Soviet power, in the present historical conditions, nothing is in a position to preserve the unity of the Russian people and their independence from outside aggression'.[66] The ideology of the *smenavekhovtsy*, which Trotskii considered to be founded on this new sort of 'patriotism', might well turn out to be 'the path along which the best elements of the old command corps will draw closer to us'.[67] The book, he said, ought to be circulated not only among Red Army officers, but also among the commissars,[68] in the party.

A passage in an article by General A. Brusilov, published to mark the Red Army's 4th anniversary, provided a clearer idea of the positions to which Trotskii was referring. Brusilov had gained renown and distinction during the World War, and a substantial part of the 'Smena vekh' movement had come to consider him a kind of 'ideal' figure.[69] The views that he expressed in his article seem to anticipate several of the features of the theory of 'socialism in one country', outlined by the leading group around Stalin between 1924 and 1931. But at the time Brusilov's article appeared, his positions must have seemed very close to the ideas that Trotskii voiced in his battle against the supporters of the 'single military doctrine'; and even closer to the isolationist theses that Trotskii was defending at the beginning of the 1920s:

> It must be recognized that [in the construction of the Red Army] many members of the command corps of the old army have played a part, taken the side of the Soviet government, and devoted all their efforts to the organization of the army. Above all one should stress the enormous energy and the colossal task undertaken by Comrade Trotskii, at the head of the Commissariat for War. Personally, I hold that Russia, whatever its political regime, cannot survive without a strong army, and I therefore think that the development and strengthening of the Red Army is thoroughly desirable for the Russian cause. I think that the Bolsheviks, whether consciously or

unconsciously I would not know, have accomplished a great deal in this direction: i.e. they have not allowed our martyr Russia to fall to pieces altogether, and, apart from a few frontier areas, they have held united those pieces that were beginning to fall apart. I believe that this has been a great state accomplishment (*ogromnoe gosudarstvennoe delo*). But without the assistance of the army, this could certainly not have come about. As a result of the propaganda campaign to promote the idea of the International, the Soviet government, in my view, has succeeded in bolstering the national consciousness of Russians, and has raised the spirit of patriotism which – to our shame – they possessed in such slight measure . . .

I am convinced that the Red Army, in its turn, will become stronger and will continue developing yet further. In order that Russia may develop freely, it is necessary that nobody interfere in our internal affairs. We must construct our internal life on our own, without any help from foreigners. And, in the end, we shall no doubt establish full state sovereignty.[70]

It is not hard to understand how Trotskii – as three years previously – continued to strike many Bolsheviks more as a politically unscrupulous statesman, with a distinct appetite for personal power, than as one of the leaders of their own party. He still appeared to seek informal and politically dubious backing from outside the party itself. In 1924–5, during the decisive battle between RKP(b) factions for control over the armed forces, Gusev summed up in canonical form the charges that Trotskii had for years been striving to evade. It was alleged that he regarded political work in the army as consisting exclusively of a struggle for general education, and not of the formation of a 'communist political conscience'. He was reproached with having 'underestimated' the relations and the peculiar 'discipline' of the party in the armed forces, 'subordinating' it to 'military discipline' and to purely military considerations. It was further alleged that in his collection of writings, *Kak vooruzhalas' revoliutsiia*, Trotskii had again deliberately 'underestimated' the role that the military political apparatus had played in the construction of the Red Army, as well as in its victories.[71] Old scores had to be settled, even if Gusev was by no means Trotskii's largest outstanding creditor.

But the conflicts that had exploded over military affairs had not been of an exclusively personal character. In particular, the debate on the 'single military doctrine' in 1921–2 revealed that despite their professional maturity Bolshevik military leaders still held stubbornly to the spirit of 'War Communism'. Meanwhile, however, the introduction and development of NEP had begun seriously to erode this outlook in the rest of the party. In the minds of the Red commanders, the revolutionary principles of class intransigence, of retaining the initiative at any cost, and of world revolution, had now been tempered with a more realistic understanding of the structure of the Red Army. These principles constituted a stock of ideals, useful for maintaining the army's morale and fighting spirit. But they were also a potential source of opposition to NEP.

The army and the party

At the end of the Civil War the Red Army was still a complicated combination of traditional military structures and of revolutionary institutions that had sprung into being from the ruins of the old Imperial Army. Over the previous three years, the experience of war, together with efforts to harmonize the various different types of organization, had failed to iron out all the points of contention. The dividing lines between the various groups were still clearly visible. This was especially true of PUR. The Red Army's political apparatus discharged a whole range of functions which in the armies of other countries were entrusted to purely administrative bodies. Yet the existence of a party structure and the institution of dual command made the Soviet armed forces quite unique. Moreover, the process of organizing the army had had an enormous influence on the future characteristics of the party itself.

In 1923 a still relatively unknown leader, V. Molotov, wrote a booklet in which he set out the political and organizational changes that the party had undergone since its seizure of power. 'The job of governing the country', he observed, distinguished the Russian party from its Western counterparts. This responsibility had meant that 'party organizations [had] forged extremely close links with the organs of the new power'. It had also led to the creation of new roles and organizational methods unknown to European communist parties. Molotov referred above all to three institutions: the political commissars, who had been set to work alongside technicians in the armed forces and in the economic and administrative sectors; party 'control commissions', whose job was to remove from the Soviet apparatus any communists found guilty of abuses of power; and, lastly, the political departments, which had accumulated sweeping political and administrative powers. Not in the slightest embarrassed by this phenomenon, Molotov stressed the functional efficiency of these bodies and their fitness for the work with which they had been entrusted:

The political departments in the Red Army are, on the one hand, the union of communists in the army; on the other, they are one of the administrative apparatuses that are totally subordinated to the military command. Through them, Red Army communists were linked to the party organization and could take part in its general life. At the same time, again through the political departments, the military command was able to reinforce the units politically, and to order with great resolve and rapidity many very tricky military undertakings. The political department is an absolutely original revolutionary party organization. It is one of the most interesting manifestations of revolutionary creativity, which, although unknown in the past, will remain necessary to the proletarian revolution for some time in the future.[72]

This is an expression of what one might call 'low key Bolshevism': at least as attentive to techniques of organization and mass mobilization as to more general political issues. Later on, L. M. Kaganovich and Stalin himself were to become renowned and tireless representatives of this current.

But the changes to the party's military structures that we have examined in the previous chapters were not the only ones to affect party life. The methods used to intervene among the population, and the types of relations between the party and the broad masses of citizens, also underwent change. This can be seen clearly in the case of PUR. The Red Army placed several thousand expert Bolshevik agitators and organizers in not always comfortable contact with concentrated masses of hundreds of thousands and of millions of people. The attempt to exert as deep and as broad a psychological and political sway as possible over these masses was dictated by the need to stiffen the discipline and fighting spirit of the troops, as well as to secure their loyalty. To this end, the threat posed by the organs of repression was not enough. Other ways of working among the masses, distinct from straightforward 'agitation', were necessary. In the words of those Bolsheviks who realized the nature of this new situation the most rapidly, it was a matter of moving from a 'craft' stage to an 'industrial' stage in the relations of the party with the soldiers and in particular with the population at large. The oratory and conspiratorial talents of tight-knit circles who until then had mainly acted in partial or total secrecy now appeared ill-suited to the new demands. They needed to be supplemented by the array of activities that only a large apparatus could organize, with a view to remodelling the attitudes and convictions of millions of conscript soldiers. By the end of the Civil War, this huge experiment in the 'mechanization' of the 'propaganda of communism' attracted even Preobrazhenskii – who in other significant ways was far from enthusiastic about the military system, or about the pre-eminence of discipline and of bureaucratic hierarchy. It was above all in the army, during the war years, that the party developed a 'pedagogic' vocation, which later became one of its hallmarks.[73] During these years, the methods of party recruitment also changed, as did the character of the typical Bolshevik militant. Enrolment into the party organization of 'platoons at a time'[74] entailed the influx of party members who had little interest in the finer points of politics, and whose main virtue was their readiness to obey orders.

The construction of PUR was accompanied by a massive increase in the number of communists in the armed forces. In December 1920, when the Red Army was at its largest, it counted over 5 million soldiers, including both front-line and rear forces.[75] Of these, 67% were registered as 'peasants', 12% as 'workers', and 20% as 'others'. From winter 1918 onwards, the mobilizations of party members in the rear began to provide sizable nuclei of combatants, and no longer only organizers, commissars, and commanders.[76] Contingents of young new members were soon recruited among the front-line units themselves. This was the main route by which thousands of peasants came into contact for the first time with the Bolshevik party.[77] Between March 1918 and March 1920, the total membership of RKP(b) in the Red Army rose from 45,000 to 300,000, although many members had died on the battlefield.[78] The number of military party cells rose from 3000 at the end of 1918 to roughly 7000 by mid-1920.[79] Over the same period, the membership of RKP(b) as a whole rose from 340,000 to 600,000.[80] These points and figures form a background against which the events that we have tried to outline here should be viewed. Above all, they help one to understand the reaction of a section of the party to the sharp changes in course effected by the Central Committee in the field of so-called 'military policy'.

The aspect of Trotskii's activity as Commissar for War that struck his party comrades most forcefully and which is best-documented was his struggle to introduce orthodox military principles into the Red Army. This brought him into conflict with the anti-militarist trends that had emerged in 1917 as well as with the traditional socialist distrust for regular armies. Many who shared the ideas of the 'military opposition' were also opposed to the emphasis that the party leadership and Soviet government placed on centralization and efficiency during the period between the Treaty of Brest–Litovsk and the constitution of the *Sovet oborony*, when the Republic was dramatically proclaimed 'a single military field'. The creation of a regular army, founded on strict discipline and compulsory mobilization, was one of the paradigmatic forms in which this emphasis was expressed. The second major obstacle facing Trotskii was the persistent and deep-rooted 'special caste' attitude of many older party members, as well as of others who had joined the Bolsheviks following the February revolution. These men were convinced that they were accountable only to the leading organs of the party. Trotskii and the War Ministry, however, were determined to force them into line, by imposing strict military order. It took a long time for the Bolshevik cadres sent to the front to find their rightful place in the ranks of the Red Army.

The disorientation and the angry reaction of the Bolsheviks were not wholly gratuitous or unfounded. Between the 6th and 8th Congresses, there were no authoritative and detailed public pronouncements on the methods and principles to be followed in the construction of the new army. The fact that most military directives were issued by bodies largely staffed by officers who had belonged to the Imperial Army could only reinforce the conviction that military policy had escaped the control of the leading organs of the party and that indeed it had virtually been handed back to the old ruling class.

The system that emerged from the clash between Trotskii and his adversaries was, however, far from being a faithful reflection of the features of hierarchical organization, efficiency, competence, and rational division of labour that he had observed at work in the bureaucracies of the West and which he would have liked to introduce into the young Soviet Republic. He had to beat a retreat before a mixed but powerful front. This embraced positions that were clearly utopian, others in defence of real or supposed political privileges, and yet others based on the most elementary pressures that had surfaced during the revolution. The 8th Congress had expressed the view that the internal regime of the military apparatus that Trotskii and his earliest collaborators had constructed was much too rigid. It operated, they felt, in an unbalanced way and was too independent of the central party and government organs. Major corrections were made. In the system envisaged by the resolutions of the 8th Congress, the party was to become a forum for political participation and to undertake a supervisory role. The degree of centralization and executive power within the army had hitherto rendered this impossible. Congress accepted discipline and centralism as norms of internal party life, but also provided for numerous compensatory mechanisms. Although the party had been transformed on an authoritarian model, and militarized, the delegates to the 8th Congress were convinced that the party was the only remaining institution that had preserved intact the democratic and revolutionary spirit of 1917. Even those leaders most hostile to the positions of the 'military opposition' stressed the importance of the party in the armed forces. Encouraged by statements from the centre, after a certain point every single group within the party had placed dramatic hopes in the political commissars. In a sense this was a logical consequence of the introduction of strict discipline. The charismatic presence of the commissars was intended to soothe the frustration felt by both militants and soldiers.

For his contribution to the creation of the Soviet armed forces, Trotskii was rewarded with the distrust and hatred of a great many of his party comrades. They accused him of attempting to 'play down the role of the commissars' and of having 'brutally trampled on human dignity with repressions, threats, and the shooting of men he disliked'. By using such means, he had allegedly 'terrified and disoriented' party men. He was even accused of having turned the political departments from 'party organs within the army' into simple 'cultural and educational institutions'. These accusations have survived a considerable length of time in Soviet works.[81] In actual fact, Trotskii never pushed certain of his positions to their extreme conclusions. Not only, as we have seen, did he display uncertainty regarding the status of the military profession as a speciality, he was also far from being an intransigent supporter of one-man command. It is of course true, however, that his behaviour and pronouncements show that the idea he had of the party's place in the Soviet system and of its functions was much more limited than that cherished by many of his adversaries during the first period of the revolution.

Even if Trotskii was the principal actor in the play, it would be wrong to suggest that he also wrote the script. The image that M. D. Bonch-Bruevich has left of Trotskii is more convincing – even if somewhat tendentious. Bonch-Bruevich was one of the 'specialists' of the Imperial Army who did the most to assist the Bolsheviks in their organization of the Red Army, endeavouring all the while to secure the collaboration of other experts of the old regime.[82] According to this source, Trotskii had no particular interest in the 'technical' side of military art. His role in the drafting of the decisive decrees that presided over the formation of the Red Army was of only relative importance. Trotskii's conviction that it was his duty to concentrate his attention on 'high politics' caused him, in the view of Bonch-Bruevich, 'to pose' as a spokesman for orthodox military demands and pressures, although in fact he did not go into the issues in any great detail.[83] To this one might add the acute verdict of R. Schlesinger, in whose view Trotskii represented 'the typical case of a leader of the opposition who, on becoming minister, discovers that he is dependent on his permanent staff'.[84]

The army was only one field, however important, in which Trotskii sought to introduce a regime and an approach that, in his opinion, were applicable to the whole of economic and civilian life. Furthermore, as often occurred with Trotskii, he was convinced that he was interpreting an objective historical tendency:

> The transition from the revolutionary struggle against the old state to the creation of a new state, from the demolition of the Tsarist Army to the creation of a Red Army, was accompanied by a party crisis or rather by a series of crises. At each step the old methods of thought and the old ways came into conflict with the new tasks. Rearmament of the party was indispensable. Since the army is the most necessary of all the organizations of the state and since during the first years of the Soviet regime the centre of attention was the defence of the revolution, it is no wonder that all the discussions, conflicts and groupings inside the party revolved around the questions of building the army. An opposition appeared almost from the moment we made our first efforts to pass from disjointed armed detachments to a centralized army.[85]

Although, as Bonch-Bruevich suggested, certain of Trotskii's character traits may have given rise to additional strains in the process of military construction, we have no reason to suppose that anyone else, in his place, would have been able to do his job with greater ease or success. On the contrary, the work in hand probably demanded precisely such a man as Trotskii. He had been in the Bolshevik party only a few months when he was appointed Commissar for War. He had no first-hand knowledge of the arduous conditions of Bolshevik underground life, nor of the crucial experiences that over many years had welded together this group of revolutionaries. As a result, he was the person best-suited to undertake the task of constructing an armed organization on principles to which most Bolsheviks felt a deep hostility. Only someone who was relatively immune to the almost morbid feelings of pride and solidarity that characterized the Bolshevik party would have the necessary resolve to face all the resistance that the process of building a regular army was bound to entail. This also involved, however, the danger that a sizable rift might open up between the claim that there existed a 'general' party line on military matters and its actual implementation by the man who bore direct responsibility for it. It was on this rift that people such as Stalin and Zinov'ev could count, when attacking the Commissar for War.

The appointment of Trotskii as the top military leader of the Republic was clearly no accident. It was an example of the Central Committee's and above all of Lenin's skill in deploying men in the posts best-suited to them. On this point, I would agree with the balanced judgement given by Danishevskii in his memoirs.[86] Only if one takes into account the point made by Danishchevskii can the alternation of censorious and trusting attitudes towards Trotskii between July 1918 and July 1919 be explained. It is likewise hard to believe that Lenin did not in part endorse the criticisms made of Trotskii at the 8th Congress and at the July Plenum. But he clearly sought to contain them within tolerable bounds. No evidence has yet come to light of any serious attempt to topple Trotskii from his position at the head of the armed forces, at least not prior to autumn 1923.[87] But it is also apparent from the documents that, after July 1919, the Central Committee and Lenin played a much greater role than during the preceding period in the decisions of the War Ministry.

In this delicate situation, it might appear that the odds were not all unfavourable to Trotskii. The presence at the head of the armed forces of a man of such powerful charisma, notoriously prone to disregard party considerations and to draw ideas from currents of thought foreign to the Bolshevik tradition, fuelled fears regarding the political role that the Soviet military machine might eventually come to play. In 1921–2, it still seemed to many Bolsheviks that the ghost of 'Bonapartism' was threatening the country's prospects for socialist development. They were bound to regard the appearance of the 'Smena vekh' movement as disquieting. It seemed to represent a potential officers' corps ideology, founded on patriotism and nationalism, and independent of party ideology. To many Bolsheviks, Trotskii appeared to be the person least able to provide the party and revolution with the necessary assurances. They viewed his tendency to put the demands of 'modernization' before every other consideration as a form of political restoration.

Notes

Introduction

1 J. Jaurès, *L'Organisation socialiste de la France. L'armée nouvelle*, Paris, 1911.
2 G. D. H. Cole, *A History of Socialist Thought*, 3 vols.: ii, *The Second International, 1884–1914*, London, 1963, 63–8, 368, 369–70. In contrast with the standing army, the 'militia' army was thought to constitute a guarantee, both for the free development of workers' political struggles in each country, and in wars of aggression from outside. On the discussion at the Congress of Stuttgart (1907), see C. Pinzani, *L'internazionale e la guerra*, Bari, 1970, 128–9.
3 V. I. Lenin *Polnoe sobranie sochinenii*, 55 vols., Moscow, 1967–70 (hereafter *PSS*), xxxiii, 8–12, 29, 38.
4 In the report to the 8th Party Congress, in March 1919; *ibid.*, xxxviii, 137–8.
5 S. M. Kliatskin, *Na zashchite Oktiabria*, Moscow, 1965, and J. I. Korablev, *V. I. Lenin i zashchita zavoevanii velikogo oktiabria*, Moscow, 1979, the two most securely based texts, offer different interpretations. In Kliatskin's view, the Red Army possessed from its inception an eminently 'militia' character, and this had been the intention of its founders. Korablev, on the other hand, considers that the features of the 'regular' army had prevailed in the Red Army's make-up right from the start. As for Western studies, see J. Erickson, in particular, on the militia debate: 'Some Military and Political Aspects of the "Militia Army" Controversy, 1919–1920', in *Essays in Honour of E. H. Carr*, ed. C. Abramsky, London, 1974.
6 B. Knei-Paz, *The Social and Political Thought of Leon Trotsky*, Oxford, 1978.
7 G. Procacci, *Il partito nell'Unione Sovietica*, Bari, 1974.

1 The disintegration of the Imperial Army

1 L. Trotskii, *History of the Russian Revolution*, 2 vols., London, 1932, 289.
2 J. Erickson, *The Soviet High Command*, London, 1962, 3.
3 R. Pethybridge, *The Social Prelude to Stalinism*, London and New York, 1974, 80–1.
4 *Izvestiia Petrogradskogo soveta rabochikh i soldatskikh deputatov*, 2 (15) March 1917; English translation, in N. Sukhanov, *The Russian Revolution 1917: Eyewitness Account*, 2 vols., New York, 1962. For the circumstances under

219

which Order no. 1 was approved, see G. Katkov, *Russia, 1917: The February Revolution*, London, 1967.

5 V. I. Miller, *Soldatskie komitety russkoi armii v 1917 g. Vozniknovenie i pervyi period deiatel'nosti*, Moscow, 1974, 25ff.

6 *Ibid.*, 163ff.

7 Trotskii, *History*, 289–90; Erickson, *The Soviet High Command*, 4; M. Gorkii *et al.*, *Storia della Rivoluzione Russa*, 4 vols., Milan, 1971, i, 126; Miller, *op. cit.*, 48ff.

8 *Izvestiia*, 8 (21) March 1917; see Miller, *op. cit.*, 52–3.

9 'Vremennoe polozhenie ob organizatsii chinov deistvuiushchei armii i flota, '30' Marta 1917' (Microfilm, St Antony's College, Oxford); Miller, *op. cit.*, 110ff.

10 W. H. Chamberlin, *The Russian Revolution. 1917–1921*, 2 vols., New York, 1960, i, 228–9. See a later regulation: P. D. Burskii, *Vybornie organizatsii v armii*, Moscow, 1917.

11 *Izvestiia Kronstadtskogo soveta rabochikh deputatov*, 9 (22) April 1917; Miller, *op. cit.*, 142ff.

12 Kliatskin, *op. cit.*, 63; Erickson, *The Soviet High Command*, 15.

13 Kliatskin, *op. cit.*, 68; Erickson, *The Soviet High Command*, 16; also see texts in *Voenno-revoliutsionnye komitety deistvuiushchei armii (25 oktiabria 1917–mart 1918 g.)*, Moscow, 1917, 68–9.

14 *Voenno-revoliutsionnye komitety*, 102 and note 95.

15 G. Bergman, *Rossiiskaia sotsialisticheskaia armiia*, (?) 1919, 10; *Razlozhenie armii v 1917 g.*, ed. N. E. Kakurina and J. A. Iakovleva, Moscow and Leningrad, 1923, 63; Erickson, *The Soviet High Command*, 40–1.

16 *Voenno-revoliutsionnye komitety*, 30–1.

17 Kliatskin, *op. cit.*, 58.

18 See, for example, in *Voenno-revoliutsionnye komitety*, 75–6, the regulation of 23 December 1917 (5 January 1918) that set up the Biuro voennykh komissarov (Office of Military Commissars).

19 *Ibid.*, 30.

20 *Ibid.*, 139.

21 *Ibid.*, 144.

22 *Ibid.*, 150.

23 *Ibid.*, 156.

24 *Ibid.*, 192.

25 'Dokumenty o deiatel'nosti voenno-revoliutsionnykh komitetov deistvuiushchei armii (oktiabr' 1917–Ianvar' 1918)', in *Sovetskie arkhivy*, no. 1, 1977, 12.

26 *Voenno-revoliutsionnye komitety*, 166.

27 *Ibid.*, 170.

28 L. Trotskii, *Moia Zhizn'*, 2 vols., Berlin, 1930, ii, 169 (English translation, *My Life*, New York, 1970).

29 *Voenno-boevaia rabota partii bolshevikov, 1903–17 gg.*, Moscow, 1973, 274–5.

30 *Ibid.*, 296–8.

31 *KPSS v rezoliutsiiakh i resheniiakh s'ezdov, konferentsii i plenumov TsK*, 10 vols., Moscow, 1970–2, i, 477.

32 *Ibid.*, 478–9.
33 *Shestoi s'ezd RSDRP(b). Protokol'*, Moscow, 1958, 289. *I bolscevichi e la rivoluzione d'ottobre. Verbali delle sedute del Comitato centrale del partito operaio socialdemocratico russo (bolscevico) dall'agosto 1917 al febbraio 1918*, introduction by G. Boffa, Rome, 1962, 59, 96; A. Rabinowitch, *The Bolsheviks Come to Power*, New York, 1976.
34 V. Morozov, *Ot Krasnoi Gvardii k Krasnoi Armii*, Moscow, 1958, 28–31.
35 This document, and the subsequent one, were published by Shliapnikov in *Pravda*, 23 February 1922.
36 *Materialy po istorii SSSR*, i, Moscow, 1955.
37 *Ibid.*, 72–5.
38 A. M. Konev, 'Deiatel'nost' partii po ispolzovanii Krasnoi Gvardii i sozdanii Krasnoi Armii', in *Voprosy istorii SSSR*, no. 7, 1977, 99; fuller information is given by the same author in his *Krasnaia Gvardiia na zashchite Oktiabria*, Moscow, 1978, 28, 192.
39 Podvoiskii, 'La Guardia Rossa e l'ottobre', in Lunacharskii *et al.*, *I giorni dell'Ottobre*, Rome, 1969, 87.
40 E. H. Carr, *The Bolshevik Revolution 1917–1923*, 3 vols., London, 1950–3, iii, 28.
41 Kliatskin, *op. cit.*, 76–8.
42 *KPSS v rezoliutsiiakh*, i, 469.
43 Kliatskin, *op. cit.*, 76–8.
44 *Ibid.*, 80–5.
45 *Voenno-revoliutsionnye komitety*, 79.
46 Kliatskin, *op. cit.*, 89.
47 Cf. the instructions issued by Krylenko on 30 December 1917 (12 January 1918) in *Oktiabr'skaia revoliutsiia i armiia, 26 oktiabria 1917–mart 1918 g.*, Moscow, 1973, 232–8; Kliatskin, *op. cit.*, 81.
48 *Izvestiia*, 19 January (1 February) 1918. On 21 January (2 February) Mekhonoshin and Krylenko were appointed from the former, and Trifonov and Iurenev from the latter; see *ibid.*, 23 January (5 February) 1918.
49 *Izvestiia*, 19 January (1 February) 1918.
50 E. N. Gorodetskii, *La formazione dello stato sovietico*, Rome, 1972, 285; Kliatskin, *op. cit.*, 98.
51 *Izvestiia*, 19 January (1 February) 1918.
52 B. Tal', *Istoriia Krasnoi armii*, Moscow and Leningrad, 1927, 42; *Voenno-boevaia rabota*, 74; Kliatskin, *op. cit.*, 91.
53 *Voenno-revoliutsionnye komitety*, 194.
54 *Ibid.*, 102.
55 *Ibid.*, 343.
56 *Ibid.*, 130.
57 Relevant information and comments in *Izvestiia*, 2, 30 March 1918.

2 The birth of the Red Army

1 *PSS*, xxxvi, 26.
2 *KPSS v rezoliutsiiakh*, ii, 27, note 2.

3 *PSS*, xxxvi, 70. This particular expression repeats almost word for word *State and Revolution*, *ibid.*, xxxiii, 91: 'organization of the armed people (such as the Soviets of Workers' and Soldiers' Deputies)'.

4 *Dokumenty vneshnei politiki SSSR*, i, Moscow, 1957, 122. Russia was, however, allowed to maintain a limited number of contingents on the frontiers with Rumania and Turkey. At the 7th Party Congress, hardly any mention was made of the treaty's tough military clauses. But by the first half of April, very broad interpretations were already circulating. In a public speech, Volodarskii said that the obligation to 'demobilize' was not equivalent to total 'disarmament'. In his view, the treaty did not rule out the reconstruction of an armed force at a pre-war level, numbering roughly 1,200,000 men; see V. Volodarskii, *Rechi*, Petrograd, 1919, 14.

5 *Izvestiia*, 2 March 1918.

6 J. Steklov, 'Ob organizatsii nashego vooruzhennogo sila', *ibid.*, 15 March 1918.

7 Carr, *Bolshevik Revolution*, iii, 63.

8 *Izvestiia*, 23 March 1918.

9 Kliatskin, *op. cit.*, 156, note 37; *Izvestiia*, 30 March 1918. The meeting was held on the 25th and 26th.

10 *Izvestiia*, 5 March 1918; Kliatskin, *op. cit.*, 146–7. Proshiian was a member of the Social Revolutionaries' Central Committee; he handed in his resignation a few days later, following his party's decision to leave the government.

11 Kliatskin, *op. cit.*, 153–5; Erickson, *The Soviet High Command*, 25–6.

12 *Izvestiia*, 6 April 1918. Reproduced in full, to my knowledge, only in an appendix to N. Savko, *Ocherki po istorii partiinykh organizatsii v KA, 1917–1923*, Moscow and Leningrad, 1928, 73–4.

13 The resolution instituting the first body is contained in *Voenno-revoliutsionnye komitety*, 75–6, dated 23 December 1917 (5 January 1918). It was abolished in mid-May 1918. The VBVK was set up on 8 April, on an order from the Commissariat for War (Trotskii and Sklianskii); see *Pravda*, 9 April 1918. Iurenev was appointed to head it. The VBVK was granted powers over both territorial commissariats and detachment commissars; see P. A. Golub, 'Kogda zhe byl uchrezhden institut voennykh komissarov Krasnoi Armii?', in *Voprosy istorii KPSS*, no. 4, 1962, 155–60. This author's thesis is that the institution of 'commissar' in the Red Army was radically different from that of any previous commissar; the view that there was rather an essential continuity is expressed by I. Kolesnichenko and V. Lunin, 'Kogda byl uchrezhden institut voennykh komissarov', in Voenno-istoricheskii zhurnal, no. 9, 1961, 123–6.

14 *Izvestiia*, 24 March 1918.

15 *Ibid.*, 13 April 1918.

16 *Ibid.*, 25 March 1918. The Soviets' *voennye otdely* were responsible for the formation of the Red Army *na mestakh*, at a local level in the rear. At the front, among the surviving units of the old army, the superior soldiers' committees, from divisional level up, were given this task. The 'Red Army general staffs' were to constitute themselves within the said committees.

The formation of the Soviets' 'military sections' is the subject also of an *instruktsiia* of 28 January (10 February), published by *Pravda*.

17 Kliatskin, *op. cit.*, 172.
18 *Izvestiia*, 25 April 1918.
19 Kliatskin, *op. cit.*, 192; Erickson, *The Soviet High Command*, 28. The VTsIK resolution is in *Partiino-politicheskaia rabota v Krasnoi Armii e Flote*, 2 vols., Moscow, 1961–4 (hereafter *PPR*), i. 23–4.
20 Gen. A. S. Lukomskii, 'Iz vospominanii', in *Arkhiv russkoi revoliutsii*, 6 vols., Berlin, 1922, v, 157. See also D. Footman, *Civil War in Russia*, London, 1961, 78.
21 Information about the course of these initial mobilizations in Kliatskin, *op. cit.*, 194ff.
22 *Ibid.*, 197.
23 For the VTsIK decree, see *Izvestiia*, 25 April 1918. On 30 March a Red soldiers' conference had voted for the abolition of elections for officers at or above battalion level; see *ibid.*, 3 April 1918. Also see Erickson, *The Soviet High Command*, 44; Kliatskin, *op. cit.*, 159, 203.
24 *Ibid.*, 159.
25 About this meeting, some of the participants have written imprecise memoirs; e.g., S. Aralov, *V. I. Lenin i Krasnaia Armiia*, Moscow, 1959, 7ff. According to this source, 'old former military specialists' also attended. This version has been championed by V. D. Polikarpov, 'O soveshchanii rabotnikov armii u V. I. Lenina v marte 1918 g.', in *Voprosy istorii KPSS*, no. 4, 1973, 98–103. In Polikarpov's account, the meeting was held on 13 March with the attendance of party members only, and confined itself to discussing the question of the former officers. Lenin openly advocated their inclusion in the Red Army. Polikarpov contends that Kliatskin (influenced by Aralov) had confused this meeting with the one held on 25–6 March (see note 9 above), which debated the entire programme to construct the new army; see Kliatskin, *op. cit.*, 160–1. Erickson has accepted Kliatskin's version of events; see 'The Origins of the Red Army', in *Revolutionary Russia*, ed. R. Pipes, Mass., 1968, 242. The opinion that seems to have gained ground recently in the USSR is that the most important meeting was the one held on the 13th, which, it is asserted, touched on all crucial points of military policy; see *V. I. Lenin. Biografi- cheskaia Khronika*, 12 vols., Moscow, 1970–82, v, 315; Korablev, *op. cit.*, 275–6.
26 *PSS*, xxxvi, 178.
27 Golub, *art. cit.*, 157.
28 *Izvestiia*, 17 March 1918.
29 *PSS*, xxxvi, 375.
30 A Central Committee resolution of 8 May made military training compul- sory for all party members; see *PPR*, i, 22. The existence of a network of party organizations in the newly constituted units is attested by numerous documents which will be referred to below. With the opening of hostilities by the Czechoslovakian Legion at the end of May, special mobilizations of party members for work among front-line units commenced; see J. Petrov,

Partiinye mobilizatsii v Krasnuiu Armiiu (1918–1920), Moscow, 1956, 18ff. Mention is made of 'party committees and (Bolshevik and Social Revolutionary) collectives' in a resolution passed by the section for agitation and propaganda of the Vserossiiskaia kollegiia po organizatsii Krasnoi Armii, dated 22 February 1918; see *Iz istorii grazhdanskoi voiny v SSSR*, 3 vols., Moscow, 1960–1, i, 115.

31 *Perepiska sekretariata TsK KRP(b) ts mestnymi partiinymi organizatsiiami*, 8 vols., Moscow, 1957–74 (hereafter *Per.*), iii, 396–7.

32 *PPR*, i, 82.

33 See *Otchet severnoi oblastnoi Konferentsii s 3-ego po 6-e apreliia*, Petersburg, 1918, 28. On the position in favour of making the commissars answerable to territorial party organizations, see also the resolution of 'the communist Red soldiers of Moscow', in *Iz istorii*, i, 136 (dated 16 June 1918).

34 'Chekhoslovaki i kontr-revoliutsiia', in *Vypuski Visshei Voennoi Inspektsii RKKA*, Moscow, 1918, 11.

35 I. Deutscher, *The Prophet Armed*, London, 1954, 408. See also *Entsiklopedicheskii Slovar' Granat, Deiateli SSSR*, 3 parts, Moscow, 1925–8, Part I, 245, where Krylenko attributes his own resignation to 'disagreements of principle regarding the formation of the Red Army'.

36 *Izvestiia*, 5 March 1918; this is an appeal to soldiers, in which the reasons for the Brest–Litovsk peace treaty are explained, and the final demobilization of the old army proclaimed.

37 *Sedmoi s'ezd RKP(b)*, Moscow, 1959, 50.

38 *Ibid.*, 104; S. Cohen, *Bukharin and the Bolshevik Revolution: A Political Biography*, New York, 1973, 68; V. Strada, 'La pace di Brest e il dibattito nel partito bolscevico', in *Tradizione e rivoluzione nella letteratura russa*, Turin, 1969, 248–9, 253.

39 *Izvestiia*, 21 March 1918.

40 *Ibid.*

41 *Pravda*, 28 March 1918.

42 *Izvestiia*, 19 April 1918. On officers' reactions, and the offensive expressions used by Zinov'ev and Lashevich during these weeks, see Deutscher, *The Prophet Armed*, 412.

43 *Izvestiia*, 21 June 1918. On this episode, see Deutscher, *The Prophet Armed*, 414.

44 *Izvestiia*, 22 June 1918. See, in particular, Krylenko's indictment.

45 *Theses of the Left Communists (1918)*, Glasgow, 1977, 16. This document was the work of Osinskii. It was also signed by Bukharin, V. M. Smirnov, and Radek; see Cohen, *Bukharin*, 71–2 and notes 46, 48. The principles of the 'left communists', regarding military organization, were also expounded in a popular booklet written by Bukharin in 1918, *The Programme of the Communists*. There is some evidence in the text to suggest that it was written prior to the Brest–Litovsk treaty. The Red Guard is held up as a model for a future socialist army.

46 *Theses of the Left Communists*, 17.

47 *PSS*, xxxvi, 283–314.

48 *Otchet*, 28.

49 Deutscher, *The Prophet Armed*, 412; V. P. Khmelevskii, *Severnyi oblastnyi komitet RKP(b)*, Lenizdat, 1970, 147.
50 L. Trotskii, *Kak vooruzhalas' revoliutsiia (na voennoi rabote)*, 3 vols., 5 tomes, Moscow, 1923–5 (hereafter *KVR*), i, 103.
51 *Ibid.*, 109.
52 *Ibid.*, 121.
53 *Izvestiia*, 23 April 1918; *Chetvertyi Vserossiiskii s'ezd sovetov rabochikh, krest'-ianskikh, soldatskikh i kazachikh deputatov, Sten. otchet, Moskva 1918*, Moscow, 1919, 179–82.
54 *Ibid.*, 192–3.
55 *Ibid.*, 182–4.
56 *Ibid.*, 178–9.
57 *Ibid.*, 184–5. From Dan's words it may be inferred that VTsIK suddenly found itself confronted with the new draft decrees on the very morning set aside for their discussion and approval.
58 *Ibid.*, 179.
59 *Ibid.*, 342–4.
60 *Ibid.*, 344.
61 *Pravda*, 25 March 1918: article signed 'E. Ia'. Dan had written an article in *Vpered*, no. 53, in which he had employed this expression.
62 'Krasnaia Armiia', in *Kommunist*, no. 2, 1918 (27 April).
63 Erickson, 'The Origins', 246.
64 *Otchet o pervom s'ezde po vseobshchemu voennomu obucheniiu*, Moscow, (?), 10. On the proceedings of Congress, see also M. I. Usakov, 'Iz istorii deiatel'nosti partii po organizatsii vsevobucha', in *Voprosy istorii KPSS*, no. 5, 1978, 104; and Kliatskin, *op. cit.*, 255–6.
65 *Otchet o pervom s'ezde*, 13.
66 *Ibid.*, 26–8.
67 *Pravda*, 6 March 1918.
68 'Chekhoslovaki', 10.
69 *Direktivy komandovaniia frontov Krasnoi Armii (1917–1922)*, 4 vols., Moscow, 1971–4, i, 239.
70 Korablev, *op. cit.*, 257–61.

3 Reorganization on the battlefield

1 *PPR*, i, 25–7.
2 *PSS*, xxxvi, 514–15.
3 Erickson, 'The Origins', 243, 245ff. In mid-October 1918, volunteers still accounted for over 16% of Red soldiers; see Kliatskin, *op. cit.*, 233. The total force did not exceed half a million men at the end of the summer; see Erickson's assessments, 'The Origins', 255–6. The first Republic-wide conscription took place following the Kazan' victory; see Kliatskin, *op. cit.*, 229.
4 Erickson, 'The Origins', 236–9.
5 *Ibid.*, 250–1.
6 *Istoriia grazhdanskoi voiny v SSSR*, 3 vols. (iii, iv, v), Moscow, 1957–60, iii, 184ff.

7 A. Geronimus, *Partiia i Krasnaia Armiia*, Moscow and Leningrad, 1928, 35; see, by the same author, 'Osnovnye momenty razvitiia partiino-politicheskogo apparata Krasnoi Armii', in A. Bubnov *et al.*, *Grazhdanskaia voina, 1918–1921*, 3 vols., Moscow, 1928, ii, 115–16.

8 Jan M. Meijer, ed., *The Trotsky Papers. 1917–1922*, 2 vols., The Hague and Paris, 1971 (hereafter *TP*), i, 70.

9 *Ibid.*, 80–2.

10 *KVR*, i, 332–3.

11 *TP*, i, 82.

12 *KVR*, i, 320, 324.

13 Kliatskin, *op. cit.*, 222–3. Trotskii was confirmed as president of the new organ. See also Erickson, *The Soviet High Command*, 56. According to Kliatskin, not only Trotskii and Vatsetis, but also Danishevskii, Kobozev, Mekhonoshin, Raskol'nikov, Rozengol'ts, and I. D. (?) Smirnov were RVSR members at the outset. According to Korablev, *op. cit.*, 370, the names of Antonov-Ovseenko, Podvoiskii, and Nevskii should be added. Erickson, probably following Deutscher, *The Prophet Armed*, 423–4, also names Rozengol'ts, Raskol'nikov, Muralov, Iurenev, and I. N. Smirnov (*The Soviet High Command*, 56). Deutscher, in his turn, had taken these names from Trotskii, *Stalin*, London, 1968, 276, doubtless identifying the 'I. Smirnov' mentioned by Trotskii as the I. N. Smirnov of the eastern front RVS. Korablev too included I. N. Smirnov in the first RVSR. But Deutscher apparently then confuses I. N. Smirnov with V. M. Smirnov, in fact two very different political figures; see *The Prophet Armed*, 410. I have not managed to find out any more about the I. D. Smirnov mentioned by Kliatskin; I am inclined to think that the initial 'D' of the patronymic is a mistake made by the author, or perhaps the result of an error in his source. Lastly, it should be noted that throughout the whole of the Civil War the composition of RVSR remained extremely fluid; no mentions can be found in the available documents or in the relevant studies that fully agree as to its composition at any particular date.

14 See Egorov's memorandum in *TP*, i, 92–6; it is also reproduced in *Direktivy glavnogo komandovaniia Krasnoi Armii*, Moscow, 1969, 51–3. Trotskii's report to VTsIK is in *KVR*, i, 320–4.

15 *TP*, i, 105–8; the telegram to Lenin is dated 24 August. The proposal that communists be substituted for former officers of the High Command was made by Larin.

16 *PPR*, i, 33–4.

17 *Dekrety sovetskoi vlasti*, ii, Moscow, 1959, 429–30. See Kliatskin's comment, *op. cit.*, 219, which I find unconvincing. The research carried out by A. P. Nenarokov, *Vostochnyi front. 1918*, Moscow, 1969, 256–7, seems, on the other hand, to support my view.

18 Kliatskin, *op. cit.*, 209; Erickson, *The Soviet High Command*, 54–5.

19 *Iz istorii*, i, 209; *Direktivy komandovaniia*, i, 411–13.

20 *KVR*, i, 235.

21 According to J. Petrov, *Voennye komissary v gody grazhdanskoi voiny (1918–1920 gg.)*, Moscow, 1956, 22, the Central Committee's criticism of the

commissars should be seen in relation to the party centre's dissatisfaction with the state of political disorganization in the detachments.

22 Kliatskin, *op. cit.*, 220–2.
23 *Ibid.*, 224.
24 *Dekrety sovetskoi vlasti*, iii, Moscow, 1964, 603.
25 *Leninskii sbornik*, tome xxxvii, Moscow, 1970, 101.
26 *TP*, i, 116.
27 Message to Lenin of 11 September, in *TP*, i, 126.
28 *Direktivy glavnogo komandovaniia*, 54–5.
29 *Ibid.*; see also I. Kolesnichenko, 'K voprosu o konflikte v Revvoensovete Iuzhnogo fronta (sentiiabr–oktiiabr' 1918 goda)', in *Voenno-istoricheskii zhurnal*, no. 2, 1962, 41.
30 See, for instance, the telling description of one of the most bizarre of the units (led by the communist Paniushkin) that arrived from Moscow for the recapture of Kazan', in V. Putna, *Vostochnyi front*, (?), 1927, 6–7.
31 V. M. Tukhachevskii, 'O tov. Kuibysheve'; and B. Chistov, 'Partorganizatsiia v gody grazhdanskoi voiny', in *1918 god na rodine Lenina*, Kuibyshev, 1936, 17, 53–4.
32 A fairly detailed account of events is given in R. C. Tucker, *Stalin as Revolutionary. 1879–1929*, New York, 1973, 190ff.
33 Stalin, *Sochineniia*, 13 vols., Moscow, 1949–51, iv, 120–1.
34 *Izvestiia*, 31 May 1918, *Leninskii sbornik*, xviii, 193–4.
35 Stalin, *op. cit.*, iv, 118–19, 122.
36 *Direktivy komandovaniia*, i, 289–90.
37 This was Trotskii's contemptuous opinion; see *Stalin*, 71.
38 This document is contained in the subsequent 'Prikaz VS SKVO . . .', of 23 September, in *Direktivy komandovaniia*, 335.
39 *Ibid.*
40 Kolesnichenko, 'K voprosu', 42.
41 *Direktivy komandovaniia*, i, 235–8.
42 *Ibid.*, 248–9.
43 Kolesnichenko, 'K voprosu', 43.
44 *Per.*, iv, 53; Kolesnichenko, 'K voprosu', 44–5.
45 *Ibid.*, 45. The text of the document is in *Dokumenty o geroicheskoi oborone Tsaritsyna v 1918 g.*, Ogiz and Gosolitzdat, 1942.
46 *Direktivy komandovaniia*, i, 297, 350.
47 *Direktivy glavnogo komandovaniia*, 82–3.
48 *TP*, i, 134–6.
49 Kolesnichenko, 'K voprosu', 45.
50 *KVR*, i, 347–8.
51 *Voennoe delo*, no. 22, 1918, 23.
52 *Direktivy komandovaniia*, i, note 85 on p. 45; *TP*, i, 164.
53 *Ibid.*
54 *Biograficheskaia Khronika*, vi, 156.
55 Kolesnichenko, 'K voprosu', 45.
56 *Ibid.*, 45–6.
57 *TP*, i, note 1 on pp. 160–1.

58 *Ibid.*, i, 158–60; *Leninskii sbornik*, xxxvii, 106. According to Meijer, the editor of *TP*, this telegram may have been written not by Lenin but by Sverdlov.
59 Trotskii, *My Life*, 441. After this conversation the *tsaritsyntsy* dispatched a number of telegrams to Lenin; see *Leninskii sbornik*, xxxvii, note 1 on p. 107.
60 Trotskii, *My Life*, 441. It is hard to determine whether this meeting took place before or after Lenin's telegram was dispatched. Meijer dates the telegram 24–5 October; see *TP*, i, note 1 on pp. 160–1.
61 It is not clear on which date. Judging by the telegram sent by Lenin cited, on 23 October, Stalin had not yet been appointed. But according to Tucker, *op. cit.*, 196, he was appointed on 11 October. According to A. V. Danilevskii, *V. I. Lenin i voprosy voennogo stroitel'stva na VIII s'ezde RKP(b)*, Moscow, 1964, 38, on 9 October Stalin resigned from both the southern RVS and RVSR, though the author does not indicate when Stalin had been appointed to the latter of these two bodies. S. F. Naida, *O nekotorykh voprosakh grazhdanskoi voiny v SSSR*, Moscow, 1958, is even vaguer. Stalin was formally 'confirmed' a member of RVSR in May 1920; *Dekrety sovetskoi vlasti*, viii, Moscow, 1976, 391.
62 Trotskii, *Stalin*, 273. According to Deutscher, *The Prophet Armed*, 424, the appointment of Stalin to RVSR sealed the settlement to the Tsaritsyn affair.
63 Again in February 1919 Sverdlov strongly recommended that discussion of military policy should not go beyond 'strictly party' circles during the period leading up to the Congress; see J. M. Sverdlov, *Izbrannye proizvedeniia*, 3 vols., Moscow, 1957–60, iii, 171.
64 *TP*, i, 150.
65 *Ibid.*, 166.
66 *Ibid.*, 168.
67 *KVR*, i, 340.
68 *TP*, i, 164.
69 Kolesnichenko, 'K voprosu', 46.
70 *Dekrety sovetskoi vlasti*, v, Moscow, 1971, 663.
71 *Direktivy glavnogo komandovaniia*, 84–5.
72 Trotskii, *My Life*, 441.
73 See, for example, Tucker, *Stalin as Revolutionary*, 197–8, who crowns a long historiographical tradition.
74 Stalin, *op. cit.*, iv, 118; I. Deutscher, *Stalin: A Political Biography*, Oxford, 1967, 196–7.
75 Stalin, *op. cit.*, iv, 131.
76 *Ibid.*, 147, 150.
77 See, for example, the account of a speech delivered by Voroshilov on 2 December 1918 to the communists of the 10th army, in *PPR*, i, 242–3.
78 Minin was perhaps the most eminent and distinguished member of the Bolshevik organization in Tsaritsyn, where in 1917 and the first few months of 1918 he had been leader of the town committee; from July 1918 onwards he had become President of the local Soviet; see Minin, *Gorod boets*, Leningrad, 1925, 85, 196ff.
79 R. Service, *The Bolshevik Party in Revolution, 1917–1923. A Study in Organizational Change*, London, 1979, 80–1.

80 Danilevskii, *op. cit.*, 37–8; S. V. Lipitskii, *Voennaia deiatel'nost' TsK RKP(b)*, Moscow, 1975, 129.
81 *KVR*, ii, tome 1, 65.
82 *Ibid.*, i, 169–73.
83 *Ibid.*, ii, tome 2, 28; tome 1, 79, respectively. The last spasms of this anti-Ukrainian loathing are discernible in Trotskii's speech to the 9th Party Congress in April 1920; see *Deviatyi s'ezd. Protokoly*, Moscow, 1970, 77: 'What is the Ukraine, divided between ten or more different regimes, between Mensheviks, Social Revolutionaries, suffering from every possible disease? We know perfectly well that the worst of our party organizations in the Ukraine display signs of these same diseases. I gathered a fairly clear idea of this when, in the Ukraine, in several different towns, I ran into every type of criticism, grumbling, and gossip; but when it came to mobilizing *rabotniki* for the front, for every 100 that enlisted 95 deserted.'
84 *KVR*, ii, tome 1, 350–1. Further evidence of the chaos that reigned among the troops in the south seems to be provided by recently published texts also; see, for instance, an 8th army report filed in winter 1918, which denounced, among other phenomena, the fact that 'everybody gives orders': *Direktivy komandovaniia*, i, 603–4.
85 *Izvestiia*, 12 December 1918. The *polozhenie* concerning the Commander-in-Chief is also in *Direktivy glavnogo komandovaniia*, 140–1. All three documents are also contained in *Direktivy sovetskoi vlasti*, iv, Moscow, 1968, 152–7. They were approved by SNK on 5 December.
86 J. Petrov, *Partiinoe stroitel'stvo v Krasnoi Armii i Flote*, Moscow, 1964, 43ff.
87 *Per.*, iii, 409.
88 *Ibid.*, iv, 418–19.
89 The unit in question was of 'militia' origin, see *PPR*, i, 267–9. A report written a few weeks later reveals that there were no commissars in this unit; see ibid., i, 276–7. The same report (dated 20 January 1919) informed the centre that a political department, with functions similar to those previously performed by the committees and cells, was being organized in that unit too.
90 See, for example, *ibid.*, 195–6.
91 *Pravda*, 2 November 1918, where the organizational structure is described. The Latvian unit was later incorporated into the western front's 15th army, whose political department proceeded to abolish its elective party organization; see *PPR*, ii, 249.
92 *PPR*, i, 235–6.
93 Petrov, *Partiinoe stroitel'stvo*, 48–9; by the same author, *Voennye komissary*, 16–17. According to M. Rudakov, I. Kolesnichenko, V. Lunin, 'Nekotorye voprosy raboty politorganov v gody inostrannoi interventsii i grazhdanskoi voiny', in *Voenno-istoricheskii zhurnal*, no. 8, 1962, 4, the first political department was founded among the forces of the northern Urals which were later gathered together in the eastern front 3rd army. See also D. Fedotoff-White, *The Growth of the Red Army*, Princeton, 1944, 76ff.; R. Kolkowicz, *The Soviet Military and the Communist Party*, Princeton, 1967, 23ff.

94 *PPR*, i, 185–6.
95 *Ibid.*, 235–6.
96 *Ibid.*, 467.
97 Petrov, *Partiinoe stroitel'stvo*, 52; Nenarokov, *op. cit.*, 163–5; V. G. Kolichev, 'Nekotorye voprosy rukovodstva TsK RKP(b) partiino-politicheskoi rabote v Krasnoi Armii (1918–1920 gg.)', in *Voprosy istorii KPSS*, no. 2, 1977, 71–2.
98 The resolutions of the meeting are in part reproduced in *PPR*, i, 194–5.
99 I. N. Smirnov was the most authoritative military leader at the meeting. Trotskii has left a warm commendation of Smirnov both as a revolutionary figure and military leader; see *My Life*, 408–9.
100 'Iz otcheta politupravleniia pri RVSR o partiino-politicheskoi rabote v Krasnoi Armii ts nachala ee organizatsii po 1 oktiabria 1920 (8 oktiabria 1920)', in *PPR*, i, 68–9.
101 *Per.*, iv, 74.
102 *PSS*, xxxvii, 123.
103 Faced with this disconcerting omission, attempts were made to assert that after the resolution had been adopted the leadership of the military cells was transferred to the party's territorial committees and that a recommendation to this effect should be regarded as implicit in the text. This version was advanced both prior to the publication of the resolution (see *PPR*, i, note 63 on p. 341), and when it appeared for the first time in a collection of documents; see *Per.*, iv, note 1 on p. 74). Petrov, *Partiinoe stroitel'stvo*, 53, on the other hand, states that the political departments, 'on the Central Committee's decision', were to become the new organs of leadership in accordance with the resolution of 25 October. This seems the most likely account. Also see Kliatskin, *op. cit.*, 249.
104 *Per.*, v, 23.
105 *Ibid.*, 354–6.
106 Petrov, *Partiinoe stroitel'stvo*, 53; *PPR*, i, 247. The meeting was held at Kozlov, the front command headquarters; this can be inferred from what one of the participants at the meeting later stated; see *ibid.*, 273.
107 *Per.*, v, 562.
108 *PPR*, i, 244–6.
109 Petrov, *Partiinoe stroitel'stvo*, 54–5; by the same author, 'Stroitel'stvo partiinykh organizatsii v period inostrannoi interventsii i grazhdanskoi voiny', in *Partiinaia zhizn'*, no. 10, 1957, 41. Also see the earliest account (dated 20 December) of the reorganization carried out in winter 1918, dispatched to the centre by the southern front political department, in *PPR*, i, 258. In particular, regarding the army commanded by Voroshilov (the 10th), see the significant report addressed to Lenin, by the same political department, at the end of November. This reveals the scant presence and poor level of organization of the party in the detachments; see *Iuzhnyi front*, Rostov, 1972, 226–41. Of the approximately 30,000 party members in the army, represented at the 8th Party Congress in March 1919, fewer than 5000 belonged to the southern front. The eastern front was the best supplied with communists; see Petrov, *Partiinye mobilizatsii*, 64.

110 *Per.*, v, 365–9.

111 *PPR*, i, 273–5.

112 *Ibid.*, 92–3.

113 Petrov, *Partiinoe stroitel'stvo*, 53. The document to which the author refers has not been republished. For some time divisional political departments had a status inferior to those of the army and front. An RVSR order of February 1919 refers to them not as *otdely* but as *otdeleniia* of the superior political departments; see *PPR*, i, note 23 on p. 93. As we shall see further on, divisional political departments acquired greater importance only following the decisions reached at the 8th Congress.

114 *Iz istorii*, 170. See also Petrov, *Partiinoe stroitel'stvo*, 63. During this period, Stalin had another opportunity to demonstrate his centralizing zeal, despite what might have been expected of him, given the role he played in the Tsaritsyn affair. At the beginning of December, the Sovet oborony gave him the task of drawing up a resolution on 'the struggle against localist tendencies and against red tape' in the state administration; see *Dekrety sovetskoi vlasti*, iv, 165–6. Stalin's text was adopted unanimously by a commission consisting of Sverdlov, Krasin, and Kurskii. On this basis, VTsIK issued a resolution: its point 5 warned that those who violated the principle of administrative centralization would be called to account, even if they were members of the party.

115 *Per.*, vi, 449.

116 The text is also given in *PPR*, i, 50–5.

117 This category is mentioned in documents drawn up by a variety of units prior to December 1918; see, for example, the regulations governing the cells of the 6th army, approved on 25 October 1918, in *PPR*, i, 309–11; and the already cited regulations of the Caucasian military *okrug*, *ibid.*, 235–6, drawn up in summer 1918. On the institution of party 'sympathizers', which fell into disuse at the beginning of 1919, see T. H. Rigby, *Communist Party Membership in the USSR. 1917–1967*, Princeton, 1968, 71; G. Procacci, *Il partito nell'Unione Sovietica*, Bari, 1974, 12.

118 Kliatskin, *op. cit.*, 242–3.

119 *KPSS v rezoliutsiiakh*, ii, 34.

120 In the platform on the role of the trade unions, of November 1920, in *Desiatyi s'ezd RKP(b). Stenograficheskii otchet*, Moscow, 1963, 819.

121 This expression crops up in a speech delivered by Frunze in 1924; see M. V. Frunze, *Izbrannye proizvedeniia*, 2 vols., Moscow, 1957, ii, 122.

122 A. S. Bubnov, 'Voennaia distsiplina i partorganizatsiia' (March 1924), in *O Krasnoi Armii*, Moscow, 1958, 131. See also *Boevoi ustav pekhota RKKA*, Part II (1927), Moscow, 1933, 67: 'The purpose of political work in the Red Army is to strengthen the Red Army's fighting capacity, as a basis of armed support for the dictatorship of the proletariat.'

123 *Pravda*, 3 January 1919. See also *Voennaia Mysl'* (organ of the eastern front RVS), no. 1, 1919, 32ff.

124 *PPR*, i, 132–5; the original document is a pamphlet: I. I. Khodorvskii, *Pamiatka kommunista na front*, Petersburg, 1919.

125 *PSS*, xxxvii, 468; quoted from an article published in *Pravda*, 28 January 1919.

4 Opposition within the party

1 *PSS*, xxxvii, 99.
2 *Pravda*, 26 November 1918.
3 *Ibid.*, 11 March 1919.
4 *Ibid.*, 16 March 1919.
5 *Ibid.*, 7 December 1918.
6 *Ibid.*, 26 December 1918.
7 *Ibid.*, 11 March 1919.
8 *Ibid.*, 14 March 1919.
9 *Ibid.*, 20 November 1918.
10 *Ibid.*, 5 January 1919.
11 *Ibid.*, 13 November 1918.
12 *Ibid.*, 24 November 1918.
13 *Ibid.*, 19 December 1918.
14 *Ibid.*, 24 December 1918.
15 *Ibid.*, 15 March 1919.
16 *PPR*, i, 284.
17 *Pravda*, 30 November 1918.
18 *Ibid.*, 3 January 1919.
19 See, for example, *ibid.*, 23 November 1918: 'Worker, peasant, go and enrol on the courses [for commander]. No one demands from you either general or military knowledge; only the desire to fight, only the desire to die in the foremost ranks of combatants for socialism.'
20 *Ibid.*, 28 November 1918.
21 Report (not published in *Pravda*) in *PPR*, i, 264.
22 *Per.*, v, 352–3.
23 *Pravda*, 13 November 1918.
24 'S'ezd kommunistov', in *Voennaia Mysl'*, no. 2, 1919.
25 *Pravda*, 1 March 1919.
26 *Ibid.*
27 For the significance of this reference to the execution of party members, see following section.
28 See below, pp. 124–5.
29 He had been a member of the Vserossiiskaia kollegiia for the organization of the Red Army in spring 1918; see V. Ignatev, *Vos'moi s'ezd RKP(b)*, Gospolizdat, 1950, 57.
30 The report of the meeting is partially reproduced in *Nizhegorodskaia kommuna*, 1 March 1919. I owe this piece of information to R. Service, who kindly allowed me to consult notes he made on examining the archives of the said newspaper.
31 *Pravda*, 4 March 1919.
32 This document was not published at the time; now in *PPR*, i, 123–4.
33 *Pravda*, 21 December 1918.
34 This too refers to episodes dealt with in the next section.
35 *Pravda*, 7 March 1919.
36 *Ibid.*, 3 January 1919.

37 *Ibid.*, 12 March 1919. Among its own delegates to the Congress, the conference also sent Smilga.

38 See the first section of the next chapter.

39 *Ibid.*, 14 March 1919.

40 This, as we have seen, is true in particular for the party's own precongressional conferences. See, for example, N. Tsvetaev, *Voennye voprosy v resheniiakh VIII s'ezda RKP(b)*, Moscow, 1960, 23.

41 *Pravda*, 14 March 1919. Part of the following passage is given in *VKP(b) i voennoe delo v rezoliutsiiakh s'ezdov i konferentsii VKP(b)*, Moscow, 1928, 243–4. It is attributed to the Conference of the communists of the northern front 6th army.

42 R. Cobb, *Les Armées révolutionnaires*, 2 vols., Paris, 1961, i, 183. Reference to Cobb's work was suggested by Erickson, 'The Origins', 226–7. Also see remarks made by Procacci, *op. cit.*, 40–1.

43 Cobb, *op. cit.*, i, 1.

44 *Ibid.*, 42.

45 *Ibid.*, 54.

46 See above, pp. 52–3.

47 Deutscher, *The Prophet Armed*, 426; Trotskii, *My Life*, 468.

48 See above, note 13.

49 Also see A. Kamenskii, 'Ot Donbassa k Tsaritsynu', in Bubnov *et al.*, *op. cit.*, i.

50 This expression alludes to a passage contained in the famous *Povest' vremennykh let*, one of the most ancient of Russian written documents (eleventh to twelfth centuries). Having recognized that on their own they were unable to form a state and to provide themselves with laws, it is said that the ancient Slavic tribes, inhabiting the territory of the historic Rus', sent for the leaders of a Scandinavian people, the legendary Varangians, to reign over them.

51 See above, pp. 79–80.

52 *TP*, i, 204–8; Deutscher, *The Prophet Armed*, 425–6.

53 *Pravda*, 26 December 1918. The editors of *PSS* (xxxvii, 718–19) do not know of a Central Committee meeting held on the 25th, at least not one attended by Lenin; the same applies to *Biograficheskaia Khronika*, vii, 349ff. It is very likely that the resolution was the work of Sverdlov, Secretary of the Central Committee.

54 This is partially reproduced in *PPR*, i, 43, in such a way that it is impossible to understand how much support Trotskii received. Deutscher is unaware of the existence of the resolution: see *The Prophet Armed*, 426. Erickson omits the entire episode.

55 *TP*, i, 252.

56 *Dekrety sovetskoi vlasti*, v, 663.

57 *TP*, i, 196.

58 Towards the end of the article, addressing Sorin, Kamenskii wrote: 'They [the commanders of Nicholas' academy] will be in a position to make use of this power in accordance with the points of the scheme that you have cited.' But, as has been seen, the final text had already appeared on 12 December.

59 *Pravda*, 11 January 1919.

60 *TP*, i, 248–50; the message is dated 11 January.

61 *Istoriia*, iii, 356.

62 *Dekrety sovetskoi vlasti*, iv, 584.

63 *Istoriia*, iii, 356.

64 The text of 13 January is in *Per.*, v, 1971, 182–3; those of 19 and 31 January in Stalin, *op. cit.*, iv.

65 *Ibid.*, 211.

66 *Ibid.*, 213: 'RVSR needs to be transformed into a small group, closely linked to the fronts, consisting, let us say, of five individuals (including two specialists)'. The three party members were to be involved in 'supervising' the supplies apparatus, the High Command, and the VBVK. On the same page, there is a call for greater 'centralization' in the leadership of the armies.

67 *Ibid.*, 209.

68 See Konev, *Krasnaia Gvardiia*, 197; *TP*, i, 122, note 2.

69 Stalin, *op. cit.*, iv, 207; see also Deutscher, *Stalin*, 213–14.

70 According to the editors of *PSS*, the first report was read by Lenin on the 14th. The Central Committee, which met on the 16th, did not address the issue; see xxxvii, 723, 729.

71 Stalin, *op. cit.*, iv, 209.

72 *Ibid.*, 203.

73 *Per.*, v, 183.

74 The appreciation of Smilga expressed by Stalin and Dzerzhinskii is probably one of the reasons why the document of the 13th was not made public for such a long time. During the Stalin years, 'the Trotskyist Smilga' was accused, among other things, of having refused to ask for reinforcements and of having driven the command of the 3rd army to intensify the campaign of terror in the town in an unsuccessful attempt to increase the troops' resistance; see P. G. Sofinov, 'Permskaia katastrofa i likvidatsiia ee posledstvii', in *Istoricheskie zapiski*, tome 30, 1949, 36.

75 Stalin, *op. cit.*, iv, 210.

5 Military policy at the 8th Congress

1 Two years later, however, we encounter Kamenskii already in the more staid role of a supporter of the platform on trade unions elaborated by 'Democratic Centralism', a politically fanciful but far from extremist grouping; see *Desiatyi s'ezd*, 825.

2 J. M. Sverdlov, *Izbrannye proizvedeniia*, 3 vols., Moscow, 1957–60, iii, 190 and 174–5.

3 *PSS*, xxxviii, note 21 on p. 39. The speech was not printed until April.

4 *KVR*, ii, tome 1, 42. This was an interview printed in *Izvestiia* on 18 March 1919, 'Otsenka sostoianiia KA'.

5 *Ibid.*

6 *Ibid.*, 42–3.

7 *Ibid.*, 44.

8 *Ibid.*, 47; this appeared for the first time in *V puti*, 1 March 1919.

9 *Ibid.*, 48–9.

10 *Ibid.*, 48.

11 The minutes of the meeting are in *TP*, i, 296–8.

12 V. M. Smirnov had been delegated to the Congress by the communists of the eastern front 5th army; see *Vos'moi s'ezd RKP(b), Protokoly*, Moscow, 1959, 471.

13 'Nasha politika v dele sozdaniia armii', in *Pravda*, 25 February 1919.

14 *Kustarnichestvo*: the term recurs frequently in Lenin's *What Is To Be Done?*, as an accusation against the 'economists'; see *PSS*, vi, 104: 'But as well as a lack of preparation the concept of *kustarnichestvo* denotes something else: a narrow scope affecting all revolutionary work in general, the failure to grasp that on the foundations of such limited work a good organization of revolutionaries cannot be established; and lastly, and this is the most important thing, the attempt to justify this narrowness by giving life to a specific "theory", i.e. the yielding to spontaneism in this field also'.

15 *PSS*, xxxviii, 81–124.

16 *Ibid.*, 113–14.

17 *Vos'moi s'ezd*, 144–52; there is a summary in E. H. Carr, *Socialism in One Country, 1924–26*, 3 vols., New York, 1958–64, ii, 275–7.

18 *Vos'moi s'ezd*, 144–6.

19 *Ibid.*, 146.

20 *Ibid.* On the reconstitution of the 11th army at Astrakhan, see *TP*, i, 263 and note 2 on p. 264. See also J. Biggart, 'The Astrakhan Rebellion: An Episode in the Career of S. M. Kirov', in *Slavic and East European Review*, no. 2, 1976, 238, and note 41. Several months later, Ordzhonikidze made a passionate reply to Trotskii's and Sokol'nikov's allegations that his units were affected by the spirit of *partizanstvo*; see G. K. Ordzhonikidze, *Stat'i i rechi*, 2 vols., Moscow, 1956, i, 91–2: the value of the 11th army had been ignored, it was claimed, by the 'War Ministry leaders'. See also *ibid.*, 95, where a defence is mounted of the viewpoint of those Bolsheviks who 'simply weren't interested in old regulations, statutes, and military specialists', i.e. of 'the bureaucratic system common to the whole of Soviet Russia'.

21 *Vos'moi s'ezd*, 148.

22 *Ibid.*

23 *Ibid.*, 148–9.

24 *Ibid.*, 150.

25 *Ibid.*, note 62. I have not managed to discover the text by Smilga that Sokol'nikov was referring to. We know that it was called *Stroitel'stvo armii* and that it requested, as well as the introduction of the one-man command of the military commander, also the abolition of the RVSs; see Smilga, 'S'ezd kommunistov'.

26 *Vos'moi sezd*, 151–2.

27 *Ibid.*, 145–6, 149, 152.

28 *Ibid.*, 153; Carr, *Socialism*, ii, 376. V. M. Smirnov, a 'left communist' in February–March 1918, had also been in charge of the party's military

operations for the Moscow uprising of November 1917; see Cohen, *Bukharin*, 53.

29 *Vos'moi s'ezd*, 155.

30 *Ibid.*, 157. These early internal statutes (the text of which is not available) appeared in December 1918 and were to a considerable extent the work of Vatsetis; see 'Iz vospominanii glavkoma I. I. Vatsetisa', in *Voenno-istoricheskii zhurnal*, no. 41, 1962, 70–9.

31 *Vos'moi s'ezd*, 156–7; I. I. Vatsetis, 'Grazhdanskaia voyna. 1918 god', in *Pamiat'*, no. 2, Paris, 1979 (Moscow, 1977), 72–4; this is a passage from Vatsetis' memoirs, written between 1927 and 1933, not published in the USSR. In fact, this seems to be the only passage of those chosen by the editors of *Pamiat'* in which Vatsetis does not appear to be very influenced by the opinions of the leading military group that became prominent at the end of the 1920s (Voroshilov).

32 *Vos'moi s'ezd*, 158; Procacci, *op. cit.*, 34.

33 *Vos'moi s'ezd*, 158.

34 *Ibid.*, 181.

35 *Ibid.*, 202.

36 *Ibid.*, 166–7.

37 *Ibid.*, 182.

38 *Ibid.*, 76; see *KPSS v rezoliutsiiakh*, ii, 47. Iurenev's intervention indicates that the military section in the new party programme, published for the first time in 1930 (see above, note 15), and available to us only in that form, is not in fact complete. A different text, containing the section that was later actually adopted, was probably circulated among the delegates; see note 80 below. It is unlikely that Iurenev would have confused the party programme with Trotskii's theses, given that there was no mention of elections for officers in the theses.

39 Danilevskii, *op. cit.*, 75, note 1. These were two sections that in commission were then approved by a majority:

1. Strict registration of the (social) class to which the mobilized soldiers belong, with the purpose of forming units that are uniform in class terms.

2. Scrupulous selection of parasite elements and kulaks, and their concentration in special work companies.

It is interesting to note that this second measure, generally attributed to Trotskii and to his 'wickedness', met with even stiffer support from members of the 'military opposition'; see Erickson, *The Soviet High Command*, 30–1. In any case, from July 1817 onwards, numerous social groups were exempted from active service and assigned to special formations in the rear; see *Dekrety sovetskoi vlasti*, iii, 69–70.

40 Danilevskii, *op. cit.*, 68–70.

41 *Ibid.*, 69; *Leninskii sbornik*, xxxvii, 140, note 1; *Vos'moi s'ezd*, 488.

42 *Ibid.*, 485–7.

43 Tsvetaev, *op. cit.*, 47.

44 *Ibid.*

45 Danilevskii, *op. cit.*, 71, 76.

46 *Ibid.*, 71, 73.

47 *Ibid.*, 73–4.
48 *Ibid.*, 70; see also N. F. Kuz'min, 'Voennyi vopros na VIII s'ezde partii', in *Voprosy istorii KPSS*, no. 6, 1958, 182.
49 Danilevskii, *op. cit.*, 76.
50 *Ibid.*, 72; this passage was quoted for the first time in *Istoriia VKP(b)*, ed. E. Iaroslavskogo, 3 vols., Moscow and Leningrad, 1930, iii, 414.
51 *Vos'moi s'ezd*, 73.
52 Tsvetaev, *op. cit.*, 53; see Kliatskin, *op. cit.*, 378ff. At the end of the Civil War, the Red Army consisted of approximately 72% Russians, 13% Ukrainians, 4% Bielorussians, plus Latvians, Tartars, Bashkirs, and other national groups in unspecified proportions; see P. Shuktomov, 'Natsional'-nye formirovaniia v gody inostrannoi voennoi interventsii i grazhdanskoi voiny', in *Voenno-istoricheskii zhurnal*, no. 4, 1962, 118–19.
53 K. Voroshilov, *15 let Krasnoi Armii*, Moscow, 1936; I have drawn the quotation from Tsvetaev, *op. cit.*, 51.
54 Danilevskii, *op. cit.*, 70, 74.
55 *Ibid.*, 74. Zemliachka had been the *nachalnik* of the 8th army political department; see *Istoriia*, iv, 259; A. I. Todorskii, *Marshal Tukhachevskii*, Moscow, 1963, 45.
56 Kuz'min, 'Voennyi vopros', 183.
57 Tsvetaev, *op. cit.*, 51.
58 Danilevskii, *op. cit.*, 75–6; see also *TP*, i, 301, note 7.
59 As reported by Aralov himself, whose memoirs, however, are markedly anti-Trotskii in character: S. I. Aralov, *Lenin vel nas k pobede*, Moscow, 1962, 96–7 (I found this piece of information in J. I. Korablev, *V. I. Lenin – sozdatel' Krasnoi Armii*, Moscow, 1970, 87).
60 Stalin, *op. cit.*, iv, 249–50.
61 *Ibid.*
62 Trotskii, *Stalin*, 304.
63 Danilevskii, *op. cit.*, 76–7.
64 *Leninskii sbornik*, xxxvii, 136.
65 *Ibid.*, 137.
66 *Ibid.*, 135.
67 In mid-February Lenin had received a telegram from V. Smirnov, informing him that the new statutes would not be enforced in the 5th army, because of their reactionary content; see *Biograficheskaia Khronika*, v, 523; *TP*, i, 323, note 4.
68 *Leninskii sbornik*, xxxvii, 135.
69 *Ibid.*, 137.
70 *Ibid.*
71 *Ibid.*, 139.
72 *Ibid.*, 136–7.
73 *Ibid.*, 135.
74 *Ibid.*, 139.
75 Danilevskii, *op. cit.*, 88.
76 *Ibid.*, 88–9.
77 *Istorii*, iv, 46; *Istoriia KPSS*, iii, 2 tomes, Moscow, 1969, tome 2, 249, 276.

78 See, for example, Erickson, *The Soviet High Command*, who first states that Congress made 'substantial' alterations to Trotskii's line (p. 47), but then immediately asserts the contrary (p. 49).
79 *KPSS v rezoliutsiiakh*, ii, 69–70.
80 The piece added took the form of a new section in the theses, section XV; see *ibid.*, 66.
81 See the theses, section XV, and the text approved by Congress, section XVI, *ibid.*, 66.
82 Procacci, *op. cit.*, p. 35, note 34.
83 *KPSS v rezoliutsiiakh*, ii, 69–70.
84 *Ibid.*, point II, p. 69.
85 See V. P. Portnov, 'Partiino-politicheskaia rabota v Krasnoi Armii v 1918–1920 godakh', in *Voprosy istorii KPSS*, no. 4, 1961, 158, 169; Kolichev, 'Nekotorye voprosy', 74–5. Sverdlov also attended the meeting, which, among other things, confirmed the subordination of political departments to their respective RVSs.
86 *KVR*, ii, tome 1, 89.
87 According to the organizational report that the Central Committee presented to the 8th Party Conference in December 1919, the creation of PUR (provided for by the 8th Congress in point VIII of the resolutions) had involved the setting up of a 'specific institution' to take charge of political work in the army, formerly performed by the secretariat of the Central Committee. This confirms just how important Sverdlov had been in this field but also raises the question of the nature of the relations between the Central Committee secretary and the VBVK that had developed prior to the 8th Congress; *Vos'maia konferentsiia RKP(b). Protokoly*, Moscow, 1961, 220.
88 'In the spring' of 1919, disciplinary powers were formally granted to commanders too: I. Kolesnichenko, 'Deiatel'nost' Kp po ukrepleniiu voinskoi distsipliny v period stroitel'stva Sovetskikh vooruzhennykh sil', in *Voenno-istoricheskii zhurnal*, no. 9, 1963, 9–10.
89 See also Geronimus, *Partiia*, 80; *VKP(b) i voennoe delo*, 239; L. Schapiro, 'The Birth of the Red Army', in *The Soviet Army*, ed. B. H. Liddel Hart, London, 1956, 29. Special Cheka detachments had been set up by SNK in the front-line area since 16 July 1918 but as a structure it was probably still largely independent of the military commands; see *Dekrety sovetskoi vlasti*, iii, 37–8. The armed forces of the Cheka and its territorial organizations were placed under the command of RVSR in November of the same year; see *ibid.*, 456–9. There had been special Cheka commissions in the combat units of the Red Army at least since October 1918. At this time a structure, independent of the territorial hierarchy, was created for the military Chekas. The Chekas depended financially on the political department and on the High Command of the unit to which they were attached; see *Ezhenedel'nik chrezvychainykh komissii po bor'be ts kontr-revoliutsii i spekulatsii*, no. 4, October 1918, 28–30. In February 1919, VTsIK issued a *polozhenie* on the *osobye otdely*. A Central Cheka OO was set up, the head of which was to be appointed jointly by the Cheka and by RVSR. The OO had its own organs with the same names attached to the front and army RVSs. One

RVS member and all commissars belonging to the RVS had the job of exerting control over the activities of the OOs. The duties of the OOs are only partially known, given that at least one section of the February 1919 regulations has never been published. It seems from the text that the OOs were principally organs of counter-espionage and that they rapidly assumed functions that had previously been discharged by the *voennyi kontrol*; see *Dekrety sovetskoi vlasti*, iv, doc. 168.

90 *KPSS v rezoliutsiiakh*, ii, 71.
91 It is not clear whether decorations only or ranks also are under discussion here. 'Anaki otlichiia po dolzhnosti', ranks in the strict sense of the word, were formally introduced in June 1919; see *Politrabotnik*, no. 2, 1920, 12. The order of the Red Flag, on the other hand, had been instituted at the end of 1918.
92 Carr, *Socialism*, ii, 378, note 1; Korablev, *Lenin i zashchita*, 443.
93 *Voennaia mysl'*, no. 3, 1919, 10–11; see also *TP*, i, 324, note 1.
94 *History of the CPSU(b), Short Course*, Moscow, 1938, 235; R. Medvedev, *Let History Judge*, New York, 1971, 14–15.
95 *Short Course*, 235–6.
96 In 1926, Kamenskii was a member of the left opposition; see *TP*, i, 208, note 1.
97 *Short Course*, 235.
98 Stalin, *op. cit.*, x, 42–3.
99 *Ibid.*, 42.
100 *Vos'moi s'ezd*, 339–40.
101 *Ibid.*, 312.
102 *Ibid.*, 220.
103 *Ibid.*, 217–18, 314, respectively.
104 Osinskii's term: *ibid.*, 166.
105 Osinskii again, *ibid.*, 304, 197.
106 *Ibid.*, 166.
107 *Ibid.*, 170–1.
108 *Ibid.*, 320.
109 *Ibid.*, 217.
110 Lunacharskii used this adjective ironically against Osinskii; *ibid.*, 317.
111 *Ibid.*, 314.
112 *Ibid.*, 219.
113 *Ibid.*, 164. On the partial convergence of views between 'Democratic Centralists' and 'Rigid Centralists' (such as L. M. Kaganovich), see the acute remarks made by Service, *op. cit.*, 108.
114 This verb was used by Osinskii, *Vos'moi s'ezd*, 184.
115 *Ibid.*, 178.
116 See the resolution entitled 'Partiinoe stroitel'stvo', in *KPSS v rezoliutsiiakh*, ii, 71–6, point 2, p. 72.
117 *Ibid.*, point 7.
118 *Ibid.*, point 6.
119 *Ibid.*, part 'B' of the resolution, p. 77.
120 *Ibid.*, points 3 and 4, pp. 72–3.

121 *PSS*, xxxviii, 148. See again comments in Service, *op. cit.*, 109–10.
122 A delegate interrupted Osinskii to point out to him that this rule still existed; see *Vos'moi s'ezd*, 313. However, the statute approved at the 6th Congress, in July 1917, required members 'to recognize the party programme, to belong to one of its organizations, to submit to all party directives, and to pay membership fees' but did not mention the obligation to take an active part in party work; see *KPSS v rezoliutsiiakh*, ii, 496.
123 *Vos'moi s'ezd*, 313.
124 *Ibid.*, 183.
125 *Ibid.*, 178.
126 *Ibid.*
127 Procacci, *op. cit.*, 17.
128 *Vos'moi s'ezd*, 312.
129 *PSS*, xxxviii, 212.
130 L. Trotskii, *The Challenge of the Left Opposition. Writings of Leon Trotsky, 1923–1925*, New York, 1975, 82. This passage is from an article which *Pravda* published on 28 December 1923. Trotskii later included it in *The New Course*.
131 The Whites had launched their attack on 4 March; see *Istoriia*, iv, 46.
132 *TP*, i, 310–12.
133 In the following weeks Smirnov was apparently appointed 'Central Committee military instructor', a position entailing undefinable responsibilities; see *TP*, i, p. 398 and note 3 on p. 401.
134 *Vos'moi s'ezd*, 322.
135 *Ibid.*, i, 324, note 1.
136 *KVR*, ii, tome 1, 313. On 29 March, Trotskii again expressed his conviction that the reason for Soviet military setbacks on the eastern front was the 'critical itching' widespread among leading Bolsheviks; *ibid.*, 50.
137 The minutes are in *TP*, i, 318–20.
138 *Istoriia KPSS*, iii, tome 2, 277–8 and note 1.
139 *TP*, i, 320.
140 Trotskii's reply is in *TP*, i, 324–34; see also Deutscher, *The Prophet Armed*, 431–2.
141 *TP*, i, 326.
142 *Ibid.*
143 *Ibid.*, 330.
144 'Osinskii' was the pseudonym of V. V. Obolenskii.
145 *Ibid.*
146 *Ibid.*

6 Rupture and reconciliation

1 Petrov, *Partiinoe stroitel'stvo*, 89.
2 *Vos'maia konferentsiia*, 220. The recent study by M. J. Deane, *Political Control of the Soviet Armed Forces*, London, 1977, names only Smilga and Beloborodov.

3 *Istoriia*, iii, tome 1, 548.
4 *Ibid.*, iii, tome 2, 282.
5 *Ibid.*, iii, tome 1, 197.
6 See above, p. 83.
7 See above, pp. 90–1.
8 *TP*, i, 339–41 and note 1 on p. 340. Trotskii's request is in a letter dated 4 April. Smilga formally became a member of RVSR on 8 May.
9 *PPR*, ii, 38–9.
10 *Ibid.*, 287. These words were spoken by a leader of the southern front 9th army. On the polemic on this issue, see above, p. 111.
11 *PPR*, ii, 37.
12 *TP*, i, 345–6, and note 1 on p. 346, message dated 4 April. See also the order to the commissars of the 3rd army, similar in content, in *KVR*, ii, tome 1, 353–5: 'Certain communists, trusting to their membership of the communist party, justify their arbitrary breach of military orders and their non-fulfilment of the same, under a variety of pretexts. It is necessary to establish a direct and real responsibility on the part of commanders and commissars for the execution of military orders' (p. 354).
13 *TP*, i, 363, 367, dated 8 and 20 April respectively.
14 *Ibid.*, 431–3.
15 *Ibid.*, 511.
16 *Ibid.*, 515, dated 2 June; *PSS*, l, 333, dated 1 June.
17 Stalin, *op. cit.*, iv, 258, note 73; *TP*, i, 438–40, note 1; Tucker, *op. cit.*, 152–3.
18 Stalin, *op. cit.*, iv, 259–60.
19 *TP*, i, 523. Okulov had probably been appointed to the *vseroglavshtab* immediately after the 8th Congress on Trotskii's proposal; see *ibid.*, 339, document dated 5 April.
20 *Ibid.*, 521.
21 *Ibid.*
22 *Ibid.*, i, 525; *PSS*, l, 338.
23 *Ibid.*, 335. The Politbiuro was composed at this time of Lenin, Stalin, Trotskii, L. Kamanev, and Krestinskii as full members, and Bukharin, Kalinin, and Zinov'ev as candidate members.
24 *TP*, i, 256.
25 *Ibid.*, 528. Minin was later appointed to the 10th army RVS; see *Biografi- cheskaia Khronika*, vii, 311. It is significant, however, that Lenin sought to avoid any responsibility for his appointment; see *Leninskii sbornik*, xxxvii, 266–7.
26 Stalin, *op. cit.*, iv, 267.
27 *TP*, i, 523.
28 Stalin, *op. cit.*, iv, 262–4.
29 *Leninskii sbornik*, xxxiv, 174: 'I am glad that your information has proved untrue'; see *TP*, i, note 1 on p. 522.
30 Trotskii, *My Life*, 423.
31 Kliatskin, *op. cit.*, 418; the Central Committee resolution is cited by Sklianskii in a message to Trotskii dated 3 June, in *TP*, i, 521.
32 *TP*, i, 566–7, note 4; Erickson, *The Soviet High Command*, 63–4.

33 See *PSS*, l, 352–3 and note 401.

34 *TP*, i, 581, note 4; Deutscher, *The Prophet Armed*, 433–4.

35 See Trotskii's malicious remark at the 9th Party Congress, at which Iurenev criticized the War Ministry (see below, pp. 160–1): 'Comrade Iurenev speaks of oligarchy and irresponsibility. But I have a whole pile of accusations against him. He used to be a member of the VBVK and went along with our policy. It is only recently that he has broken away: at the 8th Congress, which abolished the VBVK'; see *Deviatyi s'ezd*, Moscow, 1921, 76.

36 See *PSS*, l, 316–17 and note 374, according to which S. Kamenev was named front commander again on 25 May. See also the memoirs of Kamenev regarding his contacts with the centre in Moscow during those weeks: K. C. Danishchevskii and S. S. Kamenev, *Vospominaniia o Lenine*, Moscow, 1972, 55–8. Kamenev pretended he had been completely unaware of the behind-the-scenes struggle over his confirmation as front commander.

37 *TP*, i, 483.

38 This is Gusev's expression, *ibid.*, 566, note 4.

39 The view of J. M. Meijer, the editor of *TP*.

40 The minutes are in *ibid.*, 578–81. According to Naida, *O nekotorykh voprosakh*, 183, Stalin had asked for a Central Committee Plenum to be convened immediately following the discovery of a 'plot' in the 7th army.

41 The decree is in *Izvestiia*, 8 July 1919, signed by SNK.

42 *Istoriia KPSS*, iii, tome 2, 302.

43 SNK decree, dated 8 July, in *Izvestiia*, 10 July 1919. See also *TP*, i, 520–1, note to doc. no. 279. On the appointment of Smilga to RVSR see above, p. 241, note 8.

44 *TP*, i, 581–2, note 4.

45 Erickson, *The Soviet High Command*, 56.

46 *Direktivy glavnogo komandovaniia*, 129.

47 This word appears in the SNK decree published on 10 July.

48 *TP*, i, 581, note 3, and 579.

49 *Ibid.*, 580, point 4 in Plenum resolutions.

50 *Ibid.*, point 5.

51 *Istoriia*, iv, 166.

52 *TP*, i, 590–3.

53 *Ibid.*, 592.

54 *Ibid.*, 589, message from Lenin to Sklianskii, dated 4 July.

55 *Ibid.*, 594. On this affair, see pp. 596–7, note 3.

56 Trotskii, *My Life*, 398, 452. Trotskii also referred to the suspicions that led to the removal of Vatsetis, without ruling out the possibility that he was perhaps one of those who 'skipped through the biography of Napoleon' or that he may have made the mistake of airing his 'ambitions' in public. But he did not say that Vatsetis had been formally arrested. Subsequently, Trotskii distanced himself from Vatsetis, whom he accused of negligence with respect to high-ranking officers who had shown themselves to be unreliable; see Deutscher, *The Prophet Armed*, 438.

57 Trotskii, *My Life*, 452.
58 Trotskii, *The Stalin School of Falsification*, New York, 1972, 49; see also *TP*, i, 589. In fact this document merely complied with the commitment made by the Politbiuro and the Orgbiuro to give Trotskii *carte blanche* in the south.
59 Deutscher, *The Prophet Armed*, 438, note 1. As far as I have been able to discover from the Soviet literature, the arrest of Vatsetis was mentioned for the first time in M. D. Bonch-Bruevich, *Vsia vlast' sovetam*, Moscow, 1957, 340.
60 Stalin, *op. cit.*, iv, 267–8.
61 *PSS*, xxxix, 34.
62 *Ibid.*, 36, where Lenin also speaks out against *partizanstvo*.
63 *KPSS v rezoliutsiiakh*, ii, 94–109.
64 *Ibid.*, 110–15; see also *Iz istorii*, ii, 791–6.
65 *KPSS v rezoliutsiiakh*, ii, 95.
66 *Ibid.*
67 *Ibid.*, 103.
68 *Ibid.*, 104.
69 *Ibid.*
70 *Ibid.*, 105.
71 *Ibid.*
72 *Ibid.*
73 *Ibid.*
74 *Ibid.*, 112–13.
75 *Ibid.*, 114.
76 *Ibid.*
77 *Izvestiia*, 6 July 1919.
78 *PSS*, xxxix, 480, note 15.
79 See also *Biograficheskaia Khronika*, vii, 358–9, where Lenin shows that he appreciated certain of Stalin's assessments. There is no information, however, regarding any formal Central Committee session at which the 'Circular Letter' was approved; see *ibid.*, 375ff.
80 *KPSS v rezoliutsiiakh*, ii, 11.
81 *Ibid.*, 112.
82 *Ibid.*
83 *Ibid.*, 115.
84 *V. I. Lenin i VChK (1917–22)*, Moscow, 1975, 226, 236–7, and note 1, 284.
85 *KVR*, ii, tome 1, 97. The order appeared in *Izvestiia* only on 19 July.
86 *KVR*, ii, tome 1, 222.
87 *Ibid.*, 53.
88 *TP*, i, 584, note 9.
89 *KVR*, ii, tome 1, 54.
90 *Ibid.*, 56.
91 *Ibid.*
92 *Ibid.*, 324.
93 *Ibid.*, 231–2.
94 The 8th army resolution to which Trotskii alluded was probably the one reported in *PPR*, ii, 330–1: 'The assembly sees no grounds to request a

change in the position of the communist cells in the detachments. The cells must act exclusively by means of persuasion, by personal example, but without any type of special organizational rights. Whereas the commissar is the representative of authority (*vlast'*) and the commander is the military leader, the communist cell remains the organ for party agitation and propaganda.' This resolution was passed on 11 July, three days before the 'Circular Letter' was issued. Trotskii hurriedly telegraphed the news to Sklianskii on the same day, so that he could inform the Central Committee; see also *TP*, i, 596. As regards resolutions passed by the 13th army in support of Trotskii's positions, we only know of some passed the following month (dated 21 August), also in *PPR*, ii, 306–7. In content they are similar to those passed by the 8th army. This is all the more significant if one bears in mind that in June the party organs of the 13th army had assumed positions in stark contrast with the policies embodied by Trotskii, such as the request that commissars be granted authority in 'strategic' matters, and that a 'provisional party committee' be reconstituted, alongside the unit's political department; see *Per.*, viii, 628, 660–1, respectively.

95 Trotskii's article, published in *V puti*, is in *KVR*, ii, tome 1, 237–8.
96 *TP*, i, 598.
97 *KVR*, ii, tome 1, 212.
98 *Ibid.*, 259.
99 *Ibid.*, 61.
100 *Ibid.*, 60.
101 *Ibid.*
102 *Ibid.*, 64.
103 *Ibid.*
104 This coincidence did not seem noteworthy, for example, to Deutscher, *The Prophet Armed*, 477–81. Deutscher, however, commented that July 1919 was 'the lowest point in [Trotskii's] fortunes during the Civil War', *ibid.*, 435–6.
105 *Voennoe delo*, no. 10, 1918, 15.
106 *KVR*, ii, tome 1, 116.
107 *Ibid.*, 116–17.
108 Erickson, 'Some Military and Political Aspects', 207–8.
109 *Izvestiia*, 29 July 1919.
110 *KVR*, ii, tome 1, 66.
111 *Izvestiia*, 24 July and 5 August 1919.
112 Petrov, *Voennye komissary*, 85–6.
113 See *Voennoe delo*, no. 1, 1918, 14; *Sistematicheskii sbornik postanovlenii RVSR po Flote i voennomu vedomstvu ts 1 Ianviariia po 1 dekabriia 1919 g.*, Moscow, 1922, 539–40; 454–5.
114 N. Bukharin and E. Preobrazhenskii, *The ABC of Communism*, Introduction by E. H. Carr, London, 1969, 29.
115 *Ibid.*, 259.
116 *Ibid.*, 261.
117 *Ibid.*, 262.
118 *Ibid.*, 263–4.

119 *Ibid.*, 266–7.
120 *KPSS o vooruzhennykh silakh*, Moscow, 1969, 176.
121 *PSS*, li, 22, 45.
122 Deutscher, *The Prophet Armed*, 442–3.
123 Erickson, *The Soviet High Command*, 91–2; Deutscher, *The Prophet Armed*, 464–5.
124 In his report to 8th Conference, *PSS*, xxxix, 343.
125 *Izvestiia*, 6 December 1919.
126 Also in report to 8th Conference, *PSS*, xxxix, 351.
127 'K s'ezdu sovetov', in *Pravda*, 6 December 1919.
128 *Izvestiia*, 11 December 1919; Deutscher, *The Prophet Armed*, 446–7.
129 In his report to 8th Congress of Soviets, in *KVR*, ii, tome 2, 7.
130 *Ibid.*, 10–11.
131 *Ibid.*, 27–8.
132 *Ibid.*, 7.
133 *Ibid.*, 14ff.
134 *Vos'maia konferentsiia*, 33–4.
135 *Ibid.*, 39–40.
136 *Ibid.*, 67.
137 See above, p. 93.
138 *Spravochnik partiinogo rabotnika*, Moscow, 1921, 101.
139 *KVR*, ii, tome 2, 265.
140 *Vos'maia konferentsiia*, 136. See also decisions reached by the commission formed to draft amendments to the party rules, *ibid.*, 225.
141 *Ibid.*, 173. The representatives of the territorial organizations were thus apparently Sapronov, Vetoshkin, Evdokimov, Kaganovich, and Volin. Evdokimov's name, however, is not listed among those who actually took part in the commission.
142 See *ibid.*, 232, commission documents. Of the names listed, it is likely that Dzerzhinskii represented the Central Committee; Smilga PUR; Gorbunov RVSR; Volin, Sapronov, Kaganovich, Mgeladze, Vetoshkin, and Maksimovskii, the territorial organizations; Teodorovich, Poluian, and Potemkin, the machinery of political departments, and the military *rabotniki*. It thus appears that Maksimovskii (of 'Democratic Centralism') replaced Evdokimov, and that Mgeladze was included in the commission as an extra member.
143 *Ibid.*, 232.
144 *Ibid.*, 232–3. See also *Deviaty s'ezd RKP(b). Protokoly*, Moscow, 1960, 353, note 117.
145 *KPSS v rezoliutsiiakh*, iii, 308; Procacci, *op. cit.*, 110.
146 *Izvestiia*, 12 December 1919.
147 *Ibid.*, 14 December 1919.
148 *Pravda*, 13 December 1919.
149 See *Politrabotnik*, no. 1, 1920, p. 7. For Stalin's regulation, see above, p. 149–50.
150 *Pravda*, 13 December 1919.
151 See above, p. 99.

152 *KVR*, ii, tome 1, 76.

153 *Ibid.*, 78.

154 See *Pravda*, 14 December 1919: the term does not appear in the text reproduced in *KVR*.

155 According to the account in *Izvestiia*, 14 December 1919. There is no mention of the issue in the text printed in *KVR*. In the similar political apparatus operating in the armed forces of the *Cheka*, the commissars at brigade level had been discharging the functions of the *nachalniki* of the corresponding political departments since October 1918; see *Vnutrennye voiska Sovetskoi Respubliki*, Moscow, 1972, 308.

156 *Pravda*, 13 December 1919. According to the editors of *PPR* (ii, Intro-duction, 12) Congress had decided that where the commander was a communist, no commissar need be appointed: but this was not in any case followed up immediately; see I. B. Berkhin, *Voennaia reforma v SSSR (1924–1925 gg.)*, Moscow, 1958, 292, which states that the practice of not appointing a commissar when the commander was himself a communist was not widespread until 1922–3.

   The earliest known document providing evidence of the institution of one-man command in the front-line units is in *PPR*, ii, 339, dated 4 November 1919. It is an RVSR order informing the 8th army of the decision to grant its commander *edinolichnoe upravlenie*. In the place of RVS commissars, two new posts were created: *pomoshchnik po politicheskoi chasti* and *pomoshchnik po administrativnoi chasti*. The commander of the 8th army at that time was Sokol'nikov; see *TP*, i, 738–9 and note 3.

   In the armed forces of the Cheka, from August 1919 onwards, it had been decided that political commissars should work alongside comman-ders only when the latter had been party members for less than a year. If, on the other hand, the commander had been a party member for a longer period, *pomoshchniki po politicheskoi chasti* were instituted. This provision was confirmed by a subsequent order of February 1920; see *Vnutrennye voiska*, pp. 43, 293, 296, 334.

157 *Izvestiia*, 16 December 1919.

158 *Pravda*, 16 December 1919.

159 According to an account in *Izvestiia*, dated 14 December, these were Trotskii's words. This expression does not, however, appear in the text printed in *KVR*, in which there are no references to the issue addressed by Pavlunovskii.

160 Smilga's views were encouraged, besides, by the fact that the 8th Con-gress had endorsed the principle of one-man command in every other field of state administration; see *KPSS v rezoliutsiiakh*, ii, 140.

161 *PPR*, ii, 39.

162 This definition appeared in RVSR order no. 910, issued on an unspecifi-able date in 1919 and repeated in the subsequent order no. 2120 in 1920. For the political leader to be an ordinary *pompolitchasti* and not a com-missar, the commander had to have been a party member for at least a year; see A. ST-T, 'Komissar ili pompolitchasti', in *Politrabotnik*, nos. 11–12, 1921. A subsequent order of January 1922 raised the period of

party membership from one to two years; see D. Petrovskii, 'K voprosu ob edinonachalie', in *Voennaia Mysl' i revoliutsiia*, no. 4, 1922, p. 4.

163 *KVR*, ii, tome 1, 51 and note 23. According to M. Molodtsygin, 'Sozdanie mestnykh organov voennogo upravleniia', in *Voenno-istoricheskii zhurnal*, no. 5, 1968, one-man command was introduced in *guberniia* and *uezd* commissariats as early as January 1919.

164 *Izvestiia*, 24 December 1919.

165 V. Melikov, in *Izvestiia*, 1 January 1920.

166 *Izvestiia*, 10 January and 4 February 1920. Confidential reports from the fronts to PUR during the same period indicate that the reopening of the issue of one-man command provoked an attitude of 'passivity' on the part of commissars and filled the commanders with a self-confidence 'out of all measure'; see *PPR*, ii, 277–8. The prejudices of those who drew up this kind of report, however, must have influenced the description of the phenomena that they were observing.

167 *Ibid.*, 74–84.

168 *Ibid.*, 50–2.

169 This is mentioned in a circular produced by the political department attached to the 'southern group of units on the eastern front', organized in June 1919 by Frunze to unleash a counter-attack against Kolchak; see *ibid.*, 190.

170 *Izvestiia*, 27 December 1919.

171 *Deviatyi s'ezd*, on pages 52 and 124 respectively. From this point on, we shall refer exclusively to the 1960 edition of the 9th Congress records.

172 *Ibid.*, 78–9. The Podonbass was an organ of the *voenno-trudovyi sovet* of the Ukraine, which ran the local 'labour armies'. Stalin was its president; see SNK decision of 21 January 1920, in *Dekrety sovetskoi vlasti*, vii, Moscow, 1975, 120–3.

173 *Deviatyi s'ezd*, 155.

174 *Ibid.*, 331–3.

175 Geronimus, *Partiia*, 115–16; Erickson, 'Some Military and Political Aspects', 217–18.

7 Peace or war

1 Carr, *Bolshevik Revolution*, ii, 207.

2 *Direktivy glavnogo komandovaniia*, 47, document dated 15 July.

3 *TP*, i, 182–4, document dated 25 November.

4 *Direktivy glavnogo komandovaniia*, 170–1.

5 *PSS*, xxxix, 354, 407.

6 *Iz istorii*, iii, 7–10.

7 *Ibid.*, 25–6; see Carr, *Bolshevik Revolution*, ii, 208–9.

8 *KVR*, ii, tome 2, 37.

9 *TP*, ii, 8; *PSS*, li, 115. The 3rd army RVS telegram is in *Iz istorii*, iii, 16–18.

10 *KVR*, ii, tome 2, 38–42; the order setting up the '1st Labour Army', issued by the Sovet oborony, is in *Iz istorii*, iii, 20–3.

11 *KVR*, ii, tome 2, 37.

12 *Ibid.*, 62.
13 See, for example, the *polozhenie* issued by SNK in April on the structure of the 1st Labour Army RVS, in *Dekrety sovetskoi vlasti*, viii, 39–41.
14 *Zhelezno-dorozhnyi transport SSSR v dokumentakh KP i sovetskogo pravitel'stva*, Moscow, 1957, 44.
15 *Iz istorii*, ii, 22; Carr, *Bolshevik Revolution*, i, 216 and note 2.
16 There is information about this in a Central Committee letter of May–June 1919, in *Per.*, vii, 131; viii, 62–3.
17 See *ibid.*, vii, 385. At the 9th Congress Rozengol'ts said that political departments had existed in the railways 'since mid-1918'; see *Deviatyi s'ezd*, 346.
18 See the relevant *polozhenie*, dated 17 February 1920, in *Zhelezno-dorozhnyi transport*, 93; see Carr, *Bolshevik Revolution*, ii, 219.
19 *Zhelezno-dorozhnyi transport*, 96ff.
20 See above, p. 120.
21 *Zhelezno-dorozhnyi transport*, 108.
22 *Sovetskii transport (1917–1927)*, Moscow, 1927, 19.
23 *Deviataia konferentsiia RKP(b). Protokoly*, Moscow, 1972, 113.
24 See above, note 172, chapter 6; *Deviatyi s'ezd*, 124.
25 Stalin's report is in Stalin, *op. cit.*, iv, 293–302. On the clash at the Ukrainian Party Conference (17–23 March 1920), see *KP(b)U v rezoliutsiiakh i resheniiakh s'ezdov i konferentsii*, Kiev, 1958, 45; the platform of 'Democratic Centralism' is in *ibid.*, 70–1.
26 By decision of the Politbiuro; see *PSS*, li, 155.
27 *Deviatyi s'ezd*, 124. At the Congress, Trotskii weighed his words with care, but at the Moscow Party Conference, a few days earlier, he had stated that 'it is necessary to militarize the party'; see *Izvestiia*, 26 March 1920.
28 *Deviatyi s'ezd*, 152.
29 Procacci, *op. cit.*, 45ff.
30 *Deviatyi s'ezd*, 155.
31 *Ibid.*, 111–12. Menshevik positions were strongly represented among railworkers.
32 *Ibid.*, 317–18, 470.
33 Carr, *Bolshevik Revolution*, ii, 222.
34 *Instruktsiia* of 17 July 1920, in *Spravochnik partiinogo rabotnika*, Moscow, 1922, 106–7.
35 *Deviatyi s'ezd*, 118; see R. B. Day, *Leon Trotsky and the Politics of Economic Isolation*, Cambridge, 1973, 30–1.
36 *Deviatyi s'ezd*, 107–8.
37 *Ibid.*, 192.
38 *Ibid.*, 396.
39 Trotskii, *Terrorism and Communism*, Michigan, 1961, 172–3. This booklet was written in summer 1920.
40 Undated document, in *KVR*, iii, tome 2, 241.
41 Day, *op. cit.*, 44–5.
42 P. Pavloskii, 'Novii god – novaia rabota – novye trebovaniia', in *Vestnik militsionnoi armii*, no. 3 (April), 1920.

43 *Pravda*, 17 December 1919.
44 This apparent contradiction has been remarked upon both by Deutscher, *The Prophet Armed*, 478, 491–2, and by Erickson, in 'Some Military and Political Aspects', 215, and in *The Soviet High Command*, 83, 115. One of the first to notice this inconsistency was A. Svechin, immediately after the 8th Congress: 'Trotskii's theses support the militia ideal for the Red Army. But in practice the whole work of the RVSR President amounts to an effort to hinder developments towards a militia within the Red Army; yet in theory he lacks the resolve to break away from the old militia programme of the 2nd International'; see 'Militsiia kak ideal. Kritika tezisov L. Trotskogo', in *Voennoe delo*, nos. 11–12, 1919, 436–8.
45 See above, p. 95.
46 See Pethybridge, *op. cit.*, 107; Day, *op. cit.*, 22–3.
47 For a concise reconstruction of the subsequent phases of debate on the militia issue, see Erickson, 'Some Military and Political Aspects'.
48 *Doklad nachalnika GU Vsevobucha terkadrov i kommunisticheskoi chastei tov. Podvoiskii na soveshchanie nachalnikov polkovikh okrugov*, Moscow, 1920, 9.
49 Erickson, *The Soviet High Command*, 131–2; *PSS*, xlii, 130–1.
50 Carr, *Socialism*, ii, 392–3. Once the most dramatic moment of political crisis at the end of the Civil War had passed, territorial formations (*terchasti*) were set up alongside the standing units (*kadrovyi*); see the resolution of 8 August 1923, in *Spravochnik partiinogo rabotnika*, Moscow, 1924, 301–3. The proportion of permanent (*postoiannyi*) and conscript (*peremennyi*) personnel to serve in the territorial formations was also fixed. The political machinery of PUR was extended to the new territorial units; see Berkhin, *op. cit.*, 88, 89.
51 *Spravochnik partiinogo rabotnika*, Moscow, 1922, 104.
52 Naida, *O nekotorykh voprosakh*, 37–56. The OONs (or ChONs) were abolished in 1924, with the pacification of the countryside.
53 Erickson, 'Some Military and Political Aspects', 221.
54 *Ibid.*, 222.
55 *Vos'moi s'ezd sovetov. Stenograficheskii otchet*, Gosizdat, 1921, 37.
56 E. Molotkov, 'Voennyi vopros na X s'ezde partii', in *Voenno-istoricheskii zhurnal*, no. 2, 1961, 62.
57 *Desiatyi s'ezd*, 10–11.
58 *Ibid.*, 11.
59 *TP*, ii, 396.
60 *Izvestiia*, 1 January 1921.
61 *Pravda*, 12 March 1921.
62 *Izvestiia*, 26 February 1921.
63 *Ibid.*, 22 February 1921.
64 *Ibid.*, 20 February 1921.
65 KPSS v rezoliutsiiakh, ii, 264.
66 Trotskii, 'Rech na II vserossiiskom s'ezde politprosvetov', in *KVR*, iii, tome 1, 35–6: 'The militia system presupposes that there is no friction between the working class and the peasantry.'
67 *Desiatyi s'ezd*, 708–9, 710–14.

68 *KPSS v rezoliutsiiakh*, ii, 263.
69 V. Dverisheli, 'Militsionnaia armiia kak orudie osushchestvleniia politiki pravitel'stva', in *Vestnik militsionnoi armii*, no. 1, 1920.
70 The motto on the title page of *Vestnik militsionnoi armii* was attributed to Bebel: 'Not a regular army but a militia'.
71 *Ibid.*, no. 20, 1920, 11–12.
72 See the theses presented by Podvoiskii to the RVSR meetings in December, *ibid.*, no. 21, 1920.
73 Trotskii, 'Rech na II vserossiiskom s'ezde politprosvetov', 35.
74 *KVR*, iii, tome 1, 10–11, speech delivered on 17 February 1921.
75 *Ibid.*, ii, tome 2, 11.
76 Trotskii, *The Revolution Betrayed*, New York, 1937, 218.
77 See, for example, the contemporary view of Sol'ts, 'Zadachi partii v perezhivaemyi moment', in *Pravda*, 21 January 1921: 'The 9th Conference was held under the banner of democracy (*demokratizm*)'.
78 *Deviataia konferentsiia*, 117.
79 *Ibid.*, 125.
80 *KPSS v rezoliutsiiakh*, ii, 189.
81 *Ibid.*
82 *Ibid.*, 193.
83 *Ibid.*, 197; *Deviataia konferentsiia*, 137.
84 *KVR*, ii, tome 1, 83–6.
85 *PPR*, ii, 102.
86 *Ibid.*, 428–31.
87 *Politrabotnik*, no. 2, 1921, 22.
88 *PPR*, ii, 102. The *instruktsiia* did not come into force until two months later.
89 *Ibid.*, 46–7. Cf. L. Schapiro, *The Origin of the Communist Autocracy: Political Opposition in the Soviet State, 1917–23*, London, 1955, 264–6, in whose opinion the Orgbiuro and PUR still at this date deployed their staff independently of one another, in the civilian and military fields respectively; see also, by the same author, 'The Army and the Party in the Soviet Union', unpublished paper, June 1954, in the series 'St Antony's Papers on Soviet Affairs' (Oxford), 2.
90 *PPR*, ii, 47.
91 *Ibid.*, 45–6.
92 Erickson, 'Some Military and Political Aspects', 222.
93 *Desiatyi s'ezd*, 709.
94 'Some Military and Political Aspects', 222.
95 I. Smilga, *Ocherednie voprosy stroitel'stva Krasnoi Armii. 1) Militsionnaia sistema. 2) PUR i Glavpolitprosvet. K desiatomu s'ezdu RKP*, Moscow, 1921, 3–14; Erickson, *The Soviet High Command*, 117–18.
96 Smilga, *Ocherednie voprosy*, 30.
97 Smilga, 'K voprosu o politicheskoi rabote v KA', in *Politrabotnik*, no. 11, 1920.
98 Smilga, 'Vtoroe soveshchanie voennykh politrabotnikov', *ibid.*, no. 1, 1921, 1–2.
99 *Ibid.*, 14–16.

100 *PPR*, ii, 113.
101 Smilga, 'Vtoroe soveshchanie'.
102 Smilga's dismissal is reported in *Politrabotnik*, no. 1, 1921, 32. In March he was made a member of the Prezidium of the Higher Economic Council (VSNKh); see *Biograficheskaia Khronika*, ix, 217. During the Polish campaign he had been a member of the western front RVS together with Tukhachevskii, on the recommendation of Trotskii; see *TP*, ii, 168–9 and 170–1. At the end of August he was considered responsible for an initiative that the Central Committee viewed as an attempt to sabotage negotiations with Poland for an armistice; see *ibid.*, notes to documents 594 and 595. From the outbreak of hostilities, PUR had found it difficult to convince Red soldiers of the defensive nature of the war, and to curb draft evasion and desertion; see *KVR*, ii, tome 2, 425–6, document dated 9 May 1920.
103 Until this date, the PUR orders published in *Politrabotnik* were signed by Solov'ev. But see also the following, which give different dates: Erickson, *The Soviet High Command*, 117–18; M. Rudakov, 'Nekotorye voprosy rabota politorganov v gody inostrannoi interventsii i grazhdanskoi voiny', in *Voenno-istoricheskii zhurnal*, no. 8, 1962; Petrov, *Partiinoe stroitel'-stvo*, 129, note 2; biography of Gusev in *Entsiklopedicheskii Slovar' Granat*, Part 1, 109.
104 S. I. Gusev, *Grazhdanskaia voina i Krasnaia Armiia*, Moscow and Leningrad, 1925, 94; the text quoted is dated January 1921.
105 *Ibid.*
106 *Ibid.*, 95.
107 *Ibid.*, 94.
108 Gusev, 'Krasnaia Armiia', in *Voennaia Mysl'*, no. 2, 1919.
109 T. Kramarov, *Soldat revoliutsii*, Moscow, 1964, 77–8, 80.
110 Gusev, *Grazhdanskaia voina*, 84.
111 *Ibid.*, 88.
112 *Desiatyi s'ezd*, 712.
113 Petrov, *Partiinoe stroitel'stvo*, 128, note 2.
114 *KPSS o vooruzhennykh silakh*, 148.
115 *Ibid.*, 155–9; date according to Petrov, *Partiinoe stroitel'stvo*, 128, note 2; Berkhin, *op. cit.*, has 23 February.
116 *KPSS o vooruzhennykh silakh*, 158.
117 *Ibid.*, 168–9.
118 *Politrabotnik*, nos. 8–10, 1921, 55.
119 Pethybridge, *op. cit.*, 115ff. Smilga, while he was in office, seems to have encouraged 'the return of communists to civilian work'; see 'K voprosu'.
120 *KPSS o vooruzhennykh silakh*, 172.
121 *Odinnadtsatyi s'ezd RKP(b). Stenograficheskii otchet*, Moscow, 1961, 700–1.
122 Not, therefore, only 'at the top', as Schapiro asserts, *The Communist Party in the Soviet Union*, Moscow, 1960, 264.
123 *PPR*, i, 234–5, 332–4; Schapiro, *The Origin of the Communist Autocracy*, 300.
124 Schapiro, *The Origin of the Communist Autocracy*; see also Day, *op. cit.*, 36–7.

125 See above, pp. 33–4.
126 *Pravda*, 21 January 1921.
127 *Desiatyi s'ezd*, 221.
128 *Ibid.*, 245.
129 *Ibid.*, 257.
130 Petrov, *Partiinoe stroitel'stvo*, 129–30; Geronimus, *Partiia*, 127–8. According to *VKP(b) i voennoe delo*, 289, these trends were expressed by those in favour of an immediate transition to the militia system.
131 D. Degtiarev, *Partiinoe stroitel'stvo v Krasnoi Armii*, Khar'kov, 1921, 22–5. On Glavpolitprosvet, see the next section.
132 'Izvestiia vremennogo revoliutsionnogo komiteta krasnoarmeets i rabochikh goroda Kronshtadta', 1 March 1921, in *Pravda o Kronshtadte*, Prague, 1921, 17: 'Every kind of political department should be liquidated, because a single party cannot make use of privileges for the propagation of its own ideas and receive from the state means to this end. In their place, commissions for education [*sic*] must be created, elected locally, whose means must be supplied by the state.'
133 *Desiatyi s'ezd*, 257.
134 *Ibid.*, 254.
135 *Ibid.*, 259.
136 See the resolution proposed by Bukharin, *ibid.*, 649–50.
137 *Ibid.*, 315. According to Molotkov, *Voennyi vopros*, 63, a group of military delegates, in the private sessions, proposed 'the liquidation of PUR' and of commissars.
138 *Desiatyi s'ezd*, 659–60.
139 *Politrabotnik*, nos. 4–5, 1921, 30.
140 *KPSS v rezoliutsiiakh*, ii, 265.
141 *Spravochnik partiinogo rabotnika*, Moscow, 1922, 120, dated 27 June 1921.
142 M. V. Frunze and S. I. Gusev, *Reorganizatsiia Krasnoi Armii. Materialy k X s'ezdu*, Khar'kov, 1921; the document, with the same title, which Frunze and Gusev presented to the 10th Congress, is in *Desiatyi s'ezd*, 710–14.
143 Degtiarev, *op. cit.*, 28.
144 *Biograficheskaia Khronika*, ix, 191.
145 *Politrabotnik*, no. 2, 1921, 15–16, 24.
146 Petrov, *Partiinoe stroitel'stvo*, 131; see also *KPSS o vooruzhennykh silakh*, 173–82.
147 'Doklad PURa . . . po 1 oktiabria 1920', in *Istoricheskii arkhiv*, no. 6, 1959, 27.
148 *Ibid.*, 28.
149 *Ibid.*, 38–40.
150 G. M. Ganshin, 'Gazeta "Krasnyi kavalerist"', in *Vestnik Moskovskogo Un-ta*, Zhurn., no. 1, 1967, 42.
151 I. Babel, *Collected Stories*, London, 1974.
152 'Doklad PURa', 40–1.
153 *Sbornik postanovlenii i rasporiazhenii glavpolitprosveta, 1921*, Gosizdat, 1921, 3–4.
154 *PPR*, ii, 86, 6 April 1920.
155 S. Fitzpatrick, *The Commissariat of Enlightenment*, Cambridge, 1970, 243.

156 *Ibid.*, 175–6.
157 *Ibid.*, 185.
158 *Ibid.*, 243.
159 *Ibid.*
160 *VKP(b) i voennoe delo*, 294.
161 Smilga, *Ocherednie voprosy*, 19–30.
162 *VKP(b) i voennoe delo*, 295.
163 *Sbornik*, 25–8.
164 *Politrabotnik*, no. 1, 1921, 18; *ibid.*, no. 2, 1921, 24.
165 *Desiatyi s'ezd*, 140–1.
166 *Ibid.*, 146.
167 *Ibid.*
168 *Ibid.*, 174.
169 *Ibid.*, 177.
170 With the liquidation of the 'fronts' and the institution of the (territorial) *okrugi*, the corresponding political departments were also reorganized; see Petrov, *Partiinoe stroitel'stvo*, 138.
171 *Desiatyi s'ezd*, 177; see also Fedotoff-White, *The Growth of the Red Army*, 230.
172 *Desiatyi s'ezd*, 485. Several months later, Trotskii also dwelt on the reasons why political work in the army could not be 'concentrated' in the hands of the local organs of Glavpolitprosvet; see *KVR*, iii, tome 1, 31.
173 *KPSS v rezoliutsiiakh*, ii, 243.
174 See respectively *VKP(b) i voennoe delo*, 296; *Spravochnik partiinogo rabotnika*, Moscow, 1922, 125ff.
175 Petrov, *Partiinoe stroitel'stvo*, 137, note 2.

8 Continuing political tensions

1 See Erickson, *The Soviet High Command*, 127; Carr, *Socialism*, ii, 284ff; Deutscher, *The Prophet Armed*, 481–2; by the same author, *The Prophet Unarmed*, London, 1959, 25; P. Zilin, 'Diskussia o edinoi voennoi doktrine', in *Voenno-istoricheskii zhurnal*, no. 5, 1961, 62–73.
2 See the passage directed at Minin on the Tsaritsyn affair in 'Doklad i zakliuchitel'noe slovo na soveshchanii voennykh delegatov XI s'ezda RKP 1-ego Apreliia 1922 g.', in *KVR*, iii, tome 2, 260.
3 Vatsetis also intervened, arguing from positions that drew criticism from Frunze and Tukhachevskii; see Todorskii, *op. cit.*, 76.
4 This term was used by Osinskii at the 4th Congress; see *Deviatyi s'ezd*, 105. This military 'culture' was contrasted with 'civilian culture'; see also Day, *op. cit.*, 30.
5 As well as the other writings by Trotskii that will be referred to below, see also the wide-ranging theoretical article: 'Voennoe znanie i markzism, in *KVR*, iii, tome 2, 272–89.
6 *Desiatyi s'ezd*, 349–50.
7 The 'artificiality' of the debate is mentioned by Erickson, *The Soviet High Command*, 127, who attributes it to the prevalence of personal and power struggles.

8 Deutscher, *The Prophet Armed*, 482.
9 See note 142 of the preceding chapter. See also Erickson, *The Soviet High Command*, 128; Carr, *Socialism*, ii, 385.
10 M. Tukhachevskii, *Voina klassov*, Moscow, 1921, 54–61.
11 C. Rakovskii, 'Ukrainskoe krest'ianstvo i Krasnaia Armiia', in *Pravda*, 22 December 1921: this is a brief account of the debate that took place among the military leaders at the 6th Ukrainian Congress of Soviets, and at the preceding Party Conference. The Ukrainian military apparatus appears to have enjoyed some degree of autonomy. As early as its 4th Congress (Khar'kov, November 1920) the Ukrainian Communist Party (KP(b)U) won acceptance for the principle whereby a member of its own Central Committee should head the armed forces stationed in the Ukraine; see *KP(b)U v rezoliutsiiakh*, 78.
12 'Voennoe stroitel'stvo', in *Voennoe delo*, nos. 17–18, 1919, 588–9, 638–41.
13 S. K., 'Grazhdanskaia voina', in *Voennaia Mysl'*, no. 1, 1919, 2–4.
14 M. V. Frunze, *Izbrannye proizvedeniia*, Moscow, 1977, 77.
15 N. I. Podvoiskii, *Opyt voenno-revoliutsionnoi taktiki*, (?), December 1918, 8. On the ideas of Tukhachevskii regarding the formation of a '3rd International general staff', see Erickson, *The Soviet High Command*, 126, 776. This exciting proposal, to judge by Podvoiskii himself, was already popular among Bolshevik military leaders before Tukhachevskii formulated it in his famous letter of August 1920 to Zinov'ev, reproduced in Erickson. At the 8th Party Congress, a delegate from the 1st army (at the time commanded by Tukhachevskii himself) had spoken out against the section in the party programme relating to the principle of self-determination, pointing to the danger that the RKP might turn into a purely national party, and demanding that the programme be approved by the Communist International also. He argued, furthermore, that it would be wise to create 'a single revolutionary front, from both the military and the economic viewpoints' on a world scale; see the intervention from Sunitsa, in *Vos'moi s'ezd*, 86; Tsvetaev, *op. cit.*, 35.
16 On the polemic in the 1920s among the Bolshevik military regarding the defeat at Warsaw, see Erickson, *The Soviet High Command*, 99. In the view of N. Kuz'min, 'Ob odnoi nevypolnennoi direktive Glavkoma', in *Voenno-istoricheskii zhurnal*, no. 9, 1962, the men of the south-western front, and in particular Stalin, were guilty of an act of disobedience analogous to that committed by the defenders of Tsaritsyn in autumn 1918.
17 *Deviataia konferentsiia RKP(b)*, 40–1, 57, 60ff, 66, 75ff. On Trotskii's position regarding the defeat at Warsaw: Erickson, *The Soviet High Command*, 91; Deutscher, *The Prophet Armed*, 463–4. References in Trotskii's own work, at different moments in his life, oscillate between playing down disagreements on the Central Committee regarding the expedience of the 'march on Warsaw' and a frank attribution to Lenin in person of the responsibility for this 'mistake'; see 'The New Course', in *The Challenge of the Left Opposition*, 84–5; *My Life*, 456–7, 459–60.
18 *PSS*, xli, 331. On Trotskii, see previous note, and following section.
19 S. Minin, 'V chem sila Krasnoi Armii?', in *Armiia i revoliutsiia*, no. 2, 1922.

20 S. S. Kamenev, *Zapiski o grazhdanskoi voine i voennom stroitel'stve*, Moscow, 1963, 59–60.
21 See his article in *Krasnaia Armiia*, nos. 7–8, 1921, 73ff.
22 Trotskii, 'Doklad', 254–5.
23 Frunze, *op. cit.* (1977), 59–60.
24 Trotskii, 'Doklad', 252.
25 Trotskii, 'Zakliuchitel'noe slovo na 2-j konferentsii komiacheek vysshikh voenno-uchebnikh zavedenii', 10 December 1921, in *KVR*, iii, tome 1, 80.
26 Trotskii, 'Doklad', 247–8.
27 *Ibid.*, 266.
28 See above, note 8.
29 *KPSS v rezoliutsiiakh*, ii, 366.
30 *KVR*, iii, tome 2, 210–39; Carr, *Socialism*, ii, 388.
31 *KVR*, iii, tome 2, 222–3.
32 D. Petrovskii, in *Voennyi Vestnik*, no. 11, 1922, 20.
33 Day, *op. cit.*, 47ff.
34 Erickson, *The Soviet High Command*, 129–30.
35 'Politicheskaia rabota v Krasnoi Armii', in *Pravda*, 13 December 1921; the account of the meeting is in *Izvestiia*, 7 December 1921; lastly, 'Politicheskaia rabota v Krasnoi Armii', in *Politrabotnik*, no. 15, 1921, collected in Gusev, *Grazhdanskaia voina*, 147–56.
36 *Pravda*, 13 December 1921. This term had appeared in the draft resolution on trade unions presented to the 10th Party Congress by Lenin's group; see *Desiatyi s'ezd*, 664. The term 'school of communism', as is well-known, was a definition applied by Lenin to the trade unions, and is used in the same document. At the 12th Congress (April 1923), Stalin, referring to the army, used another famous expression borrowed from the same draft resolution: 'transmission belt'; see Stalin, *op. cit.*, v, 205; 'the army is the most important apparatus linking the party to the workers and peasants'.
37 *Pravda*, 13 December 1921. At the 9th Congress of Soviets, Trotskii reported that 'no fewer than 10%' of the Red Army effectives were communists; see *Pravda*, 29 December 1921. Gusev would have liked to raise this proportion to 20%. It is likely that the party centre was on Trotskii's side on this question. At the 11th Congress, Zinov'ev said that the number of communists in the armed forces (approximately 100,000) constituted an optimal proportion, which other Soviet mass organizations should adopt; at most their number might be raised to 120,000; see *Odinnadtsatyi s'ezd*, 401. This was approximately 10% of those soldiers currently serving who had remained after demobilization: at the 9th Congress of Soviets, Trotskii had given their number as 1,300,000. The figure for communists in the army in December 1921, given in Petrov, *Partiinoe stroitel'stvo*, 150, was 72,000, equivalent, according to the author, to 4–5% of effectives. Probably this figure referred to the operating army only, excluding both central bodies and rear-line forces.
38 Some of Gusev's publications on issues to do with economic planning, for example, had been greeted with considerable interest by Trotskii himself,

who expressed a positive opinion of them at the 9th Party Congress; see *Deviatyi s'ezd*, 95ff, 103.

39 *Pravda*, 13 December 1921.
40 *Desiatyi s'ezd*, 711.
41 *Biograficheskaia Khronika*, ix, 357.
42 See Minin's report to the Ukrainian military communists in summer 1922 in *Armiia i revoliutsiia*, nos. 8–9 (August–September), 1922, 211–15. Minin had already raised this question in no. 5 of the journal, and had made a polemical mention of the scant loyalty of the officers during the Civil War.
43 Trotskii, 'Rech' na II Vserossiiskoe soveshchanie Politprosvetov', 20 December 1921, in *KVR*, iii, tome 1, 29; 'Zadachi Krasnoi Armii', 25 December 1921, *ibid.*, 53; 'Perspektivy i zadachi voennogo stroitel'stva', 18 May 1923, *ibid.*, 153.
44 Trotskii, 'Zakliuchitel'naia rech' na razbore v kotiuzhanakh', 12 December 1921, *ibid.*, 22.
45 Stalin, *op. cit.*, iv, 349. This was a 'declaration to the Politbiuro of the Central Committee of RKP(b)' made on 30 August 1920, shortly after the defeat.
46 Trotskii, 'Vnimanie k melocham', in *Pravda*, 11 September 1921; reproduced in *KVR*, iii, tome 1, 17.
47 Trotskii, 'Perspektivy', 153.
48 *Ibid.*, 152.
49 Trotskii, 'Zakliuchitel'noe slovo', 80–1.
50 Trotskii, 'Doklad na konferentsii voenno-uchebnikh zavedenii Moskovskogo voennogo okruga', in *Pravda*, 19 December 1921; *KVR*, iii, tome 1, 96.
51 Gusev, *Grazhdanskaia voina*, 86.
52 *PSS*, xliv, 16. The Russian term *kul'tura* signifies both 'culture' and 'civilization', 'level of civilization'.
53 *Ibid.*, xliv, 16.
54 Trotskii, 'Rech'', 32.
55 *KVR*, iii, tome 1, 124; *Odinnadtsatyi s'ezd*, 288–9.
56 Frunze, *op. cit.* (1977), 45, 51.
57 The expression was used by Zinov'ev in his report to the 9th Congress; see *Deviatyi s'ezd*, 391.
58 Trotskii, 'Rech'', 31–3.
59 Trotskii, 'Soveshchanie voenykh delegatov s'ezda sovetov', in *Pravda*, 4 January 1922; *KVR*, iii, tome 1, 110. See also *ibid.*, 107: 'To think it is possible to turn a young peasant into a communist, by making him read the *ABC of Communism* with us for a month or two, is radically mistaken.'
60 *Ibid.*, 108.
61 Trotskii, 'Rech'', 32.
62 Trotskii, Zakliuchitel'noe slovo', 82–3.
63 *Ibid.*, 87. At the 9th Congress of Soviets, Trotskii said that in December 1920, 33.8% of all officers had belonged to the Tsarist Army. Only 66% of all officers had received regular military instruction; see *Pravda*, 28 December 1921.

64 Trotskii, 'Zakliuchitel'noe slovo', 86. Frunze was sensitive to this argument; see Frunze, *op. cit.* (1977), 63.
65 Trotskii, 'Zakliuchitel'noe slovo', 84. See also *Odinnadtsatyi s'ezd*, 291; *KVR*, iii, tome 1, 126.
66 Trotskii, 'Rech'', 30. On the attitude of Soviet power towards the 'Smena vekh', see S. A. Fediukin, *Bor'ba s burzhuaznoi ideologiei v usloviiakh perenkhoda k NEPu*, Moscow, 1977, in particular, 262ff.
67 Trotskii, 'Rech'', 39–41.
68 *Ibid.*, 45.
69 Fediukin, *op. cit.*, 267.
70 *Izvestiia*, 23 February 1922.
71 Gusev, *Grazhdanskaia voina*. Undated document.
72 V. Molotov, *Na shestoi god*, Moscow, 1923, 20–1. Part of this passage is reproduced in Petrov, 'Stroitel'stvo partiinykh organizatsii v Krasnoi Armii v period inostrannoi voennoi interventsii i grazhdanskoi voiny (1918–1920 gg.)' in *Partiinaia Zhizn'*, no. 10, 1957, 40.
73 Procacci, *op. cit.*, 112–15.
74 The expression was used by Syrtsov at the 9th Party Congress; see *Deviatyi s'ezd*, 78.
75 Report delivered by Trotskii to 9th Congress of Soviets, in *Pravda*, 28 December 1921.
76 Petrov, *Partiinye mobilizatsii*, 69.
77 Comment by Zinov'ev at 11th Congress; see *Odinnadtsatyi s'ezd*, 390–1.
78 Rigby, *op. cit.*, 241; see also Petrov, *Partiinye mobilizatsii*, 13, 187.
79 Petrov, *Partiinoe stroitel'stvo*, 31, 107.
80 Rigby, *op. cit.*, 52–3.
81 Petrov, *Partiinye mobilizatsii*, 63, 118–20.
82 Deutscher, *The Prophet Armed*, 408.
83 Bonch-Bruevich, *op. cit.*, 269–71.
84 R. Schlesinger, *Il partito comunista nell'URSS*, Milan, 1962, 135.
85 Trotskii, *Stalin*, 277.
86 Danishevskii and Kamenev, *op. cit.*, 25. Less convincing is Danishchevskii's claim that Lenin had explicitly confessed to him his deep-rooted distrust for Trotskii, at the end of summer 1918: 'He is not one of us (*on ne nash*), one cannot have complete trust in him'; *ibid.*, 22–3. It is worth noting, however, that the editors of *Biograficheskaia khronika* have collected numerous documents that show that Danishchevskii in 1918 carried out supervisory and information work under Lenin's direct orders; see *Biograficheskaia khronika*, v, 610, 618, 627; vi, 57, 60, 97. At this time Danishchevskii was a commissar attached to Vatsetis.
87 Carr, *The Interregnum*, New York, 1954, 294–5.

Index

Mensheviks, 35–6, 96, 107, 139, 167, 171, 229n83, 248n31
Mgeladze (Vardian), 70, 104, 152–3, 188, 245n142
Miasnikov, A. F., 103, 104, 149, 157
'military opposition', 3, 113–15, 121–3, 126, 147, 150, 160, 195, 208, 214, 216, 236n39
Miliutin, V. P., 103
Minin, S. K., 132, 253n2, 256n42
  Tsaritsyn affair, 44–50, 83, 87–8, 228n78
  8th Party Congress, 103–4
  on Polish campaign, 188
  on military doctrine, 195
  attack on 'military specialists', 200–1
  opposition to one-man command, 205
  appointment to 10th army RVS, 241n25
Molotov, V. M., 212
Mulin, V., 103
Muralov, N. I., 134, 226n13
Murav'ev, 41–2

NEP (New Economic Policy) 202, 203, 205, 211–12
Nevskii, 226n13
NKVD (People's Commissariat of Internal Affairs), *see* Cheka

Okulov, A. I., 47, 66, 83–4, 88, 94, 103, 105–6, 108, 131–2, 140, 241n19
one-man command, 34
  Egorov on, 40
  threat to RVSs, 82
  Miasnikov's view, 104
  Smilga's advocacy, 129, 235n25, 246n160
  debate at 1st All-Russian Congress of military *politrabotniki*, 155–7
  in civilian administrations, 165, 167, 180
  and Gusev–Frunze programme, 188
  opposition of Minin, 205, 216
  earliest evidence of, 246n156, 247n163
  effects of debate, 247n166
Ordzhonikidze, G. K., 98, 235n20
Orgbiuro, 136–7, 177, 243n58, 250n89
Osinskii (Obolenskii), V. V., 126, 127, 239n100, 240n122, 240n144, 253n4
  on the 'organizational question', 102, 118–22
  and 'Democratic Centralism', 104
  opposition to introduction of political departments in industry, 160, 165, 167
  Theses of the Left Communists, 224n45

Paniushkin, V. L., 227n30
Panteleev, 80, 83–4, 86, 130
partisan warfare, 15, 28, 32, 52, 75, 88, 95, 98, 100, 107, 147, 168, 198
Pavlov, D., 103
Pavlunovskii, 157, 246n159
Perm', 88–90, 101, 106, 112, 129, 131
Piatakov, J. L., 104
Podvoiskii, N. I., 26, 40, 66, 131, 254n15
  plans for Soviet armed forces, 22
  and Vsevobuch, 36
  and the militia debate, 168–9, 170–4, 197
  proposal to reorganize PUR, 178
  on military doctrine, 199
  composition of RVSR, 226n13
Poland, war with, 151, 157, 162, 170, 175, 181, 188, 199–201, 205, 251n102
Politbiuro, 125, 131–2, 136–7, 140, 241n23, 243n58, 256n45
Poluian, 153, 245n142
Potemkin, 153, 245n142
Pozern, B. P., 103, 105, 109
Preobrazhenskii, E. A., 66, 90, 150, 176, 191–2, 194, 214
Procacci, G., 4
Proshiian, P. P., 22, 222n10
PUR (Political Administration of RVSR), 2, 3, 212–14, 238n87, 245n142, 247n166, 251n102, 251n103, 252n137
  creation of, 129, 238n87
  apparatus, 153–5
  and demobilization, 175ff
  and territorial party organizations, 183–5
  reorganization of, 187–94, 250n89
  debate on role of, 204–5, 207–9
  extension to new territorial units, 249n50

Radek, K., 35, 224n45
Rakovskii, C. G., 129
Raskol'nikov, F., 134, 184–5, 226n13
Red Guard, 12ff, 22, 25–6, 37, 224n45
Rodzianko, General A. P., 131
Rozengol'ts, A., 103, 134, 226n13, 248n17
RSDRP (b) (Social Democratic Workers' Party of Russia), 15
RSFSR (Russian Socialist Federal Soviet Republic), 191
Rukhimovich, M. L., 103
RVSR (Revolutionary Military Council of the Republic)
  establishment of, 39–42, 226n13
  appointment of army commanders, 44
  and Tsaritsyn affair, 45–9
  powers of, 52